THE AMERICAN JEREMIAD

THE AMERICAN JEREMIAD

Sacvan Bercovitch

THE UNIVERSITY OF WISCONSIN PRESS

Published 1978

The University of Wisconsin Press
114 North Murray Street
Madison, Wisconsin

The University of Wisconsin Press, Ltd.
1 Gower Street
London WCIE 6HA, England

Printings 1978, 1980

Printed in the United States of America

ISBN 0-299-07350-5

LC 78-53283

FOR SYLVIA

Now in an artificial world like ours, the soul of man is further removed from its God and the Heavenly Truth, than the chronometer carried to China, is from Greenwich. And, as that chronometer, if at all accurate, will pronounce it to be 12 o'clock high-noon, when the China local watches say, perhaps, it is 12 o'clock midnight; so the chronometric soul, if in this world true to its great Greenwich in the other, will always, in its so-called intuitions of right and wrong, be contradicting the mere local standards and watchmaker's brains of this earth. . . . And yet it follows not from this, that God's truth is one thing and man's truth another; but — as hinted above, and as will be further elucidated in subsequent lectures — by their very contradictions they are made to correspond.

MELVILLE, *Pierre; or, The Ambiguities*

"Twelve o'clock reported, sir," says the middy.
"*Make* it so," replies the captain.
And the bell is struck eight by the messenger-boy, and twelve o'clock it is. . . .
Hand in hand we top-mates stand, rocked in our Pisgah top, the whole long cruise predestinated ours.

MELVILLE, *White-Jacket; or, The World in a Man-of-War*

I have not sent these Prophetes, saith the Lord, yet thei ranne: I have not spoke to them, and yet thei prophecied.

JEREMIAH 23:21

Contents

Preface

Rhetoric functions within a culture. It reflects and affects a set of particular psychic, social, and historical needs. This is conspicuously true of the American jeremiad, a mode of public exhortation that originated in the European pulpit, was transformed in both form and content by the New England Puritans, persisted through the eighteenth century, and helped sustain a national dream through two hundred years of turbulence and change. The American jeremiad was a ritual designed to join social criticism to spiritual renewal, public to private identity, the shifting "signs of the times" to certain traditional metaphors, themes, and symbols. To argue (as I do) that the jeremiad has played a major role in fashioning the myth of America is to define it at once in literary and in historical terms. Myth may clothe history as fiction, but it persuades in proportion to its capacity to help people act in history. Ultimately, its effectiveness derives from its functional relationship to facts.

When I wrote the first version of this study,* I felt that the state of Puritan studies warranted an analysis of the rhetoric in its own right. After all, to discuss the interaction of language and society we need to understand the language; and while students of the period had told us a great deal about social, religious, and intellectual patterns, they had generally bypassed or denigrated the Puritan modes of expression. That the situation has improved somewhat since 1970 serves only to reinforce my original premise. Because we have begun

* "Horologicals to Chronometricals: The Rhetoric of the Jeremiad," *Literary Monographs*, III, ed. Eric Rothstein (Madison, 1970), 1–124, 187–215. I have also drawn on two subsequent essays: "The Image of America: From Hermeneutics to Symbolism," *Bucknell Review*, 20 (1972), 3–12; and "How the Puritans Won the American Revolution," *Massachusetts Review*, 17 (1976), 597–630.

to see the impact of Puritan rhetoric upon our culture, we need more than ever to insist upon what Clifford Geertz calls the *shaping* influence of religious (or quasi-religious) symbols on society.* To this end, I have drawn freely on the rhetorical analysis I offered in my earlier monograph. My additions and revisions amount to a new version of the argument, but the argument itself — concerning the richness, the complexity, and the continuing vitality, for good and ill, of American Puritan rhetoric — remains substantially the same.

At the same time, I have sought to establish connections between rhetoric and history. Without trying in any sense to detail the development from colony to nation, I relate the jeremiad to what I consider to be the central fact of that development: the steady (if often violent) growth of middle-class American culture. In doing so, I hope I will not seem to have blurred the stages of growth, from agrarian society through urbanization, the transportation revolution, credit economy, industrialization, corporate enterprise, and expansionist finance. My assumption is that every one of those stages, including the War of Independence, was historically organic — that in effect the culture was committed from the start to what recent social scientists have termed the process of modernization.

By organic I do not mean monolithic. Recent demographic work has demonstrated both the diversity of American social patterns and the overlays, even in colonial New England, of various Old World forms. I see no conflict whatever between their conclusions and my own. My argument concerns an *ideological* consensus — not a quantitatively measured "social reality," but a series of (equally "real") rituals of socialization, and a comprehensive, officially endorsed cultural myth that became entrenched in New England and subsequently spread across the Western territories and the South. Insofar as my argument tends to simplify social and economic conflicts, psychic tensions, and regional disparities, it does so in order to stress

---

* A system of religious symbols, Geertz reminds us, alters the social order "in such a way that the moods and motivations induced by religious practice seem themselves supremely practical, the only sensible ones to adopt given the way things 'really' are." Hence if we concern ourselves with social-structural process at the expense of understanding "the system of meanings embodied in the symbol," we take "for granted what most needs to be elucidated" ("Religion as a Cultural System," in *The Interpretation of Culture* [New York, 1973], pp. 122, 125). The cognitive value this suggests for literary studies seems to me particularly relevant to the American Puritan jeremiad.

the growth of a certain mode of rhetoric and vision. Insofar as this book supports the notion of American exceptionalism, it does so only in terms of an increasingly pervasive middle-class hegemony.*

Technically, of course, the concept of the middle class came into use only after 1812. As a class designation it should perhaps be restricted to the sort of specialized capitalist economy that began to develop in the United States in the first half of the nineteenth century. I use it here for its ideological implications, as a term expressing the norms we have come to associate with the free-enterprise system. In America, the foundations of that system were laid in seventeenth-century New England. Puritan society was not middle class, of course, not even in the sense that most of its members had "middling" incomes. Then as always in this country (through the nineteenth century to our own times) the majority of people were "lower class." What the Puritans instituted in New England was effectually a new hierarchical order, ranging not from peasantry to aristocracy and crown, but from lower to higher levels of a relatively fluid free-enterprise structure. Not all at once but within the first half century they established the central tenets of what was to become (in Raymond Williams's phrase) our "dominant culture."† And because

---

*I use the term "hegemony" here in the sense used by Antonio Gramsci when he speaks of a "historically organic" ideology, based on genuine cultural leadership and "spontaneous consent," as distinct from ideologies imposed by "state coercive power" (*Selections from the Prison Notebooks*, ed. and trans. Quentin Hoare and Geoffrey N. Smith [New York, 1971], esp. pp. 12, 172, 376). Keith Thomas, Robert Mandrou, and others have shown that the rise of European capitalism was attended by a clash of cultures, a lingering struggle of emergent middle class values against traditions inherited from an *ancien régime*. The development of what we now call America shows no significant ideological warfare of that kind. Those Southern spokesmen, for example, who advocated anti- or pre-capitalist forms of life explicitly dissociated their region from "the values of the nation at large" (William R. Taylor, *Cavalier and Yankee* [New York, 1961], p. 17). As Louis Hartz put it, the South was as "an alien child in a liberal family, tortured and confused, driven to a fantasy life" (quoted in C. Vann Woodward, *The Burden of the South* [Baton Rouge, 1968], p. 22; see also Woodward's comments there on the South's "un-American experience").

†Quoted in Myra Jehlen, "New World Epics: The Novel and the Middle Class in America," *Salmagundi*, 36 (1977), 50–51. As Jehlen points out, Raymond Williams "distinguishes between 'the dominant culture' in the society and certain other 'practices, experiences, meanings and values' which are 'alternative' to the dominant culture or even 'oppositional' to it"; but in America, she adds, alternative or oppositional forms have characteristically been "associated with the Old World and thus rejected by the very process of national emergence."

there was no competing order — no alternative set of values except the outmoded Old World order they rapidly discarded — the ideological hegemony that resulted reached to virtually all levels of thought and behavior. The Puritan terms for this cohesiveness were always religious, often colonial, and sometimes national, or proto-national. But none of these adequately conveys the direction of the community. I have used the term *culture* instead, intending by this a society whose defining character lay neither in its territory nor in its nationhood (though eventually it incorporated both these attributes) but in its way of life, and more precisely, perhaps, in the "webs of significance" spun out by successive generations of Americans in order to justify their way of life to themselves and to the world at large. This study is an attempt to explore what I conceive to be one major thread in that process of self-justification, the myth of America.

I approach the myth by way of the jeremiad, or the *political sermon*, as the New England Puritans sometimes called this genre, meaning thereby to convey the dual nature of their calling, as practical and as spiritual guides, and to suggest that, in their church-state, theology was wedded to politics and politics to the progress of the kingdom of God. These sermons provide most of the evidence in my discussion of early New England. But I draw widely on other forms of the literature as well — doctrinal treatises, histories, poems, biographies, personal narratives — in order to place the jeremiad within the larger context of Puritan rhetoric, and, in later chapters, the much larger context of American rhetoric, ritual, and society through the eighteenth and nineteenth centuries. Let me say at once that this approach provides only one perspective on the myth. Perry Miller stressed the dark side of the jeremiad. I argue that this was a partial view of their message, that the Puritans' cries of declension and doom were part of a strategy designed to revitalize the errand. I believe that my study offers a fuller account of both their intent and their effect, but it too provides a partial view. Even when they are most optimistic, the jeremiads express a profound disquiet. Not infrequently, their affirmations betray an underlying desperation — a refusal to confront the present, a fear of the future, an effort to translate "America" into a vision that works in spirit because it can never be tested in fact.

I try to indicate something of this in chapters 3 and 6, and, indirectly, through what might be called my controlling metaphor, the passage on horologicals and chronometricals in *Pierre*, Melville's savage, brilliant, and sweeping attack on the American dream. But my focus, as I have said, is on the affirmative energies through which the jeremiad survived the decline of Puritan New England, and, in what amounted to a nationwide ritual of progress, contributed to the success of the republic. I hope it will become clear in the course of my analysis that to describe those energies is not the same thing as to endorse them.

The organization of this study is both thematic and chronological. Chapters 2 and 3 deal with Puritan rhetoric in the seventeenth century, first in its broad structural and hermeneutical aspects, then in its historical development after 1660. The next chapter, concerning adaptations of Puritan rhetoric in the eighteenth century, centers on Edwards in the Great Awakening. In chapter 5 I discuss the ritual uses of the jeremiad from the Revolution to the Civil War, with special emphasis on the establishment of the jeremiad as a national ritual during the Federalist and Jacksonian eras. The epilogue (chapter 6) treats the influence of the jeremiad upon certain of our classic nineteenth-century writers, and particularly the use of America as symbol by the major figures of the American Renaissance. My purpose in that chapter is not to offer a new literary reading of familiar texts, but to indicate, by way of conclusion, the pervasive impact upon our culture of the American jeremiad.

Finally, a word about the introduction (chapter 1), where I take issue rather directly with Perry Miller. In the earlier version of this study I muted my dissent because I was unwilling to join in the patricidal totem feast following Miller's death, when a swarm of social and literary historians rushed to pick apart the corpus of his work. It seems clear by now that the corpus remains pretty much intact, and that it will remain a towering achievement of the American mind. It is with a deep sense of gratitude for his achievement that I have tried to clarify my differences with Miller.

The English Department of Columbia University provided a grant for the typing of the manuscript. Elizabeth Evanson, of the University of Wisconsin Press, provided editorial services for which I am grateful.

I would like to take this opportunity to thank those who responded encouragingly, in letters or reviews, when my monograph on the jeremiad was published in 1970: Daniel Aaron, Quentin Anderson, James Bell, Ursula Brumm, Michael Colacurcio, Everett Emerson, Ronald Gottesman, David Hall, Earl Harbert, Leo Lemay, David Levin, Michael McGiffert, Edmund Morgan, Richard Reinitz, Jesper Rosenmeier, David Smith, Warren Susman, Alan Trachtenberg, Ernest Tuveson, and Austin Warren.

Finally, my special thanks to those who read the manuscript, or various parts of it, and who helped improve it in many ways: William Clebsch, Ann Douglas, Emory Elliott, Lyndall Gordon, Myra Jehlen, Ann Kibbey, Michael Kramer, Nancy Cott, Carroll Smith-Rosenberg, Michael Wood, and particularly (once again) H. M. Bercovitch.

Many relevant works reached me too late for me to make use of them; this study would have benefited from several of these in particular: Henry F. May, *The Enlightenment in America* (New York, 1976); Michael T. Gilmore, *The Middle Way: Puritanism and Ideology in American Romantic Fiction* (New Brunswick, N. J., 1976); Nathan O. Hatch, *The Sacred Cause of Liberty: Republican Thought and the Millennium in Revolutionary New England* (New Haven, 1977); and Henry Glassie's eloquent and brilliant essay, "Meaningful Things and Appropriate Myths: The Artifact's Place in American Studies," *Prospects*, 3 (1977), 1–50.

A Note on Sources

I use short titles throughout when referring to the sermons, narratives, histories, and treatises of the seventeenth, eighteenth, and nineteenth centuries. In order to keep references to a minimum, I cite only those works directly quoted in the text. In a few cases I omit ellipses, indicating where I do so. In quotations from sixteenth- and seventeenth-century sources, contractions have been extended and the use of *u* and *v*, *i* and *j* has been standardized. Biblical quotations are from the Geneva translation (1560), reprinted in facsimile by the University of Wisconsin Press (Madison, 1969).

THE AMERICAN JEREMIAD

1

Introduction:
The Puritan Errand Reassessed

On board the *Arbella*, on the Atlantic Ocean, John Winthrop set forth the prospects of the infant theocracy* in a provisional but sweeping prophecy of doom. The passengers were entering into covenant with God, as into a marriage bond — and therefore, charged Winthrop, they might expect swift and harsh affliction. Invoking the ominous precedent of Israel, he explained that henceforth the Lord would survey them with a strict and jealous eye. They had pledged themselves to God, and He to them, to protect, assist, and favor them above any other community on earth. But at their slightest shortcoming, for neglecting the "least" of their duties, He would turn in wrath against them and be revenged:

> if wee shall deale falsely with our god in this worke wee have un-
> dertaken and soe cause him to withdrawe his present help from us, wee
> shall be made a story and a by-word through the world, wee shall open
> the mouthes of enemies to speake evill of the wayes of god and all
> professours for Gods sake; wee shall shame the faces of many of gods
> worthy servants, and cause theire prayers to be turned into Cursses

*The term *theocracy* has been criticized, cogently, by a number of recent historians. I retain it here partly as a convenience and partly because the New Englanders themselves repeatedly used it, meaning thereby to indicate not the rule of the priest-hood, but the harmony between minister and magistrate in church and state affairs. So conceived, the term seems to me to express the confluence of the sacred and the secular, which this study tries to examine.

3

upon us, till wee be consumed out of the good land whether wee are goeing.[1]

Winthrop's grim forecast struck a familiar chord. Only several weeks before, as the passengers prepared to embark from Southampton pier, John Cotton had similarly warned them about the perils of their high enterprise. Where much is given, he intoned, much is demanded. The same God who had sifted them as choice grain from the chaff of England, and who would soon plant them in the New World, might "also roote [them] out againe." Men generally succumbed to carnal lures, leaned toward profits and pleasures, permitted their children to degenerate. Such tendencies were punishable anywhere, but among those whom the Lord favored they were grievous beyond measure — ingratitude heaped upon disobedience, natural depravity compounded by deceit. Should the emigrants fall prey to such temptations, God would surely withdraw their "special appointment," weed them out, pluck them up, and cast them irrevocably out of His sight.[2]

No doubt these threats were prompted in part by anxiety; their very stridency speaks of hardships to come in settling an unknown land. But more significant, I think, is how closely they foreshadow the major themes of the colonial pulpit. False dealing with God, betrayal of covenant promises, the degeneracy of the young, the lure of profits and pleasures, the prospect of God's just, swift, and total revenge — it reads like an index of favorite sermon topics of seventeenth-century New England. In particular, of course, I refer to the political sermon — what might be called the state-of-the-covenant address, tendered at every public occasion (on days of fasting and prayer, humiliation and thanksgiving, at covenant-renewal and artillery-company ceremonies, and, most elaborately and solemnly, at election-day gatherings) — which has been designated as the jeremiad.

The standard definition is Perry Miller's. It has become as familiar to students of the period as his classic view of New England's errand — properly so, since he made the jeremiad the proof text of his interpretation. Miller's argument, presented in its broadest sweep in his essay "Errand into the Wilderness," centers upon the ambiguity inherent in the concept of errand. An errand, Miller observes, may be either a venture on another's behalf or a venture of one's own, and

the Puritans' tragedy was that their errand shifted from one meaning
to another in the course of the seventeenth century. They first saw
themselves as an outpost of the Reformation. Their New England
Way was to be a detour (and they hoped a shortcut) on the road leading from the Anglican establishment to a renovated England. After
1660, however, with the collapse of Cromwell's Protectorate, the
colonists found themselves isolated, abandoned. "Their errand having failed in the first sense of the term, they were left with the
second." They turned inward, accordingly, to fill their venture
"with meaning by themselves and out of themselves" — and discovered there, in what was meant to be utopia, "nothing but a sink of
iniquity." Hence the vehemence of their "literature of self-
condemnation": they had been twice betrayed. Not only had the
world passed them by, but the colony itself, the city set on a hill as a
beacon to mankind, had degenerated into another Sodom. They
vented their outrage, Miller tells us, in an "unending monotonous
wail," a long threnody over a lost cause, in which they came increasingly to acknowledge that New England was sick unto death. In
1679, a synod of leading clerics listed the land's "enormities" under
twelve general "heads"; thereafter the preachers, in "something of a
ritual incantation,"

> would take up some verse of Isaiah or Jeremiah, set up the doctrine that
> God avenges the iniquities of a chosen people, and then run down the
> twelve heads, merely bringing the list up to date by inserting the new
> and still more depraved practices an ingenious people kept on devising.
> I suppose that in the whole literature of the world, including the
> satirists of imperial Rome, there is hardly such another uninhibited and
> unrelenting documentation of a people's descent into corruption.[3]

All this is well known. It is too well known perhaps, for it seems
to have fostered a series of misrepresentations both of the jeremiad
and of the Puritan concept of errand.* For one thing, the New

---

* Students of the period, in what amounts to a ritual incantation of their own, have
told us over and again about the Puritans' "sense of impending doom" (Edward K.
Trefz, "The Puritans' View of History," *Boston Public Library Quarterly*, 9 [1957],
118), and have described in detail the "many clergymen in the pulpits of 1660–
1730 . . . trying to rub the strangeness from their eyes as if they had suddenly
returned to a society which . . . was full of new ways and strange gods" (A. William
Plumstead, Introduction to *The Wall and the Garden: Selected Massachusetts Election
Sermons, 1670–1775* [Minneapolis, 1968], ed. Plumstead, p. 30).

England jeremiad was plainly the product not of the second- and third-generation colonists, but of the first emigrants. Within the first decade of settlement, the clergy were already thundering denunciations of a backsliding people. The first election-day sermon we have warns the settlers against their apparent desire to choose "a captain back for Egypt." Two years earlier, and only six after the *Arbella* had landed, Thomas Shepard mourned that "We never looked for such days in *New-England*. . . . Are all [God's] kindnesses forgotten? all your promises forgotten?" During the 1670s, Increase Mather, bemoaning his own degenerate times, recalled that *"Our Prophets have foretold us of these dayes. . . . Renowned* Hooker *would many times express his fears*, that God would punish . . . New-England" — as did John Norton, and Peter Bulkeley, and John Davenport, and Richard Mather, and John Winthrop. Even the mild and "blessed Mr. *Cotton*, did in his time . . . testify against such a spirit of worldliness and Apostasy, even in those dayes prevailing in this Country."[4] Mather might easily have extended the list of first-generation worthies. Considered as a mode of denunciation, the jeremiad was an ancient formulaic refrain, a ritual form imported to Massachusetts in 1630 from the Old World. Insofar as the Puritan clergy were castigating the evils of the time, they were drawing directly upon the sermons of fifteenth- and sixteenth-century England, which in turn derived from the medieval pulpit.*

But the Puritan clergy were not simply castigating. For all their catalogues of iniquities, the jeremiads attest to an unswerving faith in the errand; and if anything they grow more fervent, more absolute in their commitment from one generation to the next. The most severe limitation of Miller's view is that it excludes (or denigrates) this pervasive theme of affirmation and exultation. Miller rightly called the New England jeremiad America's first distinctive literary genre; its distinctiveness, however, lies not in the vehemence of its complaint but in precisely the reverse. The essence of the sermon

---

*Coincidentally, in the year of the Cambridge Synod, 1679, the Anglican Bishop Gilbert Burnet invoked this long tradition and warned Englishmen (once again) that "the wrath of God hangs over our Heads. . . . The whole Nation is corrupted . . . [and] we may justly look for unheared of Calamities" (Preface to *The History of the Reformation in England*, Vol. I [London, 1683; first published 1679], sigs. A7ᵛ– A8ᵛ).

form that the first native-born American Puritans inherited from their fathers, and then "developed, amplified, and standardized,"[5] is its unshakable optimism. In explicit opposition to the traditional mode, it inverts the doctrine of vengeance into a promise of ultimate success, affirming to the world, and despite the world, the inviolability of the colonial cause.

The traditional mode, the European jeremiad, was a lament over the ways of the world. It decried the sins of "the people" — a community, a nation, a civilization, mankind in general — and warned of God's wrath to follow. Generation after generation, from the medieval era through the Renaissance, Catholic and then Protestant audiences heard the familiar refrain. The Lord required them to walk in righteousness, not to glory in the self; to follow His commandments, not the temptations of the flesh. So it had been in Eden, when Adam fell. So it had been in Jeremiah's time, when that most eloquent of Old Testament prophets railed against the stiff-necked Hebrews. So in Christ's time, when He denounced a generation of vipers, and in the age of the apostles and at the fall of Rome. All of history proved it: humanity was naturally depraved. It was the judgment of God after the flood, at the very moment when He decided not to destroy mankind after all, that "the imaginacion of mans heart *is* evil, *even* from his youth" (Genesis 8:21). The preachers used such texts in their jeremiads as moral lessons, but the texts themselves held out little hope, if any. As Hannah More put it in 1780, it was always "the fashion to make the most lamentable *Jeremiades* on the badness of times," because the times were always bad. Even as the preacher exhorted, they knew enough about their listeners not to expect much from them. Now again, as in Jeremiah's day, the mass of mankind would stumble and slide. Now as always, many were called but few chosen; and for the many, who willfully strayed from God (though He begged them through His prophets to return), there would be wailing and gnashing of teeth. "God writes his *severe truths* with the *blood* of his disobedient subjects."[6]

This sermon form the Puritans brought with them to Massachusetts Bay. But from the start they sounded a different note. Theirs was a peculiar mission, they explained, for they were a "peculiar people," a company of Christians not only called but chosen, and chosen not only for heaven but as instruments of a sacred historical design. Their church-state was to be at once a model to the world of Reformed Christianity and a prefiguration of New Jerusalem to come. To this end, they revised the message of the jeremiad. Not that they minimized the threat of divine retribution; on the contrary, they asserted it with a ferocity unparalleled in the European pulpit. But they qualified it in a way that turned threat into celebration. In their case, they believed, God's punishments were *corrective*, not destructive. Here, as nowhere else, His vengeance was a sign of love, a father's rod used to improve the errant child. In short, their punishments confirmed their promise. The Puritans did not seek out affliction, but where they found it they recorded it as zealously, and almost as gratefully, as they recorded instances of God's mercies toward them. The two kinds of "providences" were mutually sustaining;* together they opened out into the grand design of New England's errand into the wilderness.

Appropriately, this rhetoric of mission begins with the sermons delivered by Cotton and Winthrop to the *Arbella* passengers, between April and June 1630. As several recent scholars have noted, their very threats convey a series of figural correspondences that preclude the prospect of failure. Winthrop couched his remarks about God's vengeance in allusions to an "extraordinary work and end" based on an unalterable pledge. Though he voices the usual threats, in effect his scriptural phrases locate the venture within a configuration extending from Ararat, Sinai, and Pisgah to the New World city on a hill, and thence forward — in a "golden chain" of prophecy that "can never be broken" — to Mount Zion of the Apocalypse. With this intent, too, Cotton chose for his text the seventh chapter of the Second Book of Samuel: "I wil appoint a place for my people Israel, and wil plant it, that they may dwel in a place of their owne, and move nomore" (7:10) — a passage which, as his listeners well knew, included the promise of the millennium: "And thine house shalbe stablished and thy kingdome for ever before thee, *even* thy throne shalbe stablished for ever" (7:16). America, Cotton explained,

---

*This dualism has a long tradition behind it, of course. Flood and rainbow, exile and restoration, Christ *agonistes* and Christ glorified — nothing is more commonplace in Christian homiletics than the application of this dual image to sacred history. And nothing more flagrantly violates Christian tradition than the application of these texts to a civic community, engaged in a secular enterprise.

was the new promised land, reserved by God for His new chosen people as the site for a new heaven and a new earth. *A Model of Christian Charity* announces (in Loren Baritz's phrase) that all of history is converging upon "the cosmic climax of Boston's founding." More cogently still, *Gods Promise to His Plantation*, as Jesper Rosenmeier has shown, reveals "the Puritans' hopes that their plantation would become the scene of Christ's triumphant descent to His New Jerusalem."[7]

The American Puritan jeremiad owes its uniqueness to this vision and mode of rhetoric. In Europe, let me emphasize, the jeremiad pertained exclusively to mundane, social matters, to the city of man rather than the city of God. It required not conversion but moral obedience and civic virtue. At best, it held out the prospect of temporal, worldly success. At worst, it threatened not hellfire but secular calamity (disease, destruction, death). The Puritans' concept of errand entailed a fusion of secular and sacred history. The purpose of their jeremiads was to direct an imperiled people of God toward the fulfillment of their destiny, to guide them individually toward salvation, and collectively toward the American city of God.

To some extent, Miller acknowledged this sense of purpose. The Puritan jeremiads, he wrote, register

> bewilderment, confusion, chagrin but there is no surrender. A task has been assigned upon which the populace are in fact intensely engaged . . . [Thus] while the social or economic historian may read this literature for its contents — and so construct from the expanding catalogue of denunciations a record of social progress — the cultural anthropologist will look slightly askance at these jeremiads. If you read them all through, the total effect, curiously enough, is not at all depressing: you come to the paradoxical realization that they do not bespeak a despairing frame of mind . . . whatever they may signify in the realm of theology, in that of psychology they are purgations of the soul; they do not discourage but actually encourage the community to persist in its heinous conduct. The exhortation to a reformation which never materializes serves as a token payment upon the obligation, and so liberates the debtors. Changes there had to be: adaptations to environment, expansion of the frontier, mansions constructed, commercial ventures undertaken. These activities were not specifically nominated in the bond Winthrop had framed. They were thrust upon the society

> by American experience. . . . Land speculation meant not only
> wealth but dispersion of the people, and what was to stop the march of
> settlements? . . . [The first emigrants] had been utterly oblivious of
> what the fact of the frontier would do. . . . Hence I suggest that
> under the guise of this mounting wail of sinfulness, this incessant and
> never successful cry for repentance, the Puritans launched themselves
> upon the process of Americanization.[8]

I have quoted this passage at length because it so clearly shows the
grounds of Miller's analysis. What he meant by ambiguity was opposition: the errand is either for oneself or for someone else; the
jeremiads either discourage or encourage. Clearly, this stems from a
"paradoxical realization" that somehow the errand functioned both
ways, and that the jeremiads included both threat and hope. But for
Miller the realization is an ironic one — it lies in the reader's capacity
to see conflicting elements at work in the same act. The Puritans'
sense of a failed errand, he claimed, led them to make the errand
their own. Their "cry for repentance" furthered the community's
"heinous conduct." And the reader's ironic awareness, in turn,
builds upon a series of static oppositions: content versus form, social
progress versus catalogues of denunciation, psychology versus
theology, the march of settlements versus the ideal of theocracy, and
summarily "the American experience" (manifest in land speculation,
growing wealth, population dispersion) versus the Puritan lament, a
"mounting wail of sinfulness" that issues in a self-defeating ritual of
purgation. Methodologically, this implies the dichotomy of fact and
rhetoric. Historically, it posits an end to Puritanism with the collapse of the church-state. From either perspective, in what is surely a
remarkable irony in its own right, Miller's analysis lends support to
the dominant anti-Puritan view of national development — that the
"American character" was shaped by what he called "the fact of the
frontier."*

We need not discount the validity of this frontier thesis to see
what it does *not* explain: the persistence of the Puritan jeremiad

---

*The phrase seems to me especially striking (and ironic) in that Miller, in his
prefatory notes to "Errand into the Wilderness" (1952), takes issue on Ramistic
grounds with what he calls Turner's misguided notion of the relation between
metaphor and fact. Miller adds that he himself has used *errand* and *wilderness* "as
figures of speech" (*Errand into the Wilderness* [Cambridge, Mass., 1956], p. 2).

throughout the eighteenth and nineteenth centuries, in all forms of the literature, including the literature of westward expansion. Indeed, what first attracted me to the study of the jeremiad was my astonishment, as a Canadian immigrant, at learning about the prophetic history of America. Not of North America, for the prophecies stopped short at the Canadian and Mexican borders, but of a country that, despite its arbitrary territorial limits, could read its destiny in its landscape, and a population that, despite its bewildering mixture of race and creed, could believe in something called an American mission, and could invest that patent fiction with all the emotional, spiritual, and intellectual appeal of a religious quest. I felt then like Sancho Panza in a land of Don Quixotes. Here was the anarchist Thoreau condemning his backsliding neighbors by reference to the Westward errand; here, the solitary singer Walt Whitman, claiming to be the American Way; here, the civil rights leader Martin Luther King, descendant of slaves, denouncing segregation as a violation of the American dream; here, an endless debate about national identity, full of rage and faith, Jeffersonians claiming that they, and not the priggish heirs of Calvin, really represented the errand, conservative politicians hunting out socialists as conspirators against the dream, left-wing polemics proving that capitalism was a betrayal of the country's sacred origins. The question in these latter-day jeremiads, as in their seventeenth-century precursors, was never "Who are we?" but, almost in deliberate evasion of that question, the old prophetic refrain: "When is our errand to be fulfilled? How long, O Lord, how long?" And the answers, again as in the Puritan jeremiads, invariably joined lament and celebration in reaffirming America's mission.

This litany of hope seems to me a direct challenge to Miller's concept of ambiguity. Perhaps the clearest way to show this is to recall the great election-day address which he used as proof text for his analysis, Samuel Danforth's *Brief Recognition of New England's Errand into the Wilderness*. Danforth delivered the address in May 1670, exactly forty years after the *Arbella* fleet landed, and no one at that emotional gathering felt more keenly than Danforth that the new promised land was far from won. Yet what he said then remains one of the most impassioned statements on record of the *persistence* of the founders' dream. Taking his text from Christ's "encomium of

John the Baptist" (Matthew 11:7–9), Danforth praises the errand as a migration from a "soft" civilization to the purity of the "wilderness-condition."* To forsake worldly vanities for Christ, he points out, is the mark of every believer, in any time or place, and accordingly he invests the errand with the general import of *pilgrimage*. "What went ye out into the wilderness to see?" becomes the Christian's ultimate challenge: "What must I do to be saved in the wilderness of this world?" "How shall I seek the spirit through the wilderness of my own hard heart and recalcitrant will?" The subject was wholly fitting to the occasion. Election days in the Puritan church-state were a civic affair, but an affair nonetheless reserved for the regenerate and their children. Drawn by their spiritual calling, they had gathered together and shipped for America. They had built their theocracy to serve God. Like all saints, Danforth reminded them, ' they needed constantly to rededicate themselves to the errand *within*, from self to Chrst.[9]

The rhetorical effect here may be termed ambiguous, but emphatically not in the sense of contradiction. Danforth is not posing an alternative between pilgrimage and migration, but offering a reconciliation. His terms are not *either/or* but *both/and*. They imply the union of saint and society, the spiritual and the historical errand; and in this context they lead him to still another ambiguity. The parallels that Danforth urges upon his listeners, between John the Baptist and Danforth the preacher, between the Arabian and the New England desert, develop into a sweeping prophetic comparison — of the errand then, at the birth of Christianity, with the errand now, to bring history itself to an end. In this sense, *errand* means *progress*. It denotes the church's gradual conquest of Satan's wilderness world for Christ. Significantly, Danforth's exegesis devolves neither on "errand" nor on "wilderness," but as it were beyond these on the relative merit of John the Baptist.† The question "What went ye out for to see?" is "determined and concluded," Danforth points out,

*This literalist application, with its suggestion of new beginnings — and indirectly, perhaps, its insinuation of New England's *loss* of purity — may seem to support Miller's thesis. But it is only the starting point of Danforth's exegesis, and in fact becomes part of the rhetorical strategy designed to explain away the threat.

†*Errand* and *wilderness* remain Danforth's central terms, of course, but his explication is historical and progressivist — typological rather than archetypal. The biblical text reads:

when Christ describes John as "A prophet . . . and more than a prophet." The Baptist, that is, resembles *and supersedes* his predecessors; his role as exemplum is at once recapitulative and prospective.

> John was the Christ's herald sent immediately before his face to proclaim his coming and kingdom and prepare the people for the reception of him. . . . John was greater than any of the prophets that were before him, not in respect of his personal graces and virtues (for who shall persuade us that he excelled Abraham in the grace of faith . . . or Moses in meekness . . . or David in faithfulness . . . or Solomon in wisdom . . . ?), but in respect of the manner of his dispensation. All the prophets foretold Christ's coming, his sufferings and glory, but the Baptist was the harbinger and forerunner. . . . All the prophets saw Christ afar off, but the Baptist saw him present, baptized him, and applied the types to him personally. . . . "But he that is least in the kingdom of heaven is greater than John" (Mat. 11.11; Luke 7.28). The least prophet in the kingdom of heaven, i.e., the least minister of the Gospel since Christ's ascension, is greater than John; not in respect of the measure of his personal gifts nor in respect of the manner of his calling, but in respect of the . . . degree of the revelation of Christ, which is far more clear and full . . . than in the day when John the Baptist arose like a bright and burning light . . . proclaiming the coming and kingdom of the Messiah (which had oft been promised and long expected).[10]

All the prophets saw Christ. Who could excel Abraham or Moses? — this is history seen in the eye of eternity. All the faithful, Danforth is saying, are one in Christ; the errand here in New England is that of any other saint, or group of saints; the American wilderness no different essentially from that of Moses or John the Baptist. And yet the passage makes the difference abundantly clear. Sacred history unfolds in a series of stages or *dispensations*, each with its own (increasingly *greater*) *degree of revelation*. Hence the insistent temporality of the rhetoric: *prepare, foretold, herald, harbinger, forerunner*, and summarily *types*. Finally, Danforth insists, there are crucial dis-

---

What went ye out into the wildernes to se? A reed shaken with the winde?

But what went ye out to se? A man clothed in soft raiment? Beholde, they that weare soft clothing, are in Kings houses.

But what went ye out to se? A Prophet? Yea, I say unto you, and more then a Prophet. (Matthew 11:7–9)

criminations to be made. All of the Old Testament is an errand to
the New; and all of history after the Incarnation, an errand to
Christ's Second Coming. It leads from promise to fulfillment: from
Moses to John the Baptist to Samuel Danforth; from the Old World
to the New; from Israel in Canaan to New Israel in America; from
Adam to Christ to the Second Adam of the Apocalypse. The wilderness that Danforth invokes is "typical" of New England's situation above all in that it reveals the dual nature of the errand as
prophecy. In fulfilling the type, New England becomes itself a harbinger of things to come. Like John the Baptist, though with a
brighter and fuller degree of revelation, the Puritan colony is a light
proclaiming the latter-day coming of the Messiah, a herald sent to
prepare the world to receive His often-promised, long-expected
Kingdom.

For Danforth, in short, *errand* has the ambiguity of the *figura*. It
unites allegory and chronicle in the framework of the work of redemption.* And in doing so, it redefines the meaning not only of

---

*This figural use of John the Baptist is a characteristic of the New England pulpit,
and part of the Puritan legacy to American rhetoric. For example, in a sermon on the
importance of the social covenant, Thomas Hooker explains that "John Baptist was
sent to prepare the way, that all the crooked things might be made streight. This is
nothing else but the taking away of that knotty knarliness of the heart, that the King
of Glory may come in" (*The Soules Humiliation* [London, 1637], p. 2; ellipses deleted).
Or again, Edward Johnson describes the Great Migration in terms of a conversion
experience, by picturing one of the emigrants saying: "I am now prest for the service
of our Lord Christ to re-build the most glorious Edifice of Mount Sion in a Wilderness, and as John Baptist, I must cry, Prepare yee the way of the Lord, make his paths
strait, for behold hee is comming againe, hee is comming to destroy Antichrist"
(*Wonder-Working Providence* [1654], ed. J. Franklin Jameson [New York, 1910], pp.
51–52; ellipses deleted). A year before Danforth's election-day sermon, Increase
Mather, in a treatise on the chiliad, wrote that "there was a partial and typical
fulfillment of [the errand] . . . in the Ministry of John Baptist" (*The Mystery of Israel's
Salvation* [London, 1669], p. 102); and he kept expounding this figural progression
throughout his career. "John the Baptist arose like a bright and shining light"; another,
brighter light shone forth to reveal Christ when the Reformation began; and to bring
that brighter light to its full brilliancy was "the end of our coming hither" to America
(*Morning Star*, appended to *The Righteous Man* [Boston, 1702], pp. 71, 75–76). So, too,
Jonathan Edwards explained that while "John the Baptist was the day-star to usher in
the day," American evangelicals would shortly "enjoy day-light" itself, wherein
"Christ is actually come" (*Works*, ed. Sereno E. Dwight [New York, 1830], VIII,
555). About a century later Emerson, with similar enthusiasm, acclaimed "the new
voices in the [American] wilderness crying 'Repent'" (*Works*, ed. Edward Waldo

errand but of every term in *New England's Errand into the Wilderness*. The newness of New England becomes both literal and eschatalogical, and (in what was surely the most far-reaching of these rhetorical effects) the American *wilderness* takes on the double significance of secular and sacred place. If for the individual believer it remained part of the wilderness of the world, for God's "peculiar people" it was a territory endowed with special symbolic import, like the wilderness through which the Israelites passed to the promised land. In one sense it was historical, in another sense prophetic; and as Nicholas Noyes explained, in a sermon on the errand three decades after Danforth's, *"Prophesie* is *Historie antedated*; and *Historie* is *Postdated Prophesie*: the same thing is told in both."[11] For these American Jeremiahs, and all their second- and third-generation colleagues, the ambiguity confirmed the founders' design. They dwelt on it, dissected it, elaborated upon it, because it opened for them into a triumphant assertion of their destiny, migration and pilgrimage entwined in the progress of New England's holy commonwealth.

From that figural vantage point Danforth condemns the colonists' shortcomings and justifies their afflictions. "We have . . . in a great measure forgotten our errand," he charges, invoking the familiar precedent:

> The Lord foreseeing the defection of Israel after Moses his death, commands him to write that prophetical song recorded in Deuteronomy 32 as a testimony against them, wherein the chief remedy which he prescribes for the prevention and healing of their apostasy is their calling to remembrance God's great and signal love in manifesting himself to them in the wilderness, in conducting them safely and mercifully, and giving them possession of their promised inheritance (ver. 7–14). And when Israel was apostatized and fallen, the Lord, to convince them of their ingratitude and folly, brings to their remembrance his deliverance of them out of Egypt, his leading them through the wilderness for the space of forty years, and not only giving them possession of their enemies' land but also raising up even of their own sons, prophets . . . all which were great and obliging mercies.

Emerson [Boston, 1903–4], I, 272). And later still Horace Bushnell portrayed the Bay emigrants as men "cleansed by the Baptist of the heart," who crossed "the sea in God's name only, sent by Him . . . to be the voice of one crying in the wilderness — Prepare ye the way of the Lord, make his paths straight," so that "the new kingdom of the Lord, will come" (*Work and Play* [New York, 1881], p. 139).

The ambiguities of the biblical parallel not only obviate the threat but transform self-doubt into consolation. "Apostasy" itself serves as the prelude to deliverance. For as every member of Danforth's audience knew, Moses' "prophetical song" was addressed to those who were to inherit the millennial kingdom.* And Danforth underscores this meaning by comparing New England's "howling wilderness" with that of Moses and John the Baptist. The story of all three errands was one of ingratitude, folly, and backsliding, but the progression itself, from one errand to the next, attested to a process of fulfillment. Moses' rebuke was really a "remedy," Christ's "admonition" above all a "direction how to recover," and Danforth's lament an affirmation of God's "great and obliging mercies" to New England. And the affirmation, in Danforth's case as in the others, is unequivocal, absolute. He assures the colonists of success not because of their efforts, but God's: "the great Physician of Israel hath undertaken the cure . . . he will provide . . . we have the promise."[12]

In all this, Danforth's strategy is characteristic of the American jeremiad throughout the seventeenth century: first, a precedent from Scripture that sets out the communal norms; then, a series of condemnations that details the actual state of the community (at the same time insinuating the covenantal promises that ensure success); and finally a prophetic vision that unveils the promises, announces the good things to come, and explains away the gap between fact and ideal. Perry Miller seems to have understood this form as a triptych, a static three-part configuration in which the centerpiece, considered merely as lament, conveys the meaning of the whole. So interpreted, the New England sermons embody a cyclical view of history: the futile, recurrent rise and fall of nations that sustained the traditional jeremiad. But the rhetoric itself suggests something different. It posits a movement from promise to experience — from the ideal of community to the shortcomings of community life — and thence forward, with prophetic assurance, toward a resolution that incorporates (as it transforms) both the promise and the condemnation. The

---

*The traditional interpretation of this passage was that Moses was asking the saints, Christ's spiritual Israel, to praise God for the approaching millennium and "for their deliverance from *Mystical Babylon*, that had detained them in spiritual bondage" (Urian Oakes, *New England Pleaded With* [Cambridge, Mass., 1673], p. 3).

dynamic of the errand, that is, involves a use of ambiguity which is not divisive but progressive — or more accurately, progressive because it denies divisiveness — and which is therefore impervious to the reversals of history, since the very meaning of progress is inherent in the rhetoric itself.

This errand into ambiguity, if I may call it so, speaks directly to the contrast Miller posited between rhetoric and history. What Miller meant by history was the course of events — the "process of Americanization" — that led to the theocracy's decline; by rhetoric, he meant the lament — "unremitting and never successful" — over a failed enterprise. Thus while he stressed the affirmative "psychology" of the Puritan sermons, he interpreted the sermons themselves as certain psychologists interpret wish-fulfillment dreams. What counts is not the happy ending but the conflicts that prompted the need for fantasy in the first place. The conflicts are "real," the happy ending transparently a means to something else — avoidance, compensation, substitute gratification, or simply self-delusion. Now, the fact of the theocracy's decline is incontrovertible. But we need not interpret it as Miller does. His "Errand into the Wilderness" is a hail and farewell to the Puritan vision. Danforth's *Errand into the Wilderness* attests to the orthodoxy's refusal to abandon the vision, and the fact is that the vision survived — from colony to province, and from province to nation. The fact is, furthermore, that it survived through a mode of ambiguity that denied the contradiction between history and rhetoric — or rather translated this into a discrepancy between appearance and promise that nourished the imagination, inspired ever grander flights of self-justification, and so continued to provide a source of social cohesion and continuity. In fact, that is, the New England orthodoxy succeeded, precisely through their commitment to the Puritan ideal, in transmitting a myth that remained central to the culture long after the theocracy had faded and New England itself had lost its national influence.

So perceived, the evidence presents us with a different perspective on the relation between rhetoric and history. Even if we grant that the jeremiads were a form of wish fulfillment — even if we agree with Miller that their rhetoric served as a "guise" for "real" conflicts

— we need not see them in opposition to the course of events.* Suppose, for example, that the wish fulfillment or disguise is in fact profoundly relevant to those conflicts. What if it actually offers a resolution of sorts, a *realistic* way to deal with crisis and change, and so becomes a source not only of revitalization but of rededication as well? Miller likened the second-generation Puritans to a husband who, while on an errand for his wife, discovers that his wife has forgotten all about her request — or worse still, denies she ever made a request at all. The analogy is accurate so far as it goes. But suppose the husband simply refuses to acknowledge the mistake. What if he persuades himself that his errand has nothing to do with his wife — and that in fact *he is correct*? What if, moreover, he does not harbor that "fantasy" in secret, like Walter Mitty, but proudly declares it to others, and for sound, pragmatic reasons — reasons that conform to the "real" course of events — *persuades them too*?

I am suggesting that "the process of Americanization" began not with the decline of Puritanism but with the Great Migration, and that the jeremiad, accordingly, played a significant role in the development of what was to become modern middle-class American culture. I hope that in suggesting this I do not seem to be overstraining the worn links between Puritanism and the rise of capitalism. My point is simply that certain elements in Puritanism lent themselves powerfully to that conjunction, and precisely those elements came to the fore when the Bay emigrants severed their ties with the feudal forms of Old England and set up a relatively fluid society on the American strand — a society that devalued aristocracy, denounced beggary, and opened up political, educational, and

---

*Part of my disagreement with Miller in this respect stems from our different sense of the Puritans' use of language. According to Miller, the Puritans "strove with might and main to chain their language to logical propositions, and to penetrate to the affections of their auditors only by thrusting an argument through their reason"; therefore, "any criticism which endeavors to discuss Puritan writings as part of literary history . . . is approaching the materials in a spirit they were never intended to accommodate" (*The New England Mind: From Colony to Province* [1953; rpt. Boston, 1961], p. 12; *The New England Mind: The Seventeenth Century* [1939; rpt. Boston, 1961], p. 362). My own view is closer to that of William Haller: "the strength of the Puritan pamphleteers did not lie . . . in a greater power of lucid and coherent thought but in their command of the art of suggestive, provocative, poetic speech" (*The Rise of Puritanism* [New York, 1957], p. 256).

commercial opportunities to a relatively broad spectrum of the population.

The argument has been demonstrated elsewhere so persuasively as hardly to need comment here. Tocqueville's well-known views on this matter are representative of a host of others, from Adam Smith through Friedrich Engels down to a variety of historians in our own time.

It was in the states of New England, that the two or three main principles now forming the basic social theory of the United States were combined. . . . [These] colonies as they came to birth seemed destined to let freedom grow, not the aristocratic freedom of their motherland, but a middle-class and democratic freedom of which the world's history had not previously provided a complete example. . . .
The foundation of New England was something new in the world. Puritanism was almost as much a political theory as a religious doctrine. No sooner had the immigrants landed than they made it their first care to organize themselves as a society . . . [through which] a middling standard has been established in America . . . [in all areas —] religion, history, science, political economy, legislation, and government. In England the nucleus of the Puritan movement continued to be in the middle classes, and it was from those classes that most of the emigrants sprang. The population of New England grew fast, and while in their homeland men were despotically divided by class hierarchies, the colony came more and more to present the novel phenomenon of a society homogeneous in all its parts. Democracy more perfect than any of which antiquity had dared to dream sprang full-grown and fully armed from the midst of the old feudal society. . . . [In this sense,] the whole destiny of America [is] contained in the first Puritan who landed on these shores, as that of the whole human race in the first man.[13]

Tocqueville was making the point by hyperbole, but the point itself is valid enough to suggest a fundamental truth about our culture. The economists Douglass North and Robert Thomas have shown that "the colonization of [Anglo-]America was a direct outgrowth of . . . the decline of feudalism." The philosopher Ralph Barton Perry has argued the "affinity" of "Puritan individualism . . . with laissez-faire capitalism." The historian Robert E. Brown has pointed out that "property was [so] easily acquired" in New England that "the great majority of men could easily meet the requirements" for political franchise.[14] These and many similar quantitative differences between Old and New England are symptomatic, I believe, of a sweeping qualitative distinction between America and all other modern countries. In England (and the Old World generally), capitalism was an economic system that evolved dialectically, through conflict with earlier and persistent ways of life and belief. Basically New England bypassed the conflict. This is by no means to say that conflict was avoided altogether. On the contrary: the first century of New England history is a remarkable instance of rapid social change, involving widespread moral, psychic, and political tensions. The emergent structures of a free-enterprise economy did not all at once transform the guild and craft mentality; for a time mercantile capitalism actually helped maintain aristocratic privilege; for an even longer time pre-modern modes of social and familial relationship resisted the commercial revolution underway in the Northern Anglo-American colonies. But by and large the resistance was as ineffectual as it was anachronistic. It signified not a contest between an established and an evolving system, but a troubled period of maturation. The emigrant leaders did not give up their class prerogatives when they landed at Massachusetts Bay, and yet the forms they instituted tended to erode traditional forms of deference. They restricted opportunity in commerce and property ownership, yet social power in the colony increasingly shifted to the commercial and property-owning classes. In all fundamental ideological aspects, New England was from the start an outpost of the modern world. It evolved from its own origins, as it were, into a middle-class culture — a commercially oriented economy buttressed by the decline of European feudalism, unhampered by lingering traditions of aristocracy and crown, and sustained by the prospect (if not always the fact) of personal advancement — a relatively homogeneous society whose enterprise was consecrated, according to its civic and clerical leadership, by a divine plan of progress.

I think it can be said without hyperbole that the process of consecration began with the two prototypic American jeremiads of 1630. Winthrop's "Model" of social cohesion derived from a doctrine of vocational calling which (by implication at least) undermined the tenets of feudal hierarchy by its appeal to self-discipline and self-sufficiency.* Cotton defended "God's Promise to His Plantations" through analogies to commerce for "gaine-sake":

> *Daily bread may be sought from farre.* Yea our Saviour approveth travaile for Merchants, when hee compareth a Christian to a Merchantman seeking pearles. . . . Nature teacheth Bees . . . when as the hive is too full . . . [to] seeke abroad for new dwellings: So when the hive of the Common wealth is so full, that Tradesmen cannot live one by another, but eate up one another, in this case it is lawfull to remove. . . . God alloweth a man to remove, when he may employ his Talents and gifts better elsewhere, especially when where he is, he is not bound by any speciall engagement. Thus God sent *Joseph* before to preserve the Church: *Josephs* wisdome and spirit was not fit for a shepherd, but for a Counsellour of State.[15]

---

*In discussing the "radical criticism" involved in the theory of vocational calling, Michael Walzer notes that the Puritans excluded unproductive or parasitic classes, and that they tried to motivate the "godly poor" into becoming "self-sufficient and presumably self-disciplined men" (*The Revolution of the Saints* [Cambridge, Mass., 1965], pp. 215–17). Compare Franklin's account of "the general Mediocrity of Fortune in America" (*Writings*, ed. A. H. Smyth [New York, 1905–7], VIII, 603–14), or the anonymous account of "independency," "industry," and self-advancement in New versus Old England, in *American Husbandry* (London, 1775), I, 61–62, 187–88; or again, Crèvecoeur's famous description of the pre-Revolutionary American farmer, "honest, sober and industrious," "exalted" by independence and "the bright idea of property," and secure in the sense that America is the land "for men of middle stations" and the aspiring poor (*Letters from an American Farmer*, ed. Warren B. Blake [New York, 1957], 73, 30, 63; see also p. 46). Franklin's work shows how "the conservative tradition" of vocational calling could reinforce the "progressivist" tradition of open competition (John Cawelti, *Apostles of the Self-Made Man* [Chicago, 1965], p. 5). In all three works, the idea of "American husbandry" contrasts forcefully with the European idea of peasantry — a contrast that may be traced from the earliest descriptions of colonial agrarianism, at least in the Northern Anglo-American settlements. This is not to deny the dramatic social and economic changes from the seventeenth to the eighteenth century. Richard Bushman, who has examined those changes in Connecticut, specifies 1690 as a dividing line between Puritan and Yankee New England; but he also tells us that "the situation began to change" in "the last quarter of the seventeenth century," that the changes represented a broad "impulse [already] present but checked in 1690," and that "No sudden mutation caused them to appear." In sum, the Yankee was not so much a "new man" as a "freer man than his Puritan progenitors, for he could acknowledge to himself and to the world more of what he was" (*From Puritan to Yankee: Character and the Social Order in Connecticut, 1690–1765* [New York, 1967], pp. 37, 288).

Cotton's analogies, like Winthrop's concept of vocation, bespeak a moment of cultural transition: they reflect an earlier ideal of class deference while foreshadowing later developments toward free enterprise. But in both cases the direction is unmistakable. All of Cotton's examples, from nature and the Bible, are geared toward sanctifying an errand of entrepreneurs whose aim is religion, or, *mutatis mutandis*, legalizing an errand of saints whose aim is entrepreneurial.

In this respect a direct line may be traced from the first emigrants to the latter-day Jeremiahs. It runs from John Cotton to (say) Cotton Mather, who used Joseph as a model for his rags-to-riches stories of famous New Englanders,* and who defended "regulated *Usury*" by reference to nature, to the Old and New Testaments, and to "the *Law of Necessity* and *Utility*" whereby "a man should expect something for [his own] support and comfort . . . from the *profitable use*, which other men make of those things whereof he is himself the proprietor." Danforth too espoused these assumptions. In fact, they are intrinsic to the message of *New England's Errand into the Wilderness*. "John preached in the wilderness, which was no fit place for silken and soft raiment," Danforth observes, because the Baptist's "work was to prepare a people for the Lord." How could he do so amidst the "superfluous ornaments," the "delicate and costly apparel [of] . . . princes courts"? This is neither a plea for the sanctity of poverty nor a summons to some ascetic retreat from the world. Nor is it merely a denunciation of the rich, in the manner of the Old Testament prophets. In effect, Danforth is urging upon New Israel the middle way of the Protestant ethic, reinforcing Cotton's analogies

---

*For example, the biographies of Theophilus Eaton and Sir William Phips in the *Magnalia*. The theory behind these biographies is Mather's famous proto-Franklinesque sermon on the business vocation: "Would a man *Rise* by his Business? I say, then let him *Rise* to his Business. It was foretold. Prov. 22. 29, *Seest thou a man Diligent in his Business? He shall stand* before Kings; He shall come to preferment. . . . *Young* man, work hard while you are *Young*: You'l reap the effects of it when you are *Old*. . . . Let your *Business* ingross the most of your time" (Cotton Mather, *Two Brief Discourses* [Boston, 1695], p. 48). The parallels are plentiful in John Cotton's writings, including even his apocalyptic sermons — as in the threats he draws from Revelation 16: "the Lord will powr out a Viall upon [our cattle], that from 25^1. they shall fall to 5^1. price" (*The Powring Out of the Seven Vialls* [London, 1642], p. 26).

and Winthrop's model of vocation by reminding his audience that the prophecies they inherited, their promised future, entailed "the values of piety, frugality, and diligence in one's worldly calling." Economically as well as figurally, it was their mission to leave a "soft" Old World order, with its "courtly pomp and decay," for a "purer" kind of society, one that would provide them with the proper means for both "respectable competence in this world and eternal salvation in the world to come."[16]

So understood, the nature of the errand goes far toward explaining the distinctive form and function of the American Puritan jeremiad. The European jeremiad developed within a static hierarchical order; the lessons it taught, about historical recurrence and the vanity of human wishes, amounted to a massive ritual reinforcement of tradition. Its function was to make social practice conform to a completed and perfected social ideal. The American Puritan jeremiad was the ritual of a culture on an errand — which is to say, a culture based on a faith in process. Substituting teleology for hierarchy, it discarded the Old World ideal of stasis for a New World vision of the future.* Its function was to create a climate of anxiety that helped release the restless "progressivist" energies required for the success of the venture. The European jeremiad also thrived on anxiety, of course. Like all "traditionalist" forms of ritual, it used fear and trembling to teach acceptance of fixed social norms. But the American Puritan jeremiad went much further. It made anxiety its end as well as its means. Crisis was the social norm it sought to inculcate. The very concept of errand, after all, implied a state of *un*fulfillment. The future, though divinely assured, was never quite there, and New England's Jeremiahs set out to provide the sense of insecurity that would ensure the outcome. Denouncing or affirming, their vision fed on the distance between promise and fact.

*Clinton Rossiter offers an excellent overview of this system from within the ideological premises of the culture: "Classes in America are stages rather than castes. . . . In specific terms, this means the steady growth, relative to all other classes, of an ever more prosperous and secure middle class. . . . The best of all classes — in many ways, the only class that counts — is the middle class. The performance of any institution is to be judged finally in terms of how well it serves to expand or strengthen or reward this class" ("The Relevance of Marxism," in *Failure of a Dream? Essays in the History of Socialism*, ed. John H. M. Laslett and Seymour M. Lipset [New York, 1974], pp. 474–75).

I need hardly say that they were not reveling in crisis for its own sake. Anxiety was one result of the ritual, its day-by-day aspect. The other aspect, equally crucial to the concept of errand, was direction and purpose. Together, these two elements define the ritual import of the jeremiad: to sustain process by imposing control, and to justify control by presenting a certain form of process as the only road to the future kingdom. The emphasis on control speaks directly to the tensions I mentioned earlier, underlying the *Arbella* sermons by Cotton and Winthrop. As Christopher Hill points out, in arguing the connection between Cromwell's revolution and the growth of the English middle class, Puritanism served in important ways to harness "the turbulent force of individualism." That force was nowhere more turbulently manifest than in Puritan New England, a colony of radical dissenters — militant, apocalyptic, "irrepressibly particularistic and anti-authoritarian."* In 1630, Edmund Morgan notes, "emigration offered a substitute for revolution."[17] But the hazards of settlement required the colonial leaders to seek a more permanent substitute. They found it, after a precarious beginning, in the New England Way of church-state, a sort of institutionalized migration, consciously modeled on the pattern of exodus. And they sought to enforce their Way through what proved to be perhaps their most durable creation, the ritual of the jeremiad.

Danforth's sermon testifies eloquently to its distinctive qualities. In contrast to traditionalist rituals, the New England Puritan jeremiad evokes the mythic past not merely to elicit imitation but above all to demand progress. The fathers, says Danforth, were mighty men, as were Moses and John the Baptist — unexcelled in their piety, wisdom, and fervor — but the errand they began leads *us* toward a *higher, brighter dispensation*. Precisely because of their greatness, we have a sacred duty to go beyond them. To venerate and emulate is to supersede; in God's New Canaan all of life is a passage to something greater. This outlook obviously derives from Protes-

---

*Herbert Lüthy presents a powerful, if rather extreme, image of such "Calvinist communities," from Geneva to Puritan New England, inspired by an "incorrigible Republican spirit," which became "the most dynamic factor in the rise of Western society" (*From Calvin to Rousseau*, trans. Salvator Atmosis [New York, 1970], p. 52). The complementary side of this was, of course, the Puritan emphasis on order in family, church, and commonwealth.

tant ritual. One need only think of Bunyan's Pilgrim, Christian, whose lifelong progress is shaped by a series of crises that point him forever forward toward a single preordained goal. But Christian's crises, like those of every Reformed Christian, are personal and eschatological; they involve the conflict between the "temptations" of society and the demands of faith, between temporal commitments and last things. More often than not, therefore, Christian finds himself defying social authority. The society to which he conforms instead is the community of the elect, wherever they happen to be, journeying from a wicked world to their heavenly home. And the journey, moreover, is essentially retrospective — an *imitatio Christi*, patterned after the completed and perfected progress of the biblical Jesus. Christian advances with his eyes fixed on the past. The New England Puritans fixed their gaze on the future. Christ's victory over Satan, they stressed, was itself a shadow or type of His greater victory to come, when He would usher in the millennium; and accordingly they grounded their covenant in prophecies still to be fulfilled. Even as they strove individually to imitate Christ, they invested their hopes in the success of their venture. In short, they absorbed the personal into the social errand. What for others was an ideational structure — the *New World* of regeneration, the *promised land* of heaven, the *wilderness* of temptation, the *garden* of the spirit — was for Danforth and his colleagues a political reality, the civic, religious, and economic structures of a covenanted New World society.

The contrast has far-reaching implications. Both Bunyan's Christian and the New England saint are on an errand — constantly "betwixt and between," forever at the brink of some momentous decision — but *as rituals* their errands tend in opposite directions. The ritual that Bunyan adopts leads Christian into what anthropologists call a "liminal state," a sort of cultural no-man's-land, where all social norms may be challenged.[18] And given the Calvinist tenet that salvation is a lifelong enterprise, it is an errand fraught with all the religious and economic dangers of unfettered individualism: the excesses both of antinomianism and of self-interest. The American Puritan jeremiads seek (in effect) to prevent these excesses by turning liminality itself into a mode of socialization. Their errand entails a ritual that obviates the traditional distinctions between preparation for salvation and social conformity — a carefully regulated process in which the fear for one's soul is a function of historical progress, moral discipline a means simultaneously to personal and social success, and success a matter of constant anxiety about the venture into the future. And more than that. The ritual of errand enforces an identity that is at once transitional and representative; it identifies the community's "true fathers" not by their English background but by their exodus from Europe to the American strand; it establishes a mode of consensus by calling and enterprise rather than by (say) national tradition or genealogical patterns; and it implies a form of community without geographical boundaries, since the *wilderness* is by definition unbounded, the *terra profana* "out there" yet to be conquered, step by inevitable step, by the advancing armies of Christ.

In all this, as it turned out, the Puritan concept of errand was well suited to the process of Americanization.* I am speaking, of course, of implication and effect. According to Huizinga, "the factors that have dominated European history are almost absent from American history. . . . No stumps from a feudal forest remained, still rooted everywhere in the soil, as in Europe." Again, the formulation seems to me too strong. In one sense, the Massachusetts Bay theocracy *was* a stump transplanted from a feudal forest. In many of its specific attributes, the Puritan state was obviously transitional, the substance of a new social order encased in squirearchical and quasibiblical forms. By 1670, when Danforth delivered his election-day address, the New England Jeremiahs were already on the defensive. The aspiring merchant class and the landholding "lay brethren of the congregation" were challenging clerical control with increasing success — or better, increasingly assuming control in face of the in-

---

*In a recent essay, Michael Zuckerman has argued that in the early colonies "both the self-assertion that inform the modern psyche and the coercive mutuality that marks the modern community achieved something of their subsequent scope. . . . Communities made excessive claims of concord for themselves and then fell into a dismayed sense of declension whenever they failed to sustain such ideological aspirations" ("The Fabrication of Identity in Early America," *William and Mary Quarterly*, 34 [1977], 184–85). I would add that this dual tendency is particularly a Puritan characteristic, and that the New England Puritans contributed in particular to modernization through a rhetorical mode specifically devised to transform a "dismayed sense of declension" into a ritual of cultural aspiration.

adequacy of theocratic forms. In 1669, a Third Church of Boston was formed by a group of tradesmen who dissented from the orthodox First Church. Shortly after, Richard Bellingham, the "sternest" of the Old Guard magistrates that followed John Winthrop to the post of governor, expressed his fear of "sudden tumult," and his council warned against "an invasion of the rights, liberties, and privileges of churches."[19] Only twenty of the fifty deputies in the General Court of 1669 were reelected in 1670. The issues of the Halfway Covenant threatened a widespread generational rift. Whether or not all this indicated a decline in piety, as Danforth and his colleagues wailed, the colonists were forcing the institutions they lived under to comply openly with the political and economic realities of their New World society.

In this sense, there is some justice in Perry Miller's ironic image of the Old Guard "backing into modernity," at the end of the seventeenth century, in "crablike progress" from an "aristocratic" order to "a middle-class empirical enterprising society." But his irony tends to obscure the fact that the New England Way was above all (to recall Huizinga's image) a plant of a modern new world. The Halfway Covenant, which served to secularize the colony, was less a departure from old ideas than it was an effort (as I try to show in chapter 3) to extend and adapt those ideals to new conditions. The freemen who elected a new government in defiance of Governor Bellingham in 1670 were covenanted members of the visible churches of Massachusetts. The Third Church was built on land donated for that purpose by the widow of John Norton, a pillar of the first-generation orthodoxy; among its first members was Sarah Cotton Mather, the widow of John Cotton and Richard Mather;[20] and these widows were not betraying the "grand design" their husbands had sought to realize. Despite their allegiance to theocracy, the emigrant Puritans were part of the movement toward the future. Their rhetoric and vision facilitated the process of colonial growth.* And in sustaining that rhetoric and vision, the latter-day Jeremiahs

---

*Their achievement therefore may be seen as a massive irony. To restate Miller's insight (though from a very different perspective) it was an exemplary case of self-deception in the service of one's own and society's best interests, where the self-deception works precisely because self-interest *seems* to be opposed to society's interests.

effectually forged a powerful vehicle of middle-class ideology: a ritual of progress through consensus, a system of sacred-secular symbols for a laissez-faire creed, a "civil religion" for a people chosen to spring fully formed into the modern world — America, the first-begotten daughter of democratic capitalism, the only country that developed, from the seventeenth through the nineteenth centuries, into a wholly middle-class culture.

It is a long way from Danforth's sermon to the flowering of civil religion in America, and we shall see that the jeremiad was considerably affected by a variety of social and intellectual changes. But through all change the persistence of the rhetoric attests to an astonishing cultural hegemony, one that the rhetoric itself reflected and shaped. Perhaps the most incisive critique we have of this development is Melville's great novel *Pierre; or, The Ambiguities*. The novel opens with a eulogy to the American Way ("Out of some past Egypt we have come to this new Canaan; and from this new Canaan we press on to some Circassia"), and then proceeds to unveil ambiguity after ambiguity, until it ends in a solipsistic void, like a movie reel of the Puritan ritual run backward at top speed. The very reversal of movement suggests the continuity of the errand, even a madcap inevitability to it all. Pierre Glendinning, "nature's aristo-crat," "noble American," and "thorough-going Democrat" — descended from the fabled heroes of colonial and Revolutionary days, and "fated" to bring their work to fruition — migrates from a paste-board "paradise" to the republican Babylon, where he finds himself the fool of prophecy, messenger of a God whose only voice is silence, ranting to no one about a New Revelation that remains forever unrecorded, unfulfilled, except in the mock apocalypse of his self-destruction. It is a satire of violence nourished by self-deceit, a tragedy of rhetoric turned relentlessly upon itself. But there is a momentary pause at its center, where Melville inserts a coolly ar-gued discourse, entitled "Chronometricals and Horologicals." Its author, Plotinus Plinlimmon, contrasts our imperfect "horological" time with the "chronometrical" time of heaven — God's permanent and universal Truth, unaffected by "relative, worldly, human truths." Never, Plinlimmon warns, impose the ideal upon experi-ence; never confuse New Jerusalem with "the general Jerusalem of this world": "the absolute effort to live . . . according to . . . the chronometrical is, somehow, apt to involve those inferior beings eventually in strange, *unique* follies, unimagined before."[21]

It is precisely this effort to fuse sacred and profane that shapes the American jeremiads. Their threats of doom, derived from Christian tradition, imply a distinction between the two realms; their language itself, expressing their special sense of mission, incorporates the threats within the broader framework of the absolute. This rhetorical synthesis of man's time and God's was first outlined by John Cotton and John Winthrop, the chief spokesmen for church and state in early Massachusetts. It was developed by their colleagues and heirs into a comprehensive definition of New England's errand into the wilderness, a dream of a society in which "the fact could be made one with the ideal."[22] When in the last decades of the century they came to feel that history had betrayed them, they clung all the more tenaciously to their dream; and they managed to bequeath their peculiar form of the jeremiad to subsequent generations because in some basic sense they were responding to actual social needs. Drawing on the very precariousness of their experience, the American Puritans, as we shall see, forged what was to become a framework for national identity.

Plinlimmon's pamphlet has usually been read as a counterstatement to all this — as a jeremiad, we might say, against American jeremiads. But we learn that Plinlimmon is a leader among a motley group of "Teleological Theorists, and Social Reformers and political propagandists . . . [dedicated to] the hasty and premature advance of some unknown great political and religious Millennium"; and his pamphlet's heaped-up ambiguities invite us to consider a prospect quite different from that of the European jeremiad. Its title, we recall, is conjunctive, not divisive: "Chronometricals *and* [not *or*] Horologicals."* And though Plinlimmon insists on the discrepancy

---

*The full title reads: "*EI* by Plotimus Plinlimmon, (In Three Hundred and Thirty-Nine Lectures). Lecture First. Chronometricals and Horologicals, (Being not so much the Portal, as part of the temporary Scaffold to the Portal of this New Philosophy)." Several critics have noted that "EI" is a multilingual pun on "God" and "if" (the last word of the truncated treatise). If so, the pun reinforces the ambiguity I have been discussing: it suggests that chronometricals and horologicals are mutually sustaining *and* contradictory elements in a (therefore) endless process of self-definition;

(essential to the European jeremiad) between heaven's time and ours, he slyly shows us a way out of the dilemma. We do not really have to choose between the two worlds, he insinuates. We have access to both, providing that we embrace the realm of experience while giving priority, in rhetoric and imagination, to the realm of the ideal. We live well in our "artificial world" insofar as we acknowledge its distance from the higher Truth — and having acknowledged this, devise a "virtuous expediency" that allows us to ignore the difference. Unquestionably, Plinlimmon explains, the heavenly is as distinct from the earthly as "the chronometer carried to China, is from Greenwich. And, as that chronometer, if at all accurate, will pronounce it to be 12 o'clock high-noon, when the China local watches say, perhaps, it is 12 o'clock midnight; so the chronometric soul . . . will always . . . be contradicting the mere local standards and watchmaker's brains of this earth. . . . And yet," he continues,

> And yet, it follows not from this, that God's truth is one thing and man's truth another; but — as hinted above, and as will be further elucidated in subsequent lectures — by their very contradictions they are made to correspond.[23]

Melville offers us none of Plinlimmon's subsequent lectures, but we may follow them for ourselves in the jeremiads of seventeenth-century New England and beyond.

Pierre, the novel's antiheroic hero, embodies this ambiguous mutuality, as does every aspect of his story, while the author himself, who is ambiguously Melville and not-Melville, both scoffs and endorses: admires and ridicules Pierre, disclaims Plinlimmon's lecture even as he validates it.

2

The Blessings of
Time and Eternity

Considered in Plinlimmon's perspective, the term jeremiad is an apt one. Jeremiah is at once a historian of horologicals and a chronometer of the future; he both laments an apostasy and heralds a restoration. In Hebrew tradition this dual function is something of a paradox. The chosen people had sinned and continued in sin, had been punished with exile and were being threatened with more severe punishments unless they reformed; but they remained chosen nonetheless, still the keepers of the ancient promise to Abraham. And Jeremiah asserts the fulfillment of the promise as the very telos of history. The exile, he announces unequivocally, will end; eventually, Israel will return to a second paradise, a Canaan abounding in blessings beyond anything they had had or imagined. But he never clarifies the relation between means and ends. As he envisions it, the restoration is sometimes a reward for performance, sometimes a gift. Israel's redemption, it would seem, will come by miracle, though its deeds are to justify the miracle. Although restoration depends on service, it is already a foregone conclusion in God's mind and will. It may be, as modern commentators have argued, that Jeremiah's emphasis on miracle provided him with a way out of despair — that his reliance on "the unique divine initiative at the end of history"[1] grew in proportion to what seemed to him the nation's irreversible moral deterioration. Whatever the case, his testimony is problematic. No prophet stressed repentance as much as Jeremiah did, and none so fervently foretold the gratuitous spiritual transformation in store for the house of Israel.

The Christian solution was as simple as it was sweeping. Jeremiah, according to the Church Fathers, was addressing two different peoples. One was the literal Israel, whose story of disobedience and decline was a commonplace of secular history. To them Jeremiah spoke "like unto a *Sonne of Thunder*." The Israelites had entered into a "national covenant," agreeing to keep the law and obey God's commandments — "which my covenant they brake," Jeremiah thunders, speaking for God, "althogh I was an housband unto them" (31:32); and John Cotton, speaking for Jeremiah, explains the consequence: "the Lord cast them off," to "laugh at their Calamities until He has *consumed them utterly, so that there shall be no Remnant, nor escaping*." Yet there *was* to be a remnant. In the verses (31:31, 33) immediately preceding and following this prophecy of doom, Jeremiah changes his tone entirely. Speaking now with "the still, and soft voice of a . . . *Sonne of consolation*, (for their sakes whom the Lord had appointed to bee heires of salvation)," he announces a new covenant, absolute and immutable. Here, the Christian commentators observed, Jeremiah was addressing a different audience — not the Israelites before him, but the *spiritual* Israel, the entire community of the elect, past, present, and to come — and what he said concerned not temporal affairs, but the promise of *"Christ the Messiah* . . . and their eternal deliverance . . . Typicall from Babylon."[2] In these consoling verses, Babylon represented the world, and Jerusalem the kingdom of God. By the types and figures of heaven's chronometer, Jeremiah was specifying the sole, sufficient condition of sacred history: the covenant of grace, unchanged from the protevangelium in Eden through the Incarnation, pledging that Christ's church would triumph over Satan.* Whatever their horological blemishes, the saints would in the end rejoice in Zion.

---

*This developmental view of the covenant of grace — "from *Adam* to *Noah*, from *Noah* to *Abraham*, from *Abraham* to *Moses*, from *Moses* to *David*, from *David* to CHRIST, from CHRIST to the end of the world" (Peter Bulkeley, *The Gospel-Covenant* [London, 1651], p. 113) — is a commonplace of the literature. The passages from Jeremiah to which I refer read as follows:

Beholde the daies come, saith ye Lord, that I wil mak a newe covenant with the house of Israel, and with the house of Judah,

In Christian terms, then, Jeremiah was a Janus-like prophet, facing secular and sacred history alike. On the one hand, he laid the foundation of the European jeremiad: the conditional pact between God and a civic community for certain temporal ends. On the other hand, he outlined the terms of unmerited redemption for the elect. So understood, the two covenants stand as sharply divided from one another as Augustine's two cities. It became the motive and substance of the New England Puritan jeremiad to obviate that division. My purpose in this chapter is to clarify the ways in which the Puritans managed to circumvent tradition and establish a rhetoric commensurate with their vision of errand — commensurate, that is, with their sense of themselves as a chosen people under a covenant that was at once provisional and absolute, temporal and sacred. In doing so, I range at large through the political sermons of three generations. It goes without saying that many ministers changed their minds about basic issues during this period, that not all of them thought alike, and that their relation to the colony at large shifted rather drastically between 1630 and 1700. In the next chapter, I discuss what I consider the most important of these shifts. Here I would like to describe the structure of the Puritans' language and outlook — to provide an anatomy of their rhetoric which may serve as a framework for assessing continuity and change.

The framework is rooted of course, in sixteenth- and early seventeenth-century England. Between the period of the Marian exile and the Great Migration, from Bloody Queen Mary to "persecuting" William Laud (as the Puritans dubbed the Anglican archbishop under Charles I), English Protestants advanced the doctrines of Congregationalism and national election. The two doctrines had certain parallels. Both attracted dissenters of all kinds; the adherents of both movements identified to some extent with the blessed rem-

---

Not according to the covenant that I made with their fathers, when I toke them by the hand to bring them out of the land of Egypt, the which my covenant they brake, althogh I was an husband unto them, saith the Lord.

But this shalbe the covenant that I wil make with the house of Israel, After those daies, saith the Lord, I wil put my Law in their inwarde partes, & write it in their hearts, & wil be their God, and thei shalbe my people. . . .

They shal aske the waye to Zion, with their faces thetherward, *saying*, Come, and let us cleave to the Lord in a perpetual covenant that shal not be forgotten. (31:31–33; 50:5)

nant of Jeremiah 31:31, 33; and (coincidentally perhaps) both movements selected as their main text Jeremiah's description (50:5) of a group which at the close of Israel's seventy-year exile would "aske the waye to Zion . . . *saying*, Come, and let us cleave to the Lord in a perpetual covenant." The fundamental difference between Congregationalists and the adherents of national election lay in the distinction between the two covenants. On the surface, it seems a difference of degree: the Congregationalists were more overly concerned with the covenant of grace, and were relatively unconcerned with temporal "agreements of the people." But the implications ran much deeper. Let me suggest these by reference to the exegetical problem concerning the Babylonian captivity, the subject of all Jeremiah's prophecies, and particularly of Jeremiah 31 and 50.

The problem was inherent in the very origins of Reformed thought. For Calvin, the Babylonian captivity signified the bondage of sin. Quoting Augustine, he went so far as to deny altogether the possibility of a temporal commitment on God's part, and explicated Jeremiah 50:5 and 31:31–33 (including even 31:32) purely in terms of grace. The return from exile was for him a promise outside time of the believer's release from the *regnum satanae* into the *regnum spirituale*. Ever since the "natural covenant made . . . in Paradise, was violated," he argued, "the covenant which remaineth, is wholly to be ascribed unto grace"; the so-called new covenant merely brought to light "whatever had been shadowed forth under the Law"; God's frequent threats to "utterly reject" His people were not meant literally. They were simply metaphors or hyperboles, stylistic devices by which He wished to impress upon those He would *not* reject the importance of reformation.[3]

For his part, Luther sought to attach a concrete, worldly significance to the captivity. In an effort to explain the long dominion of the Roman Catholic church, he undertook a wholesale reexamination of biblical prophecies, and found in Jeremiah's new covenant a momentous foreshadowing of current political and social events. The thirty-first and fiftieth chapters of Jeremiah, he proclaimed, "instruct us in what manner the end of the world is approaching." They predict through the type of Babylon the reign of the papacy, and, through the type of Israel's deliverance, the flight of the true church from Rome, its victory over "this Babylonish beast," and the final descent of New Jerusalem. No wonder, Luther concluded, that Catholic priests had always kept the Bible from their flocks: the rise of Protestantism and the fall of Catholic Rome were a main subject of the prophecies![4] In all this he was not really in conflict with Calvin. Both men believed that Catholic Rome was Antichrist incarnate, both saw the Reformation as an intrinsic part of sacred history, and both maintained that the sacred contradicted the secular in all ways. Still, differences remained in outlook and emphasis — Calvin's approach was personal and presentist, Luther's historical and developmental — and the differences opened in seventeenth-century England into two mutually opposed concepts of a visible people of God.

The more popular of these concepts, that of national election, stems from the identification of Babylon and Rome. Though English theologians agreed that "mystically" Babylon signified the postlapsarian world, they were eager to adopt Luther's position. Swept up as they were in a high tide of nationalism, they discerned in their own past the dawning of the Reformation, and rewriting Britain's history to match the apocalyptic timetable, they claimed that their "noble and puissant Nation" was destined to head the universal battle against Antichrist. Their millennial fervor spread steadily from the period of the Marian exile to become a motive of revolution. At all stages it reflected a belief in the imminent end of history; but the fact that it was a national undertaking confined the movement itself in secular affairs. New Jerusalem belonged to the saints, after all, and not even the extreme English patriot-chiliasts doubted that in their land as elsewhere many were called but few chosen. The martyrologist John Bale, for example, who inspired a generation of his countrymen to expect momentarily the fall of Babylon, followed "the true opinion of St. Austin" concerning the two cities, limited atonement, and the need to seek salvation in one's heart, rather than in external events. So, too, Oliver Cromwell's schoolmaster reminded his "happy favoured brethren" that the final conflict meant the destruction of sinners, among whom he numbered most Englishmen. From John Foxe to Thomas Fuller every historian who extolled the prospects in store for England's green and pleasant land hastened to add that in the "higher" sense "it is not fit that good men should live long on earth." Even Britain was "too bad for his servants to live in."[5]

So the adherents of national election concentrated perforce on reforms relevant to the city of man. When they boasted of being a "new chosen people" or an "army of saints" they spoke metaphorically, supposing at most a vague analogue to the progress of the church. Their specific associations were with the institutions of the secular past, such as the medieval state-compact and the covenant of Jeremiah 31:32. The sum of our duties, Robert Dowglas told the members of Parliament in 1651, is "*To walk after the Lord & keep his commandments.*" We hope thereby at last to find "Peace and Safety" — not for our souls but in our daily lives. We also recognize that we have the "terrible liberty" to defy God and so justly to "*be divided and cut in pieces,*" as his "sword is now devouring Germany."* Accordingly, most English Puritans appealed to natural law and secular reason, in explicit antipathy to the Congregationalists' "Church-oath," with its pretensions of assurance about grace. What they offered differed only in degree from the condition of other nations: an exemplary community in more or less direct contact with God concerning the people's welfare. Accordingly, too, their view of history centered upon secular affairs. In asserting that God manipulated every event, they meant no more than to explain in Christian terms the vicissitudes of fortune. Sacred history, they acknowledged, belonged to theology, not historiography, and they focused instead upon "mundane happenings" in the story of men and nations. What morals they drew applied to outward rewards and punishments, teaching "for what virtue . . . God made prosperous; and for what vice . . . he made wretched" for what apparent causes he would "[en]courage and discourage, raise and throw down kings, estates, cities."[6]

*Perhaps the most forceful single statement of this outlook appears in Edmund Calamy's authoritative sermon of 1645. Calamy argues the necessity for a national covenant on the grounds that, according to "our *English Chronicles, England* was never destroyed, but when divided within it self." In this sermon, too, he explains that Jeremiah 50:5 — as the basis for the "union" of Scotland, Ireland, and England — stands for "*a covenant of nature,*" and that this natural or "*National Covenant* hath been a long time as it were dead and buried. . . . And therefore it is high time to raise it out of the grave" (*The Great Danger of Covenant-Refusing* [London, 1646], title page, pp. 8, 18). This is also the message of the anonymous *Covenant-Interest and Priviledge* (London, 1675), pp. 1–2, and the various "agreements of the people" in *Leveller Manifestoes of the Puritan Revolution*, ed. Don M. Wolfe (New York, 1944), pp. 225–34. Significantly, the royalist position on this issue is substantially in agreement with Calamy's: e.g., Henry Leslie, *A Sermon at the Publique Fast* (Oxford, 1643), pp. 38–39.

The English Congregationalists took the contrary course; they linked their movement to the city of God. To be sure, they equated Babylon with Rome, anxiously awaited the apocalypse, and even, for a short time, accepted the idea of England's calling. But fundamentally they sought separation from the kingdom of sin. They came out of Babylon as a remnant fleeing from spiritual exile, "not by bodely remooving, but unlikeness of maners." Like the apostolic Christians, the earth seemed to them "the sphere of uncleanness," and they gathered into small vineyards of Christ as into oases in the wilderness. Before 1640, as Brethren of the Separation, they condemned the Anglicans for their indiscriminate church membership policy. After 1640, as proponents of the Congregational Way, they suspected the state church of being a "popish device." "The prophet Jeremiah," wrote the great Separatist John Robinson,

> speaking of the new covenant, testifieth that . . . [God] would re-
> member . . . [the chosen ones'] iniquities no more, Jer. xxxi. 31, 33,
> 34. But your national church never came within the compass of this
> promise. It is [therefore] Babylon, though much purged and repaired.
> Now as the people of God in old time were called to come to Jerusalem
> and there to build anew the Lord's temple, so are the people of God
> now to go out of Babylon spiritual, and as lively stones to couple
> themselves together by covenant . . . [so as to constitute] a spiritual
> building, the Lord's temple, . . . [having] for an inheritance the
> kingdom of heaven.[7]

The image of temple and kingdom in this passage stands not only beyond the domain of secular history, but deliberately opposed to it. It reminds us that New Jerusalem cannot be built in England or anywhere else, not even by analogy to that blessed state. Indeed, according to the Congregationalists, such analogies most dramatically reveal the incompatibility of the two realms. This "fair field of England," sneered Robinson, "of whose beauty all the Christian world is enamored," what is it but a weed patch with a "few kernels of wheat scattered among the tares here and there" — "a small sprinkling of good men amongst the great retchless rout of wicked and graceless persons" — and hence, even under its national covenant, merely another form of the captivity from which Jeremiah summoned the people of God?[8] It may be, as these arguments imply, that the Congregationalists came to place an undue trust in their sense of election. But if so, they carefully divorced that personal assurance from the providence guiding the mass of mankind. Insofar as church covenant intimated sainthood their kingdom was not of this world. It had to do with the journey to redemption, with chronometricals.

The Great Migration owes its unique character to its inheritance of both these strains in its English background. The settlers, in William Haller's words, felt they had inherited "the mantle of Israel, lost by England's Stuart kings"; they also felt they were an exclusive band of saints, called by God into a church covenant that separated them from the mass of humanity. In short, they were children of an improbable mixed marriage — Congregationalists on a historic mission for mankind. They took with them when they left a sacred and a worldly view of their errand, both a conviction that they were elect and an expectation of the great things they were to do on earth. On the one hand, they conceived of their flight, with the Plymouth Pilgrims, in spiritual and inward terms, as a means of self-improvement. On the other hand, they saw themselves leaving a real Babylon, in another (and final) act of the drama of human history. Unlike their Plymouth brethren, they were determined from the beginning not to withdraw from the world but to reform it.* If they saw their migration, in the words of Thomas Shepard and John Allin, "to be . . . a heavenly translation from corrupt to more pure churches," they also thought of it as "the establishment of the Holy Commonwealth . . . preparatory to the great event." England had forfeited its national covenant; the leading English dissenters, men like William Preston and Thomas Brightman, were forecasting as well-nigh

---

*This is perhaps to distinguish too sharply between the Plymouth and the Massachusetts ventures. The contrast does hold true, I believe, in the early decades; but it would seem that the Pilgrims came by and large to share the Bay settlers' outlook. In part, perhaps, the Bay clergy's influence was augmented by the ambiguities implicit in the position taken by Separatists like William Ainsworth and John Canne, who linked the Babylonian bondage typologically with the saint's state under the Church of England, and admitted at least the theoretical viability of a state-church modeled upon the Israelite theocracy. In part, too, the Plymouth leaders may have been driven in reaction against Roger Williams to identify more closely with their neighbors, an identification no doubt enforced by the "wilderness-condition" they shared with their nonseparating brethren and by various ideological pressures and crosscurrents. For whatever reasons, it seems evident that the historiographic and doctrinal lines demarcating Boston from Plymouth became increasingly blurred after 1650.

inevitable an "apocalyptic . . . lamentable calamity." For their part, the emigrant leaders viewed the prospect with a grim joy. No doubt they felt troubled about leaving the comforts of England, and guilty about abandoning their families, friends, and congregations. But they found ample compensation in their sense of things to come. "Truth," they announced, was being driven out of Europe altogether," and the Lord had "chosen New England as her residence"; "I am veryly perswaded," Winthrop wrote his wife in 1629, that God will bringe some heavye Affliction upon this lande [England], and that speedylye." He also, in the same year, reasoned out the migration in traditional Separatist language, by reference to the woman in Revelation, chapter 12, forced to fly the world's "coldness, carnality, contention." That rationale complemented and enforced the other; together they demonstrated (as Winthrop further noted in his 1629 "Conclusions for the Plantation in New-England") that "It appeares to be a worke of god. . . . He hath some great worke in hand wch he hath revealed to his prophets among us." Thus doubly protected by the national covenant and the covenant of grace, they set out as a holy remnant to complete a predetermined historical design.[9]

Nowhere does this dual legacy show itself more lucidly than in the prototypic jeremiads of Cotton and Winthrop. Puritan scholars have analyzed the *Arbella* sermon as a model of social discipline, the "city on a hill" it extols "knit together" by authority, charity, and reasoned consent. And so, clearly, it is. Yet the same terms apply just as clearly to the ecclesiastical order. A city is the "Title given to the Church," as Richard Mather observed, and specifically to "a Church by Covenant," "knit together by voluntary consent." Such "Fellowship . . . is a *City set upon a Hill*" as a shelter for the soul rescued out of Babylon, as a "model" of heaven, and as a promise of the millennium to come. The nationalist John Milton, using the concept in its social sense only, spoke in 1643 of England "holding up, as from a Hill, the new Lampe of *saving light* to all Christendome." Somewhat earlier, the Separatist John Robinson maintained, from his spiritual viewpoint, that the saints must "resort to the place where [God] hath put his name, for which they need not go either to Jerusalem, or to Rome, or beyond the seas; they may find Sion the Lord's mountain prepared on the top of every hill." Winthrop and

Cotton use both meanings of the term simultaneously; and that double meaning of their "city on a hill" pervades their discourses. It recurs in their blessings and threats and in the scriptural allusions that thread their arguments. When John Cotton speaks of America as "the ends of the earth" he is referring not only to a specific locale, but also to Christ's Second Coming. When he tells the prospective immigrants that "God plants us when he gives us roote in Christ," he does so in order to fuse the concepts of civic and spiritual planting. Winthrop's rhetoric serves the same purpose. The social covenant, as he explains it, becomes interchangeable with the covenant by which the elect join together in the Body of Christ. His closing reference to Moses' farewell exhortation evokes the promised land both of Massachusetts and of heaven.[10] Like Cotton, in short, Winthrop sets out a prophetic view that unites sacred and secular history.

In England, the elect nation remained earthbound because the final rights to the millennium rested with the church. The English Congregationalists held their church-states aloof from the world. It was reserved for the American Puritans to give the kingdom of God a local habitation and a name.

In general, Protestant Europe turned a deaf or incredulous ear to the American Puritans' claim. Those who took them seriously could consider them nothing short of blasphemous — "Colluvies of wild Opinionists, swarmed into a remote wilderness to find elbow-roome for [their] phanatick Doctrines and practices."[11] But several conscientious Calvinists charitably tried to argue the orthodoxy out of its strange, unique folly. One of these was Roger Williams, who addressed his appeal to John Cotton in a series of lengthy letters and treatises, which (Williams correctly said) set forth the elementary truths of the faith. That God once summoned His people to a holy land, Williams pointed out, had no bearing whatever on the Puritan migration. The Old Testament differed from all other histories in two respects: first, it pertained exclusively to sacred history; and second, its heroes and major events were above all prefigurations of Christ. So understood, the story of the Hebrews applied to Christians only in spiritual terms, as stages of the saint's pilgrimage to heaven. The wilderness now meant the world, Jerusalem the celestial city, Canaan the kingdom of God. These and other sacred places were by definition confined to sacred history — to the Bible, the true believer, and the progress of the church. By definition, therefore, anything outside that sphere — any person excluded from the church, any place that lay temporally or geographically beyond the boundaries of Scripture chronicles — was profane. To understand the things of this world in any other sense was to deny the very meaning of faith. For Williams the entire issue was as plain as it was incontrovertible: "*America* (as *Europe* and all places) lies dead in sin." As citizens, we may consider ourselves Englishmen or Dutchmen or New Englanders, and even take pride in that identity. As Christians, "we are all, in all places, strangers and pilgrims." How then, Williams demanded, could the New England saints propose the "Nationall State of the *Jewes*" — the type of heaven — "as the Type of the . . . [American] Kingdome of Christ Jesus"? Were they mad enough to claim that "the very Land of England [was] literally Babel . . . and the Land of New England, *Judea, Canaan*?" How dared they "mingle *Heaven* and *Earth*, the *church* and *worldly state* together," as though the Incarnation had not separated those areas once and for all?[12]

Williams's acerbity may come from his Separatist convictions, but the argument itself, let me emphasize, was wholly traditional. Its source may be traced to (say) Book XI of Augustine's *Confessions*, which anticipates Plinlimmon's distinction between horologicals and chronometricals (but without the American's insidious ambiguity). In his famous discussion here of the meaning of time, Augustine directs man toward an indivisible present that includes past and future. The history of nations — the arena of human time, and the national covenant — is reduced to a series of meaningless moments in a drama of the absurd.* Time in its absolute sense, as it conforms

---

*For a short time, during the Constantinian empire, Augustine did espouse a vague form of political millennialism. But when he rejected this he rejected all sacral conceptions of society. Ever "since the coming of Christ, until the end of the world, all history is homogeneous," he maintained. "Every moment may have its unique and mysterious significance . . . but it is a significance to which God's revelation does not supply any clues. . . . There is no sacred history of the last age: there is only a gap for it *in* the sacred history" (R. A. Markus, *Saeculum: History and Society in the Theology of St. Augustine* [Cambridge, 1970], pp. 167–68, 20–21). Significantly, modern religious reaction against theories of progress often expresses itself in this Augustinian mode — for example, in the comments of the Catholic Jean Daniélou and the Protestant Theo Priess on "Christian Faith and History," *Journal of Religion*, 30 (1950),

to the heavenly chronometer, reveals every object or event as an emblem of eternity. In this light, the Old Testament prophecies type out the believer's journey to God: the whole story of Israel becomes the background for the act of will which transforms geography into eschatology.

The New England settlers of course retained the Augustinian framework. But they deliberately adopted a double focus, social as well as private, on the kingdom of God. And though John Cotton diverged in other respects from his colleagues, he heartily complied in this. In his replies to Williams he confirmed Christ's "antitypal" role, and all that this implied about the "wilderness of the world" and the "heavenly Canaan." But he refused therefore to relinquish the correspondence between Canaan and New England. Indeed, it was exactly by formulating a synthetic "middle way" that he defended the theocracy. As a "Nationall Civil State," he wrote, adhering to the Mosaic laws out of faith in Christ, the colonists fulfilled "the type of Israel materially." As the remnant that would inaugurate the millennium, they fulfilled the type spiritually, in terms of the progress of sacred history. Upon this conviction, Cotton acclaimed the special figural status of New England, specified its moral and historical importance in God's plan, and expounded his millennial expectations, for America first and then the world.[13]

Upon this conviction, too, his contemporaries and successors built their political sermons. Even as they urged each man to search into the minutest details of his life, they insisted upon the overarching plan which explained the social pattern of their lives, and so allowed them to fuse the particular, the social, and the cosmic. To this end, they described the progress of their church-state in terms of the process of conversion and sanctification. The same prophecies that they used to expound the believer's way of grace they also used in their political sermons to expound New England's role in redemptive

---

157–79, or in the meditation on "Christian Culture" by the Greek Orthodox Nicholas Berdayev: "The impossibility of terrestrial perfection constitutes the peculiarity of the Christian culture. By its very nature the latter could not ultimately fulfill itself. It symbolizes the principles of an eternal search, longing, and aspiration; and it is but the symbolic reflection of the possibilities beyond the limits of this earth" (*The Meaning of History*, trans. George Reavey [Cleveland, 1936], p. 122).

history. Their biographies repeatedly assert the identity of the exemplary life and the colonial venture. Both explicitly and implicitly (through the metaphors, for example, which bind the ocean crossing to the rites of baptism and the wilderness trials to the temptations of the soul), the individual becomes a "representative man" in a way that attests at once to his own and his society's divine calling.* And the American Puritan jeremiads, reversing this technique, proclaim the colony to be the fulfillment of the biblical types, like the saint made perfect in Christ.

Through such rhetorical ambiguities the clergy explained the meaning of the American wilderness. What seemed merely another worldly enterprise, financed by English entrepreneurs, was in reality a mission for "the *Generall Restoration of Mankind from the Curse of the Fall*, and the opening of [the last stage in] that Scheme of *the Divine Proceedings*, which was to bring a blessing upon all the *Nations of the Earth*." Hence their special prerogatives, which men like Roger Williams could never appreciate: the Old Testament promises be-

---

*Sometimes the relation between literal and spiritual is made transparent, as in Peter Bulkeley's *Gospel-Covenant*, p. 350: "faith takes the soule aside . . . in a solitary desart place. . . . [God] will allure us, and draw us into the wilderness . . . when he will speak to our heart, and when he prepares our heart to speak unto him." Sometimes it issues in a complex configuration, involving history, prophecy, and *peregrinatio*, as in Cotton Mather's description of the Puritan victory over the Indian King Philip: "Og, the king of the woody Bashan, encountered by Joshua, with his armies passing into Canaan, was the Python destroyed by Apollo. [Now,] 'twas unto a Shilo, that the planters of New-England have been making their progress, and King Phillip is the Python that has been giving them obstruction, in a fatal enterprize [against] our Lord Jesus Christ, the great Phoebus [Apollo]" (*Magnalia Christi Americana*, [1702] ed. Thomas Robbins [Hartford, 1853–55], II, 578–79; ellipses deleted). One function of American Puritan biography is to make explicit this connection between saint and society. Correspondingly, the pervasive plea of the jeremiads, that "the heart of this people might be moved, as the heart of one man," is generally accompanied by the explanation that "Israel are often called collectively God's son . . . as if the whole multitude of them were one person" (Samuel Torrey, *Exhortation unto Reformation* [Cambridge, Mass., 1674], p. 35). And in both personal and political writings, the New England Puritans generally mingle comments from authorities on the morphology of conversion (like William Ames and William Perkins) with comments from the early Christian progressivists, like Eusebius, and especially the leading seventeenth-century English millenarians (Thomas Brightman, John Owen, William Twisse), all of whom interpreted the prophets in practical, political terms to explain current events.

longed to all true Christians spiritually, but to God's New Israel historically and geographically as well. From one election day to the next, on one day of humiliation after another, the colonists heard how for them Jeremiah came with a "comfortable Vision" — "with milk and honey in his mouth" — to remind them that God had promised "the *Removal* of the Glory and of his Kingdom from [the Hebrews] to another people," in America. Their church-state attested to the correspondence of the human and the divine; in a sort of celestial ambiguity, it proved that "*Prophesie* is *Historie antedated*; and *Historie* is *Postdated Prophecie*." And prophecy now disclosed, in the "sober sense of many of our Divines," "a certain Prognostick that happy times are at hand, even at the Doors." Now that the last days were approaching, "No changes nor injuries of Time can stop the course . . . *For the set time to favour Sion is come*, . . . the time prefixt by the Prophet Jeremiah."[14]

Most directly, the Puritans expressed this union of the disparate realms of community and grace in their theory of church covenant. All accounts now indicate that before emigration they had not worked out the details of congregational polity; had not, that is, confronted the problem of visible versus spiritual calling. Their solution is evident in the New England Way of church-state (or state-church). It was a community at once purer and more political than its Old World counterparts, effecting a social cohesion more profound than that of national groupings and, simultaneously, raising the church's spiritual authority beyond the limits of the most militant English congregations. Both these developments have received a good deal of attention in recent years. Larzer Ziff has shown how the church covenant "served as the basis of a new cultural identity . . . broader than religious practice and deeper than political rights." Edmund Morgan has traced the orthodoxy's transformation of the idea of visible sainthood into a union of the seen and the unseen, wherein the outward act reliably evinces the inception of grace. In both cases, the way of salvation was made into a mode of socialization. *Our* church covenant, announced Richard Mather, "is not another Covenant contrary to the Covenant of Grace . . . but an open profession of a man's subjection to that very Covenant." It signifies nothing less, said Peter Bulkeley, than that "solemne Covenant" in which "God tooke Abraham and his seede to be his Church and people . . . separating *Ishmael* from *Isaac* . . . *Esau* from Jacob," those under the law from "the children of promise," and, to speak plainly, the damned from the elect.[15]

The English national covenanters were bound to object. As Roger Williams had decried an excessive literalism, so now they decried the colonists' excessive claims to the spirit. Samuel Hudson, for one, protested that "Mr. *Cotton* tels us, that a *visible Church is a mysticall body, whereof . . . the Members* [are] *Saints . . . and united together . . . by a holy Covenant,*" whereas this definition obviously belongs to the *"invisible Church.*" And the great John Owen, expostulating against Thomas Hooker with all the high authority at his command, denounced even more emphatically the newfangled New World attempt to "make particular Churches to be a species of the Universal Church." But the emigrant divines stood fast. In their eyes it was New England's unique prerogative to make visible what elsewhere remained invisible. Hypocrites would now and then deceive them, yet as a rule, they maintained, "The Covenant of Grace is cloathed with Church-Covenant in a Political, visible Churchway." Elsewhere church membership might or might not indicate a true believer; here it was plain "evidence that God hath chosen us and taken us to be his." Expressly joining Jeremiah 50:5 and 31:31–33 (including 31:32), they proceeded as though godliness could be truly detected, institutional forms could guarantee eternity, and the covenant of fraternity could be made one with the covenant of heaven:

[In] Jeremiah, L. 5 be the words which foretold [that] the people of God returning out of captivity of Babel should bind themselves in Church covenant with the Lord. You read the like expression, Jer. xxxi, 31, 32, 33. *This shall be my covenant with the house of Israel, I will forgive their iniquities and remember their sins no more*. The covenant of grace doth make a people, a joined people with God, and therefore a church of God. In such a covenant the Lord is content to take you by the hand and become a husband to you, Jer. xxxi, 32. You have [thus] entered into such a covenant, wherein Christ is yours, and all the promises yours.

.   .   .   .   .

Although that which is foretold [in Jer. 50:5] was in part fulfilled when the people of God returned from Captivitie in *Babylon* at the end of the seventie years: yet we must not limit the place to that time only. For as some passages in this Scripture were never fully accomplished, so many things that literally concerned the Jewes were types and figures, signifying the like things concerning the people of God in these latter dayes. And this place seemes not onely to be meant of personall conversion, but also further, of the open and joynt calling of a company, so noting the joyning of a company together in holy Covenant with God.[16]

Experience later modified the theory, but this implicit yoking together of social identity and the claim to election became a cornerstone of the American jeremiad. One of its most remarkable aspects is the expansion of Cotton's and Winthrop's ambiguities into a cultural commonplace. Over and again the colonial Jeremiahs portray the settlers as a people of God in terms of election, the body politic, and the advancing army of Christ. Their descriptions of the "temple-work" in progress refer alternately, and sometimes simultaneously, to the soul, the actual flourishing of plantations, and the work of redemption. Recurrently, their allusions to *wilderness, vineyard, Canaan*, and *Zion* blur the distinction between the historical, moral, and spiritual levels of meaning. They blur them further still by equating the literal and mystical blessings for sainthood. The theocracy, said William Hooke in 1645, will beautify the land with "not onely a spirituall glory . . . but also an externall, and visible glory."[17] He did not mean that prosperity rewards piety. Individually, he knew, saints might suffer as much or more than others. But collectively, as a historic enterprise, God's American people had His pledge that the desert would blossom like the rose. It was "rare," the ministers acknowledged, for "religion and profit [to] jump together," but New England was a rare place.[18]

The distinction is a crucial one. With all other Christians, the New England Puritans believed that what the Old Testament described as material rewards were to be understood as spiritual blessings.* They had only one reservation: the case was different in

---

*Let me repeat that this outlook involves a drastic reversal of Christian hermeneutics. Theoretically if not practically, European Puritans of all convictions denied any link between profit and grace. When Christ, they explained, fulfilled the Law He unveiled once and for all the transcendent spiritual significance of the Old Testament. The Bible taught that Canaan was a land of abundance, but if we interpret *abundance* in its common earthly sense, "What is this," cried the Separatist John Robinson, "but

New Canaan. Here, as nowhere else, the wheel of fortune and the wheel of grace revolved in harmony. Here, "the gospel hath brought in its right hand Eternal Salvation. And in its left hand, Riches with Protection and Deliverance from Enemies."[19] And lest any "be possessed with doubts because we are suffered to prosper so much," the ministers seized every occasion to explain that, through the "Mercy of the *New-Covenant*," New England fell heir to "Promises of Converting and Sanctifying Grace; and thereunto . . . an addition of Promises respecting *Temporal Blessings*." The elect of other lands might expect the blessings of heaven, but meanwhile they had to endure deprivation and ill-treatment. The Protestant countries of Europe, inspired by God's latter-day church, might covenant for temporal blessings, but individually their inhabitants could expect no special dispensation of grace. New England alone had the high advantages, heralded in thunder and sweetness by Jeremiah, of both covenants. Of all communities on earth, only the new Protestant Israel had "the Blessings both of the *upper and nether Springs*, the Blessings of Time and of Eternity."[20]

Fortified by their double blessings, the American Puritans enlisted the covenant of grace as a vehicle of social control. The promises they inherited had been granted from eternity, but the process of fulfillment, they stressed, required the believer's active cooperation, both in the colonial venture and in his own regeneration. The result was a doctrine of "preparation" that European Calvinists promptly condemned as "a veritable doctrine of works." Modern scholars have by and large accepted that verdict. Perry Miller called preparation Arminianism clothed in orthodoxy. Norman Pettit has seen it as a "conscious ambivalence;"[21] the Puritan leaders, he ar-

---

to make the Lord's people an herd of oxen which are promised to be brought into a fat pasture, there to feed at ease?" (*Works*, ed. Robert Ashton [Boston, 1851], III, 202–3). So, too, the Protestant authorities on the apocalypse stressed that Jeremiah's predictions pertained to the realm of the soul. "The enjoying of these *outward* things, unto the Jews was a pledge of the *Spiritual* as it were inwrapped in them . . . according to the economy of that time" (Thomas Brightman, *The Revelation Illustrated* [Leyden, 1616], p. 173) — a pledge of "*Everlasting Life* . . . not deliverance from Temporal enemies, worldly prosperity, nor the land of Canaan, nor long life in the land the Lord hath given us" (Joseph Mede, *Works*, ed. John Worthington [London, 1677], pp. 252–53).

gues, were trying to meet two very different needs at the same time: to acknowledge the sovereignty of God and to encourage human initiative.* I would suggest that they were being neither hypocritical nor ambivalent, but (in the manner of their concept of errand) ambiguous. What others saw as contradiction they described as complementary aspects, absolute and conditional, of the New England Way. Their covenant had a twofold nature, they observed. In one sense, it was predetermined, a decree "established before the foundation of the world . . . in the mind and will of God." In another sense, it was a contract in time, expressing a fallible human enterprise. For Scripture and experience alike taught that personal salvation, like the worldwide work of redemption, was a matter of growth by degree. It was a process of "living to God," involving a mutual obligation (since Christ is never "actually ours till he be received by us"), entailing struggle and temptation at every stage ("Consider how we are said sometime to *keep* Covenant [Jer. 31:31, 33] and sometime [Jer. 31:32] to *break* Covenant"), and so allowing at best for a provisional sense of security. And this provisional contract, far from subverting the terms of grace, "actually" reinforced the absolute decree. The "way of tryall by conditionall promises," as Peter Bulkeley put it, in a major colonial treatise on preparation, "provokes us to be faithful." By making us aware of shortcomings, it quickens our understanding of God's design and leads us to the right

* Recently, Michael McGiffert has described this dualism in terms of covenant and contract. He notes that for American Puritans "covenant" meant an involuntary and sacred relationship, whereas contract meant something legal, limited, and conditional; and though he concedes that they absorbed "the covenant of the community into the covenant of grace," he contends that the idea of contract nonetheless exerted "a subversive influence . . . like a great undertow," tending toward legalism and voluntarism ("The Problem of the Covenant in Puritan Thought: Peter Bulkeley's *Gospel-Covenant*," *The New England Historical and Genealogical Register*, 130 [1976], 125). My analysis, like McGiffert's, draws heavily on Peter Bulkeley's *Gospel-Covenant*, since the colonists' covenant theory appears there in its fullest form. And like McGiffert, I think that Bulkeley (a) "is committed to a pure form of covenant"; (b) believes in "New England's stellar role in the drama of redemption" and advocates "the utmost exertions of the saints in preparing for Christ's return"; (c) stresses "the deadly conditionality" of the New England Way; and (d) tends to hold these divergent views in "tension" (pp. 125, 128, 122). My point is that the tension signifies not confusion but a deliberate interchangeability of terms. In effect, Bulkeley invokes contradiction so as to offer, through the concept of preparation, a unique resolution of opposites.

conduct which may in some small measure repay our involuntary debt.[22]

As the colonists developed their sense of mission, preparation became a mainstay of the New England Way.* It provided them with a middle ground not only between right- and left-wing Protestants but more broadly between Arminians and Catholics. Against the Arminians they argued that God "giveth himselfe first in order of nature, before he giveth any thing else accompanying Salvation." The "Papists," they charged, "who build upon their works," wrongly "teach a doctrine of doubting; No man (they say) can come to be assured . . . of his own salvation." Their own position was less an effort to steer clear of either extreme than a means of drawing in both, precisely as the idea of theocracy encompassed both teleology and day-by-day discipline. Thus Danforth, in *Errand into the Wilderness*, speaks of the man with the withered arm (Matthew 12:10, Mark 3:1–3, Luke 6:6–8): the invalid himself had to stretch forth his arm, though he first needed God's help to do so. Thus Bulkeley connects divine and human willing: "*For my owne sake will I do thus and thus unto you*," God had said, but "*He that believeth shall be saved*" — or rather not *but*, but *and*, "for the conditional promise is absolute in its effect," intending "faith in whom it shall be fulfilled." Ultimately, "the absolute and the conditionall promises are both one in substance . . . springing from the same fountaine, even from the purpose of his grace." Thus, too, Thomas Hooker describes the Israelites' conquest of Canaan: "It was the Lord's power and gift that give them possession of the land. . . . Yet notwithstanding they

---

*By "mainstay" I also intend to include ritual function — the use of preparation as a means of socialization. What I would suggest is that preparation was a sort of personal analogue to the tribal concept of the errand. Perhaps the most striking account of its application is the poetry of Edward Taylor, with its obsessive use of process as a means of control. Taylor's "Preparatory Meditations," a model of indefinitely prolonged crisis — intended to harness the wild inclinations of the self by *resisting* any resolution of conflict — are the poetic fruition of the great doctrinal works half a century before. Preparation was part of a social as well as spiritual process; it led outward from self to society. The errand, as Danforth explained it, was a corporate venture, leading ritually from society to self. What conscience meant to the preparationist was for Danforth the conscience of the tribe — the Great Migration, the founders' city on a hill, the sacred communal past. But in both cases, the object of the ritual was to link saint and society in the framework of New England's destiny.

were fain to fight for it, before the Canaanites were dispossessed."[23] In all cases, what seemed to others to be two different approaches to salvation became simply a difference in perspective, or in manner of expression.*

For the American Puritans, then, unlike other Protestants, eschatology posed no threat to social discipline; in theory at least, they succeeded in bridging Augustinian piety and Reformed progressivism. The elitist nature of their church-state precluded Arminianism even as their concept of mission encouraged human initiative. When John Cotton, for example, argued with an apparently democratic zest for the layman's participation in government, he meant not "the liberty of the people," but the "rights of saints." When he and his colleagues taught gospel responsibilities, they did so not for the heathen but exclusively within the confines of a "church designed for the saved," a "holy commonwealth" intended primarily to "protect themselves and their children."† And they found the proper means of protection in the doctrine of preparation. No tenet was more basic with them than that "grace may be interrupted in the saint . . . for a season"; no remedy for that dark period came more readily than Peter Bulkeley's in 1651:

conditionall expressions have in them the force of a quickening exhorta-

---

*The relation between human and divine willing was a matter of emphasis and degree, of course. As Christopher Hill observes, Puritans generally tried to interrelate faith and works: "Men fought for God's cause and expected it to prevail because it was God's"; or, in the words he quotes from Thomas Taylor: "We teach that only Doers shall be saved, and by their doing though not for their doing" (*The Century of Revolution, 1603–1714* [Edinburgh, 1961], pp. 169, 82). But in New England the difference in degree escalated into a qualitative difference both in theory and in practice.

† The elitist nature of early New England preaching deserves special emphasis. Edmund Morgan notes that Thomas Hooker of Connecticut was an exception, since he reached "beyond the narrow bounds of the Puritan tribe" (*The Puritan Family: Essays on Religion and Domestic Relations in Seventeenth-Century New England* [Boston, 1944], p. 184). But it was an exception that proved the rule. By and large, the exclusiveness of the American Puritan church-state posed the problem, to quote Morgan again (*Visible Saints: The History of a Puritan Idea* [New York, 1963], pp. 122–23), of "How would the gospel be spread to the heathen . . . with a church designed [as it was in New England] only for the saved? . . . John Cotton, for example . . . could only ask of his critics: '. . . when an Indian or unbeleever commeth into the Church, doe not all the prophets . . . apply their speech to his conviction and conversion?' The honest answer . . . was probably no."

tion for every one that standeth [in Christ] to take heed lest he fall; and so they make us stand more cautiously and sure. They serve to keep the Saints more watchfull, by which watchfulness they are helped to stand more firmely. [Thus] the same thing is promised both absolutely, because it shall certainly be fulfilled, and with condition, because it shall not be brought to passe but by meanes, in which mans care is required. Truly, such is the mercy shewed us in making this Covenant with us, that we might live unto eternity.[24]

The early Separatists acted as if they were saved while acknowledging that they might be damned; the New Englanders acted as if they were damned while presuming they were saved. On that basis, the clergy outlined two separate, though complementary, ways of trial. One was the way of affliction. As the doctrine of works reminded the saints of their need for faith, so conversely the doctrine of grace served as a torture instrument to make them behave. With it, the ministers taught the believer who stumbled in taking hold of his inheritance about the nature of damnation. In their hands the covenant became a "halter" to restrain "slippery and unstable hearts," a "hammer" with which "the soul can be broken," an "Image of fear" to make "thee see plainely, that thou art become the heire apparent of hell." At the same time, remembering their dual role as Jeremiahs, they offered a "kind, loving, easie" form of provocation. God was also pleading for repentance by unveiling His intention to restore His people. This trial by mercy, the clergy explained, showed plainly that for the colonists backsliding was not a matter of crime and punishment, but of regeneration through suffering.* How could such tenderness on God's part *not* bring them gratefully

*The concept of trial by mercy proved especially conducive to the mingling of traditional pulpit genres. The Puritans' sermons on grace often undertake to remedy temporal ills. Their sermons on state affairs — relating social, political, and even military duties to the process of redemption — teach that "we do all commit this cause [of our "suffering country"] unto the Lord, even in the same way as we do every one commit unto him the Salvation of our Soules" (John Higginson, *The Cause of God* [Cambridge, Mass., 1663], p. 19). Peter Bulkeley's use of "the city on a hill" is characteristic in this regard: "we should in a speciall manner labour to shine forth in holinesse above other people; wee are as a City set upon a hill, in the eys of heaven and earth, Angels and man. Let us study [so] to walk [i.e., behave] that they may be constrained to say of us, onely this people is holy and blessed, the seed which the Lord hath blessed" (*Gospel-Covenant* [London, 1651], pp. 425–26; ellipses deleted).

to obedience? It turned His wrath itself into an act of love, giving "encouragement to such as are smitten downe with the terrors of the Almighty" — for precisely when "the soule seeth the flashes of hell, [then] God intends to doe good to a man." Our "faith may be exercised for a season, yet Gods promise," the ministers insisted, "is faithfull and sure."[25] And they proceeded, accordingly, to transform adversity into hope under the overriding metaphor of a "season of trial" and *"solemn divine Probation."*[26]

The clergy patterned their view of New England's declension on God's merciful trial of the saints. The problem, as they formulated it here, related only superficially or symptomatically to misbehavior. What really mattered was the state of the soul. Richard Mather's *Farewel-Exhortation* (1657) pictures an upright community which must nonetheless fear for its salvation, and most political sermons echo his analysis. Though they detailed a long list of carnal excesses, they acknowledged that in their outward comportment New Englanders surpassed all other peoples. As Richard Mather put it, "in this country [unlike others] profession is somewhat common, Authority through the goodness of God countenancing Religion, and ministring Justice against all known ungodliness"; or, in the words of his son and grandson (some forty years later), New England's "Blameless Morality" is so far "beyond what is to be found with any other people" that "there are Practices which . . . would [elsewhere] be a step toward Reformation that [here] . . . would deserve the Name of great Degeneracy and Apostasy" — for "New England has one thing that will weigh down more than forty of the best things that other countries can brag of: that is, religion, religion, religion! . . . Impostors have but seldom got in and set up among us; and when they have done so, they have made a short blaze, and gone out in a snuff."[27] But all three Mathers knew that there remained a more insidious form of fraud within their ranks: the show of godliness without a corresponding conviction. The very "weight" of religion in the colony encouraged such imposture, and it was precisely the concern with "profession" and "practices" that the ministers most virulently denounced.

"*Because* the Word of God is plentifully and powerfully dispensed throughout this Land," said Richard Mather, and Increase after him, "You have *therefore* so much more need to take heed and beware,

least your Religion reach no further [than the] . . . *form thereof*"
— "*least a promise* of eternal life . . . *being left you* in Christ Jesus any
of you should seem to come short of it." The rest of the orthodoxy
joined in chorus. That "You are a Professing People," they pointed
out, "will signify and come to nothing, if this spirit be wanting."
What "vain Confidence, to rest on any external signs of Gods presence!" — to feel comfortable "when the Word is lodged onely in the
porch, and never cometh into the House" — as though it were
enough just to "live under the Gospel, and enjoy the clear and
convincing Dispensations of it!" "Do you think that God liveth on
goat's blood"? Others could aspire to no more than a "visible regular
course of Obedience"; the elect distinguished themselves by their
dread of failure. Hence, as "*a people near unto the lord* . . . we have
greater cause *not* to be secure." The ministers, in short, knew "how
much weight [God] lays upon his fear, in that he hath made it one of
the main grants of the Everlasting Covenant," and to that end they
directed their appeal for reform. They showed, on the one hand, a
people "grown customary, formal, superficial," "fawning upon
God" with faces like "painted Sepulchres." On the other hand, they
pictured the Lord "*pleading a controversy with this Land.*" They depict
Him in this guise as a rejected and suppliant lover: longing to reclaim
His beloved, "*waiting that he may be gracious,*" eager to forgive all
injuries and insults. Despite our hardheartedness, "Gods compassions are *moving*, his bowels are *sounding*, his *repentings* are kindling,
his *heart is turning within him*, towards New England. . . . After all
our backslidings he is crying after us, *I am married unto you, I will heal
your backslidings. Open unto me, my Love.*"[28]
This emblem of sainthood is a familiar one — but familiar in a
very different way from that in which the New England ministers
used it. By all tradition, it was an emblem of the *difference* between
believers and society at large. The clergy made it instead the basis
for an appeal for social revitalization. Having pleaded so long in
vain, God, they warned, had every right to abandon the colony.
And yet He was offering a last chance. "God hath set New-England
between *Ebal* & *Gerazim*" and announced: "here is life and death set
before thee; choose which you will." As an omniscient God He
knew the outcome; on the human level, He left it to them "what *exit*
we shall make upon this trial." The jeremiads took their direction
from the discourses on grace. To the extent that they "flourished in

dread of success," as Perry Miller claims, the preachers were trying to stress that the proper exit would be reached by *in*security. "The spirit of the law," they knew, "fills a man with rejoycing . . . but the spirit of grace will make us vile in our owne eyes"; and to the "*Children of the Kingdom*" in the election assemblies they intoned: "Consider your selves who you are, and of what consequence it is that *righteousness be rained* down on you." The "awful, considerable" alternative was firstly personal. "Though you may be *Justified*, yet . . . God will not let you see that you are so. . . . God being sadly *Grieved* by your Sins, will Retire from you . . . [and His] burning Indignation . . . [will] break forth upon you"; He will "*change from a faithful* Monitor into [a] . . . *furious Enemy*, Avenger and Tormentor," threatening no "*escape if we neglect so great Salvation*." [29]

Secondly, the alternative to self-abasement meant the collapse of the colony. Since the errand was part of sacred history, the progress of saint and society became identified: one reflected, and verified, the other. When he rebuilt Jerusalem after the Babylonian captivity, Nehemiah could claim that what he had done for his people would redound to his own perpetual good. How much more should this hold true for each inhabitant of New Israel, of whom Nehemiah (like John the Baptist after him) was a type! If we would have the privileges of heaven, the clergy urged, should we not "be *found* already Initiating our selves at the works of that [millennial] *Kingdom*" in America? Instead, "*The land mourns and fades . . .* [because we] *have broken the everlasting Covenant.* . . . Wherefore if we would be recovered out of our Condition, 'tis the *Covenant . . .* that must Recover us." The issue had enormous implications: "Our *Everlasting Recompenses* will be very much adjusted, by the Regards which we had for . . . New-England." Those who came to the colony's aid would find their reward both on earth and in the afterlife; those who failed the cause "shall in the *other* World be Losers too." (So, too, by extension, with regard to fellow travelers or foes abroad: he "*whose heart doth indeed travel with . . . the Lord Jesus in these Ends of the Earth*" will share in the kingdom, but as for him who would harm it, "Woe to that person, whoever he be"; "it were better . . . that a mill-stone were hanged about his neck, and he thrown in the midst of the sea.") By this standard, Samuel Torrey in 1683 summed up the orthodoxy's plea:

May we not with fear and trembling apprehend our selves: even this *whole People, New England*, as it were standing before God, upon our great Trial for *Life and Death* [?] You have been set in this your day of Grace in a way of *probation and trial*. O it is high time to make that great, comprehensive, unchangeable, eternal Choice, upon which depends not only the Salvation of your own Souls, but even the deliverance and salvation of this People, and these Churches: If you do thus chuse Life, all will be well with *New-England*, but if you should refuse, you will likely, not only to destroy your selves; but all.[30]

The nature of the choice indicates a deep, stubborn optimism in the clergy's appeal. It suggests that by 1683 the orthodoxy had found in the rhetoric of probation a way to combine the role of visionary with that of social critic. As prophets of probation, they could describe themselves as isolated representatives of the people — historian-seers whose representative qualities were enhanced by their hostility toward those they represented. Alienation and engagement: *by their very contradictions these terms were made to correspond*; and the correspondence explains what must otherwise appear as a pervasive paradox, the Jeremiahs' insistence that God would *not* forsake His people. From the early sixties through the synod of 1679, they virtually guaranteed success. "Be strong, O Zerubbabel, and be strong all ye people," for "God hath good things yet in reserve for New-England." He "is not only ready . . . but desirous" — "as willing as able" — to pardon our sins: the "great Mountains standing before you . . . shall become a Plain."* Recall that we "of these Ends of the earth have long since made our choice" — that "*N-Englands* true & main Interest . . . is a fixed unalterable thing."

*The allusion to mountain and plain recurs throughout the political sermons, in reference either to the leveling of the mountains in Isaiah 40:4 — where it signifies universal deliverance — or else to Zerubbabel, the postexilic king of Israel who had a vision of the seven-branched candlestick that symbolizes the New Zion (Zechariah 4:2). It may be well to stress that such promises, obviating the conditional (or optional) aspect of New England's future, appear in every form of the literature. In the poetry, as Kenneth Silverman notes (*Colonial American Poetry* [New York, 1968], pp. 128–29), however bleak the picture of present decay, the message is "that the Wilderness Errand *will* be performed." Even Michael Wigglesworth's *God's Controversy with New England* (1662), usually cited as the prime example of clerical despair, ends with the promise that God's "heart is with you all / And shall be with you maugre Sathan's might" (*The Puritans: A Sourcebook of Their Writings*, ed. Perry Miller and Thomas H. Johnson [New York, 1963], II, 616).

God "hath engaged himself . . . to pardon us, to purge us, to convert us, to heal us."[31]

The prospect of ultimate triumph in these sermons is embedded in the very terms of trial. Even as Samuel Torrey acknowledges God's wrath, he asserts unconditionally that the Lord will, after all, "keep Religion alive with us in these ends of the Earth, which we believe God hath given to his Son *for an Inheritance* and for a firm Possession. . . O, when God thus saves *New-England* we shall rejoyce and triumph. . . . Then will be fulfilled in us, and for us, what is prophesied and promised." So also Samuel Willard, John Oxenbridge, and Samuel Whiting, having recited the predictable catalogue of declension, assure their audiences that "no matter how far New England had declined . . . God would revive the country." Did He not promise Jeremiah that "the close of the greatest day of *Jacobs* trouble is, that he shall be saved out of it, *Jer.* 30.7"? Then "let this be our comfort," that amid "the Hurricano's of tempestuous times . . . the cause of God and Israel is Committed to the Lord himself that he would *maintain* it." And thus Urian Oakes — who portrays New England as a sailor drowsing (like Melville's Ishmael) "*on the Top of a Mast in the midst of the Sea* . . . over-born by Security in the mouth of danger" — concludes for the assembly's "*Advantage and Comfort*" that "*God will not make an utter end of us.*" "All is well that ends well," he observes, and it is "the Lords design in humbling and proving you that he may do you good at your Latter End. Though *the Earth should tremble and reel to and fro* . . . yet . . . *it shall be well.*"[32]

Other ministers, in much fiercer denunciations than Oakes's, reaffirm and elaborate upon his conclusion. It was "obvious that God hath a Controversy with us," and it had been their sad duty to communicate his "wrath with his Inheritance." Yet they had "not spoken these things that we should Despair, but that we might be *Awakened*." A period of probation was for them also a season for implantation, and "when he hath prepared the Soyle . . . he will cast in the precious Seed." Preparation entailed harsh measures — breaking up, overturning, remolding the dry earth — because it signified the cultivator's loving care for the harvest to come. God simply "knows not how to give thee up . . . O N[ew] E[ngland]." He "*hath chosen this for his habitation*, He is your God . . . and re-

member it is in a Covenant of Grace he is yours.   If he seems as
if he would be gone, it is but to try your love." Remember, then, the
great distance between a *"sinner foresaken and a saint foresaken."* Sinners can do nothing but await their just doom. Saints must do everything to show themselves worthy of God's love; and when they fail
to comply, He "withdraws himself . . . yet so that he draws their
hearts after him." His thunder itself spoke sweetly to them: *"Fear
thou not, O my servant Jacob, and be not dismayed O Israel, for behold I will
lift thee up . . . above all afflictions."* [33]

These ambiguous images of consolation find their counterpart in
the emblem of the colony as the justly afflicted saint. The emblem
is shadowed forth in the settlers' earliest writings. The emigrant
leaders had known from the outset that their special appointment
would bring special troubles — and that these troubles were a badge
of grace. The familiar text read, "As manie as I love, I rebuke and
chasten" (Revelation 3:19); its meaning was plain enough: "So many
as I love I rebuke earnestly, lest they should perish with the wicked.
And those that I favour I chasten in this life, lest they should be
damned forever. Who is that man that hath of me here neither
chastisement nor rebuke, but is left without restraint, wallowing in
the concupiscence and desires of the flesh? A great sign it is of the
indignation of God; whereas the other is an evident token of love."
God's lightning wrath, in short, which lit up the saints' way of trial,
and so called attention to the pitfalls before them, also revealed New
Jerusalem at the end of the road. With this end in view, the ministers
painted (alongside their image of a pleading God of Mercy) the image
of an avenging God of Justice. "Have you not observed," they asked
after every setback — drought, Indian attack, outburst of crime or
dissension or heresy — "that there have been more . . . tremendous
dispensations of divine Providence in New England than in any
place where you have been?" Why was it that "no place under
heaven . . . will so highly provoke and incense the displeasure of
God as . . . New-England"? Why were there *"no persons in all the
world unto whom God speaketh as he doth unto us* [by His] . . . most
awful Providences"? The reason was obvious. Because New England was God's country, its inhabitants must expect His lash. *"God is
terrible out of his holy places."* [34]

On these grounds, the ministers distinguished carefully between the lesser "vindictive" punishment meted out to other nations and their own "corrective affliction." The former was the wages of sin, the latter of grace. In New England, God chastised His people more severely — "so as purely to *Purge away their Dross*" — and more lovingly, to draw them close to Himself.[35] In either case, He was turning their suffering to His and their glory.* So it was that when the clergy detailed the colony's afflictions they did so proudly and, as a rule, in the phrases of grace. The emigrant theorists of preparation, for example, had written that God visits sorrows upon the saint in order to "knocke off his fingers from base courses," thus "to do [him] good in the latter end": "that which God ayms at" in the "*blackness* of your *trouble*" is "to fit you for your [heavenly] Mansion-place," where He will "mend all." The jeremiads tell us of King Philip's War that "God is knocking the hand of New Englands people off from . . . new Plantations . . . [so] that he may doe us good in the latter end"; therefore, "the *Blacker* you see the *Troubles* to grow, the sooner and surer" it is that He will "perform his whole

---

*They pointed out, of course, that it was vile on New England's part to put God to such trouble. "Our Lord Jesus Christ from Heaven may thus Argue with us; *If other People do Wound me by their Sins, 'tis not such a Wonderful and horrible Thing. But for you, O my People of* New England, *a People that . . . I have known above the other Families of the Earth*" it was heinous beyond expression. And yet in the long run the very wonder and horror of it all was a testament to God's plan. How "marveilous [it will be] in the eyes of the world . . . that grace should be shewed in pardoning such sins!" (Urian Oakes, *The Soveraign Efficacy of Divine Providence* [Boston, 1682], pp. 23–24; Cotton Mather, *Things for a Distressed People to Think Upon* [Boston, 1696], p. 15). The use of "grace" here is revealing of colonial Puritan hermeneutics. Traditionally the word *woes*, like *judgments*, had a double meaning — signifying either *punishment* (for the unregenerate) or else *victory* (for the elect) — and the New England clergy strove with all the rhetorical skill at their command to turn this double meaning into the ambiguity of grace. What Calvin applied only to saints they applied to the errand at large. There was a "need of many evils," wrote Calvin, speaking of God's chosen, "because [God] would heal those wounds which He himself had inflicted. . . . As the Prophet [Jeremiah] saw that . . . the Jews . . . disregarded all God's promises, he added terror to the hope of mercy. Hence he said, 'Ye shall perish, thou and thy people' [Jer. 27:13; cf. 31:32]. He was, no doubt, constrained by necessity to speak in this severe way; for the kind of exhortation which he had used availed nothing; and yet God shewed at the same time by his threatening how much he loved the people" (*Commentaries on the Prophet Jeremiah*, ed. John Owen [Grand Rapids, Mich., 1950], I, 87, and III, 371).

work upon our Zion" and "all will be mended." Such parallels persist from Chauncy's Harvard address of 1655 through the earthquake crises of the 1720s. Taken together, they form a sort of teleology of tribulation. "The reason why Jesus Christ doth not come immediately to judge the world," the colonists were told, "is because of *his long suffering toward us Israelites*." They were not quite ready, not yet pure or contrite enough, and so he was punishing them: "*we are judged of the Lord that we might not be condemned with the World.*"[36]

The jeremiads support this argument with a variety of scriptural analogues. They present the settlers as a prodigal son whose father was hedging his ways with thorns to confine his sinful inclinations. Or they paint them as a patient receiving treatment from "the great Physician of *Israel*." Or again, they picture them as a biblical hero in his moment of temptation: Moses at the rock, David in adultery, Peter denying Christ, and, repeatedly, "*Job* in the midst of his plunges," begging for pity, though his "Deliverance out of trouble will not arise untill the Lords Time be come."* Perhaps the dominant comparison is to the rebuilding of Jerusalem. Consider, said the ministers, the "faults, evils, and distempers" of the "Jews upon their return from Babylon. . . . You must not think it strange, if you be tryed" even more severely, for your mission supersedes theirs. Consider also that "every *Tragedy* they passed through, had a glad *Catas-*

---

*The image of New England as Job is characteristic, and characteristically it is rendered in the following manner (my examples come respectively from Increase Mather, *The Times of Man* [Boston, 1675], p. 5; John Higginson, *The Cause of God* [Cambridge, Mass., 1663], p. 18; Samuel Sewall, *Phaenomena quaedam Apocalyptica* [Boston, 1697], p. 60; Cotton Mather, *The Serviceable Man* [Boston, 1690], pp. 45–46; and William Stoughton, *New-Englands True Interest* [Cambridge, Mass., 1670], pp. 23–24): "As Satan said concerning Job, when God boasted as it were to him of his integrity, . . . Put forth thine hand and touch all that he hath, and he will curse thee to thy face, . . . so now we find [Satan] . . . tempting and saying concerning us, Let that people of so much Profession in the Wilderness be but thus and thus proved and tried." Accordingly, we may turn to the "Holy Counsell given to Job in . . . [his] distresses." Although at present evil events are "compassing and afflicting us on every side" — although "poor . . . New-England [is now] stretching out her Trembling Hands . . . and [pleading:] . . . *Have pity on me, O yee my Friends, for the Hand of the Lord hath touched me!*" — nonetheless we may safely predict "that the End of the Lord with *New England* will be such as was with *Job*": restoration with the doubled blessings of time and eternity.

trophe, every stress had a comfortable issue," and that now, even "more universally and gloriously" than then, "the Lord of Hosts will be gracious to His remnant." [37]

The most complete statement of this position appears in Increase Mather's *The Day of Trouble Is Near*. Written by the foremost American Puritan in his bid for clerical leadership, and bringing together as it does the various images of saintly affliction in an especially dark period of the country's history, it deserves to be cited at length:

> *Christ himself was exposed to sufferings*, [and] *David speaking* as a Type of Christ saith, *Thou hast showed me great and sore troubles*. [Thus] God hath Covenanted with his people that sanctified afflictions shall be their portion, that they shall have Physick as well as Food, [both] ordered according to the Covenant of Grace.
>
> *When glorious Promises are near unto their birth, we may conclude that a day of trouble also is near*. Hereby the children of God *learn* to know more of God, and of themselves too: as we see in Job.
>
> The Lord hath been whetting his glittering Sword a long time [over New England]. The sky looketh red and lowring. The clouds begin to gather thick in our Horizon. *Without doubt*, [therefore,] *the Lord Jesus hath a peculiar respect unto this place, and for this people*. This is *Immanuels Land*. Christ by a wonderful Providence hath dispossessed Satan, who reigned securely in these Ends of the Earth, for Ages the Lord knoweth how many, and here the Lord hath caused as it were *New Jerusalem* to come down from Heaven; He dwells in this place: therefore we may conclude that he will scourge us for our backslidings, [for as said] a Jewish Writer who lived in the dayes of the second Temple [i.e., after the return from Babylon]; "the dealings of God with our Nation and with the Nations of the World is very different: for other Nations may sin and do wickedly and God doth not punish them, until they have filled up the Measure of their sins, and then he utterly destroyeth them; but if our Nation forsake the God of their Fathers never so little God presently cometh up on us with one Judgement or other, that so he may prevent our destruction." So [with other places] it may be he'll reckon with them once for all at last; but if *New-England* shall forsake the Lord, Judgement shall quickly overtake us, because God is not willing to destroy us. [38]

The coherence of Increase Mather's statement — blending the theocracy's views on grace and church-state, history and eschatology, blessing and affliction — bears witness to the coherence of the founders' dream, and particularly, to the force of the rhetoric mar-shaled to protect it.* In this respect, the jeremiads develop from year to year, and from one generation to another, in a self-conscious, self-perpetuating tradition. In 1719 William Williams informed his election-day audience that "This *Exhortation* has been many times urged from this Place." Thirty years before, Cotton Mather had buttressed his discourse by invoking the whole range of election addresses, as had Samuel Torrey a decade before *him*. Specific cita-tions, allusions, and mutual commendations abound throughout the political sermons. This does not mean that the outlook of the American Jeremiahs became irrelevant to the country's development. Nor does it even mean that they tended increasingly "to devaluate the contemporary situation."[39] To say that they lamented a growing discrepancy between fact and ideal is not, after all, to describe a historical position, but to explain a mode of rhetoric. Their lament was a strategy for prodding the community forward, in the belief that fact and ideal *would be made* to correspond. Ironically, it was their intransigence — their unshakable commitment to the New England Way — that allowed the Old Guard Puritans to retain their hopes, to develop the implications of their rhetoric and vision, and so to make their version of the jeremiad a vehicle of cultural continuity.

*Briefly, the stylistic strategy entails: (a) the interrelationship of types (David, Job, Jacob, and Joseph); (b) the unity of disparate images (food, "physick," birthpains, refining furnace, and sword), both through the logic of the argument and through interlinking biblical texts; (c) the sustained connection between the darkly "lowring" present and the approaching millennium, which constantly looks forward to the climactic parallel between New England's remnant and the remnant returned from Babylon — a climax prepared for earlier by the emphatic reference to New Jerusalem. Throughout, Mather carefully weaves together the personal (absolute) level and the collective (temporal) level.

3

The Genetics of Salvation

The American jeremiad was born in an effort to impose metaphor upon reality. It was nourished by an imagination at once defiant of history and profoundly attuned to the historical forces that were shaping the community. And in this dual capacity it blossomed with every major crisis of seventeenth-century New England: doctrinal controversy, the Indian wars, the witchcraft trials, the charter negotiations. From the start the Puritan Jeremiahs had drawn their inspiration from insecurity; by the 1670s, crisis had become their source of strength. They fastened upon it, gloried in it, even invented it if necessary. They took courage from backsliding, converted threat into vindication, made affliction their seal of progress. Crisis became both form and substance of their appeals. In the last chapter I described this process in terms of the logic of Puritan rhetoric, as the gradual unfolding of a distinctive style and outlook. Here I would like to deal with some of the ways in which experience affected the course of that unfolding. My purpose in doing so is largely heuristic. I do not intend to explore the complex relationship between social and ideological change in seventeenth-century New England, but simply to outline several turning points in the evolution of the rhetoric.

Perhaps the major turning point was the mid-century debate on baptism. Puritan scholars have called the Halfway Covenant (1662) the *locus classicus* of the orthodoxy's decline. The first emigrants, we have seen, restricted civic as well as religious power to "visible saints" — that is, to those among them who had experienced conversion, testified persuasively to that effect, and continued to behave in a way which indicated, "within the reach of reasonable charity," that they were truly elect. When, therefore, many of the children of the saints did not qualify for visible sainthood, their failure seemed to erode the very basis of the errand. The Halfway Covenant was an effort to prevent erosion. While retaining the premises of visible sainthood, it granted provisional church status to the still-unregenerate children on the grounds that, in their case, baptism alone conferred certain inalienable covenant rights. In retrospect, we can see how much the compromise deflated the founders' "holy pretence." We may even agree that in the long run it proved to be an act of self-betrayal. Undoubtedly, the Halfway Covenant encouraged a laxness of church controls that prepared for the triumph (toward the end of the century) of an "open church" policy. Undoubtedly, too, we can trace from 1662 the secularizing movement that was eventually to extend the prerogatives of visible sainthood to the entire American electorate.

But this is only one view of the matter. The ministers who instituted the Halfway Covenant denied discontinuity. And the fact is that they were very impressive in demonstrating their unity with their forebears. Increase Mather's compilation of *The First Principles of New-England* shows beyond doubt that Hooker, Norton, Cotton, and virtually all the other founders had placed an immense emphasis on baptism in New England. Pointing to the crucial passage in Genesis where God makes His pact not only with Abraham but also with Abraham's posterity, they felt they could safely assume that "our children" — unlike others — *"Confederate in their Parents*, because to the Children of Parents in Covenant, that promise Gen. 17.7 doth belong."* The promise, in short, assured those children of

*Moreover I wil establish my covenant betwene me and thee, and thy sede after thee in their generacions, for an everlasting covenant, to be God unto thee and to thy sede after thee.

And I wil give thee and thy sede after thee the land, wherin thou art a stranger. (Genesis 17:7–8)

This text was often associated in the New England Puritan jeremiads with the prophecy of Isaiah 44:

membership by birth in the elect community. "Even if [they] showed no visible signs of grace, there was still good reason to believe that they would finally be saved." And even if that assurance might not pertain to every child, its overall probability permitted the elders to look upon baptism (restricted as it was to the saints' offspring) as a reasonable guarantee of conversion, and hence as a valid premise for their children's participation in the church-state. The "persons in Question," explained Increase Mather, in a characteristic blend of figural and Ramistic argument,

> are either belonging to the visible Church, or of the world only. The Scripture speaketh of those two terms, *Church* and the *world*, as opposite and Contradistinct . . . [and since our] visible Church is gods house, of which the Israelites' Temple was a Type . . . [therefore all those] within the Pale of the visible Church have the right to Baptism, and consequently may transmit the right to their children. The Lord promised to give grace to our Children that he should extend his Covenant, not only to Parents, but also their Offspring.[1]

This genetics of salvation, as I have called it, may be seen as the doctrinal counterpart of the concept of errand.* It confirms the Puritan mission from within — adds to the assurance of Scripture

---

I wil powre my Spirit upon thy sede, and my blessing upon thy buddes;
  And thei shal growe as among the grasse, & as the willowes by the river of waters.
  And who is like me, that shal call, and shal declare it, and set it in order before me, since I appointed the ancient people? . . .
  Rejoyce, ye heavens: for the Lord hathe done it: shoute, ye lower partes of ye earth: brast forthe into praises, ye mountaines, O forest and everie tre therein: for ye Lord hathe redemed Jaakob and wilbe glorified in Israel. (3–4, 7, 23)

*Here, as elsewhere, I do not mean to say that the ministers had no fears about the future, or that their expressions of despair were merely strategies of affirmation. Undoubtedly, some ministers felt less optimistic than others, and many of them must have wondered at times if this new generation of New Englanders really *was* God's elect people. Their threats expressed real anxiety, a genuine sense of bewilderment and outrage. My assumption, as I said in the Preface, is that this dark side of the rhetoric does not contradict the logic of the jeremiad itself, any more than it does (say) in the case of the Puritans' argument about preparation and predestination. Emory Elliott has argued in *Power and the Pulpit in Puritan New England* (Princeton, N.J., 1975) that the sermons shift in the 1670s to a relatively pessimistic stance, but he also points out that the orthodoxy never abandoned the errand, and that during the 1690s they returned once more to the optative mood.

prophecy the "internal evidence" of generational succession. And like the errand into the wilderness, the genetics of salvation is a distinctive product of American Puritanism. It blends the heterogeneous covenants of community and grace; and it adapts the rhetoric to new conditions without abandoning the founders' vision. For Increase Mather's argument about continuity, let me repeat, is a persuasive one. Indeed, the tenets of the Halfway Covenant are foreshadowed in many other early documents besides those which he assembled. It seems safe to say that the majority of first-generation divines believed that New England's venture was "not the *business of one age*," but the issue of a promise made *in perpetuum*. Speaking of the covenant of grace, the first planters announced that "All the rich blessings of that Covenant shall be [our] *Inheritance for ever*" — ours and our children's alike. By heaven's time, our children *already* "bear the name of God upon them." Was it not the word of God Himself that through the mercy granted to the fathers the sons "also may obtain mercy," despite their apparent "ungodliness" (Romans 11:31)? Did He not vow, through His prophet Jeremiah, that "their children also shalbe . . . established before me" (30:20)?[2]

"In the latter daies ye shal understand it," Jeremiah had announced (30:24). Now that those days were come, the emigrants could have no doubt about the matter. Since God gave "himselfe to be a God unto *Abraham*, and to his seed . . . it must of necessity follow, that . . . he will perform both his owne part of the Covenant, and *Abrahams* part also . . . from one Covenant to another; by all which things it doth appear that the Lord will keep our part of the Covenant also." All this in no way implies that the first settlers anticipated the problems of the 1660s. On the contrary, their belief in what they called the "Praeingaged" holiness of their children was based on the conviction that no problems would arise. In their view, no "Essential Alteration" could obtain between the generations; it could not be otherwise than that "the Branches would be answerable to the root." Since they were called en masse to a historic undertaking, it followed that the spiritual legacy from father to son would continue to the final victory. The ministers of the second and third generations took up these arguments with a vengeance. Their sermons glow with visions of parents and "their Off-spring with them partak[ing] of Eternal Life and happiness." Sometimes, in fact, they suggest that the offspring, being nearer to victory, will not only *"Inherit* the *Glory* of the Ancestors" but shine with a "Double Glory," since in temporal terms at least God "will do *more* for us than ever He did for them." As history draws towards its close, the *"Covenant-Mercy* of God unto [His people] . . . the *further* it Rolls, the bigger it grows."[3]

Most English Puritans, despite their enormous diversity of opinion, regarded baptism to be a *"means* of grace." That is, baptism was for them the form as distinct from the substance — a human aid toward belief without any attendant claim upon salvation. The New England clergy could simply not allow for such uncertainties to stand between the promise and its realization. The very ambiguity of their errand militated against this. But they could not dismiss the problem out of hand, since it expressed a basic tenet of the Reformed movement, of which they claimed to be the vanguard. Accordingly, they turned in this dilemma, as in others, to their theory of exceptionalism. Elsewhere, they conceded, the covenant of grace probably *was* no more than a personal matter between man and God. In England or Germany or France, it might well "take in the Parent, and *leave out the child."* But their case was different. Baptism in New England was also a social and historical matter. In their American Zion, the sacred place reserved for the end-time remnant, "the line of Election doth for the most part run through the loyns of godly Parents."[4] *For the most part* was their notion of compromise: the qualification was both a gesture toward common sense and a reaffirmation of their vision, a plea for unity couched in a declaration of uniqueness. For themselves alone, and among themselves *for the most part*, they asserted that baptism was a reliable sign of grace.*

---

*Although this was the general view of baptism in New England, colonists were not of one mind on the subject. Their treatises are sometimes contradictory, and now and then they seem rather reticent about declaring a fixed opinion. Joy Gilsdorf has speculated that their intense millennialism led the emigrant divines to equivocate on the meaning of baptism: if the new age was at hand, "there was obviously no need to decide the worrisome question" ("Puritan Apocalypse: New England Eschatology in the Seventeenth Century," Diss. Yale 1964, p. 146). Furthermore, their views on the "line of election" clearly built upon the Reformers' developing concept of baptism (through Tyndale and the Zurich theologians). But the European Calvinists stressed that "few of any class or nation were of the elect" (C. J. Sommerville, "Conversion versus the Early Puritan Covenant of Grace," *Journal of the Presbyterian Historical*

Rhetorically, their solution secured the uneasy transition from one generation to the next, until their errand would be accomplished. And the rhetorical solution, be it noted, had significant historical implications as well. For it was precisely through the "ironic" links between the Halfway Covenant and Solomon Stoddard's open church policy that the Puritans managed to bequeath their vision to Yankee America. What began, perhaps, as a measure of desperation — their pleas with the "rising generation" to claim salvation through a national covenant — turned out in the long run to be a reassertion of the colony's grand design.

Most dramatically, they expressed their vision through the legend of New England's golden age. Following the logic of their genetics of salvation, the Puritan Jeremiahs made ingratitude their main case against the unconverted. It was a breach of filial duty, they thundered, not to embrace the God of the fathers. The children were obliged to *demand* grace by virtue of their parents' mission. And to sustain their case, they proceeded to elevate the emigrants into mythic tribal heroes — a race of giants in an age of miracles — imposing on the tiny, barren American strand of three decades before the archetypes of scriptural and classical antiquity. "If my weakness was able to show you," said John Higginson in 1663, "what the Cause of God and his People in *New-England* is, according to its *divine Originall* and *Native beautie*, it would dazzle the eyes of Angels, daunt the hearts of devils, ravish and chain fast the Affections of all the Saints." As a rule, the ministers overcame their weakness through the most florid stylistic flights in the literature. "Our Fathers were Clothed with the Sun . . . the Moon was under

Society, 44 [1966], 187). In New England the principle of hereditary election "reduced to a minimum the uncertainty of living under an omnipotent and arbitrary God" (Edmund S. Morgan, *The Puritan Family: Religion and Domestic Relations in Seventeenth-Century New England* [Boston, 1944], p. 184). Thus while English Puritan views of baptism remained "excessively tangled" and "thorny" (Geoffrey Nuttall, *Visible Saints: The Congregational Way, 1640–1660* [Oxford, 1957], pp. 118, 135), New England preachers insisted that the rising generation fell under a "necessity to be New born": "Scripture Prophecies & Promises," bringing us "advantages for the obtaining Grace & Salvation . . . as others have not," *required* "persons, to say . . . *He is my God*, who can say, *He is my Fathers God*" (Cotton Mather, *The Duty of Children* [Boston, 1703], pp. 32, 49, 22).

their Feet. . . . God Rode upon the Heavens for their help" and "ran to . . . fall on their necks and kiss them." No land under heaven had seen "such rich overflowing of Compassions," or enjoyed "the uniting glory then manifest from the shine of mercy from the Throne, Grace Ruling and Ordering both Rulers and People under the Glorious Banner . . . of Love." "If we look abroad over the face of the whole earth, where shall we see a place or people brought to such perfection?" Never, in sum, had God so "wonderfully owned and exalted" a people as he did this "precious Remnant." Their city on a hill bodied forth the hopes and fantasies of mankind. It was a greater Latium, a dream of earthly paradise made real, recovering from the "disguises of mythology" and the chimerical Eldorados of Renaissance writers, the actual (and more splendid) benefits God intended for His peculiar people. "Such great Persons as *Budaeus*, and others, who mistook *Sir Thomas Moor*'s UTOPIA; for a Country really existent . . . might now have certainly found a Truth in their Mistake; *New England* was a true Utopia."[5]

As a backdrop for this age of wonders, the clergy set out an apocalyptic history of America. The framework for that history derived from the emigrant divines; but it was elaborated after 1662 into a full-scale vision of the prophetic meaning of the New World. I repeat the date, 1662, not only to recall the Halfway Covenant but to contrast the fate of Puritanism in Old and New England. Indeed, nothing more sharply reveals the force of the New England Way than the fact that the Halfway Covenant coincided with the return in 1660 of Charles II. The contrast might be made even earlier, before the fall of the Protectorate, when in the 1650s many English millennialists became disenchanted with Cromwell, and increasingly dissociated their hopes for the Second Coming from the course of British history. In any case, the dissociation was complete after the Restoration. Whatever the prospects for civic progress or church reformation, Christ's kingdom, they felt sure, was not of this world. It amounted to a bitter reversal of the English Puritan dream; but as I mentioned earlier, the fact that the dream itself was rooted in secular (not sacred) history must have facilitated their adjustment to a "more prosaic day."[6] They compensated for their lost Holy Commonwealth on the one hand by emphasizing the inwardness of grace, and on the other hand by a renewed pride in national antiquities. The

New World ministers suffered what might be considered similar disappointments; but they had committed themselves to a view that precluded the separation of sacred from secular. When, accordingly, they felt that history was undermining their ideal, they had no choice but to explain history away. They did so by asserting the priority of prophecy over appearances, by absorbing a backsliding generation into their myth of ordained progress, and, in a daring "application" of their genetics of salvation, by extending the legend of the fathers to the story of America itself.

According to the second- and third-generation orthodoxy, the New World at large — not just New England but the entire continent — was destined for an errand in sacred history. Like Canaan of old, America was the child of prophecy and promise. It had remained so long unknown, controlled solely by Satan and his minions, in order that Christ could more awesomely reveal His power when, in "the fulness of time," He undertook the renovation of the Church. Connecting Jeremiah's predictions with those concerning "the ends of the earth" — a phrase which through a variety of scriptural texts intimated the Second Coming — the clergy observed that God had vowed (Psalms 2:8) to give his remnant "the heathen for thine inheritance, and the endes of the earth for thy possession." What else could He have meant by that but "a *New* Heaven in the *New* World"? Moreover, America clearly denoted the fourth and last of the round earth's imagined "ends." The apocalyptic number (see Revelation 6:2–8, 7:1) had been traditionally linked to the Four Horsemen as types of the spread of the gospel, each of the first three Horsemen representing one of the continents then known, and the fourth Horseman representing the last stage of time. In the Reformation, all this took on another, more concrete meaning. If a fact "so great and considerable as America is," wrote John Goodwin in 1642, "was yet unknown . . . for so many generations together," does not its discovery in these last days mean that new "secrets of the scripture [will] see the light of the sun?" During the last third of the seventeenth century, the New England Puritans seized upon these implications. They pointed out that "*Asia, Africa,* and *Europe* have, each of them, had a glorious Gospel Day," so that by the end of the fifteenth century, the "Barrier *Solum* to the millennium lay across the Atlantic. Hence Columbus providentially called the continent "ST. SAVIOR," and the two highest achievements of modern *"humane affairs . . . Literature* and [Reformed] *Religion . . .* dawned upon the miserable world, one just *before*, the other just *after*, the famed navigation hither" — a voyage directed by God for "the great issue . . . of the . . . Hopes* of his people."[7]

Hence, too, the settlement of New England followed directly upon the revival of interest in the Book of Revelation. Ever since the Marian exile, English Protestants had maintained that "this heavenly book" revealed all the mysteries, of "every Age and Generation . . . untill this last and utmost Prophetical Period." Ever since the turn of the seventeenth century, English Puritans had argued with growing excitement that as history advanced, more and more light would be thrown on the veiled symbols of the Apocalypse. Then in 1627 Joseph Mede published his famous *omnium-gatherum* of Protestant apocalyptica, *The Key of the Revelation*. In retrospect the colonial clergy realized the momentous order of events: Columbus, the printing press, the Reformation, and, in 1627, *"Mr. Medes Clavis . . .* which was a notable means to revive the thinking and Speaking of *New Jerusalem*. And this was the year wherein the Design for . . . *New England*, began to be ripened"! The meaning of this correspondence could hardly be mistaken. "When the *Seventy years*, for the Churches confinement in *Babylon*, were almost out, Good Men might have *Known* that they were so: Holy Daniel did Know it," as did Jeremiah. It was so also before the deliverance from Egypt and before the Incarnation. Surely, then, the recent and multiplying speculations about the vision of St. John — who, the emigrants pointed out, was like them exiled, like them "carried away into the wilderness" (for "such of us as are in an exiled condition . . . shall know what God is doing, and about to do in the world, though others know nothing of these matters") — surely, those speculations proved that *"the Twelve Hundred & Sixty years* assigned unto the Reign of the *Antichristian Apostasy*, draw towards *their Period*." Considered together with all other aspects of American history, it constituted "not meer *Conjecture*, or *Opinion*, but . . . Demonstration [that] . . . an *Age of Miracles* [is] now *Dawning* upon us," one in which the inhabitants of "this *New-England Israel . . .* are concerned more than any other men Living."[8]

From this vantage point, the latter-day Jeremiahs showed the colony through a mirror reflection of past and future. Standing (as it were) at a meeting of two eternities, they perceived that the Great Migration, in all its divine original beauty, was but the first stage of an errand to the end of time. As the story unfolded in the late seventeenth-century sermons, the migration opened with a "Divine Call," in an "incomparable Minute," to "a people separated and set apart by God to be the Subject of a very great and glorious Work of Reformation." This new Israel the Lord brought "by a mighty hand and an outstretched arm over a *greater* than the Red Sea," and gave them "*these Ends of the Earth* . . . for the *Bounds of their Habitation*." How He had subsequently preserved and prospered them there, was a matter of common knowledge. "Ask now of many of the Ages that are past, and ask from one side of Heaven unto the other, whether there hath been any such . . . almost unexampled unparall[el]ed mercy" shown to man. The desert had bloomed into another garden of God — not the lost land of milk and honey but the miraculously rejuvenated home of the blessed remnant. In phrases drawn from Isaiah, Psalms, and Jeremiah (interwoven with those from Revelation), the jeremiads exult in a miraculous and instantaneous transformation. "When he planted these Heavens and laid the foundation of this Earth," His vow to create in "Sion . . . *a Tabernacle not* [ever to be] *taken down* . . . hath in an eminent degree [been] fulfilled before our eyes." "In a day" — with a "wonderful alteration" such "as was never heare[d] of in the world" — the "remote, rocky, bushy, wild-woody wilderness" became "for fertilness . . . the wonder of the world," a second Eden, "*rejoycing and blossoming as a Rose*," and spiritually "*Beautiful as* Tirzah, *Comely as* Jerusalem, *Terrible as an Army with Banners*." Its inhabitants God had guarded as "*the Apple of his Eye*" and "dandled in the lap of his providence." He drove out the heathen to make room for them; He shielded them from enemies; He blessed their crops and their offspring. Against all schemes of Satan, "God himself hath been a Wall of fire to us. . . . *He hath fenced us . . . about as his peculiar garden of pleasure*" and "enclosed [us] . . . to be a *City of Righteousness*" and a "*Valley of Vision*." [9]

This heroic era the jeremiads project into the American city of God. The point was not just to arouse the sons to emulate the fathers, but to assert progress through continuity. Urian Oakes's often-quoted remark about "our great duty to be the Lords *Remem-*

brancers" is taken from Isaiah's prophecy of the last days (61:2–12), when God would bring salvation "unto the end of the world." Earlier in the same sermon, Oakes had applied the text at length to the colonists' accomplishments. "As a City upon a hill," he recalled, "you have, to a considerable Degree enlightened the world as to the pattern of Gods House." Indeed,

> if we cast up the Accompt, the Summe of all our mercies, and lay all things together, this our Common-wealth seems to exhibit a *little model of the Kingdome of Christ upon Earth*, wherein it is generally acknowledged and expected. This work of God set on foot and advanced to a good Degree here, being spread over the face of the Earth, and perfected as to greater Degree of Light and Grace and Gospel-glory will be (as I conceive) *the Kingdome of Jesus Christ so much spoken of. When this is accomplished*, you may then say, *the Kingdoms of this World are become the Kingdome of our Lord*, for you have been *as a Candle in the Candlestick that giveth light to the whole House.*

On these grounds, Oakes and his colleagues confirmed "Dr. *Twiss* his Opinion that when New Jerusalem should come down from Heaven *America* would be the seat of it" and urged prayer to hurry its descent.* "'Tis the prerogative of New-England above all the Countries of the world" because "the *New English* Churches are a preface to the New Heavens."[10] It was a prerogative that enabled the second- and third-generation preachers to transform the Janus-

---

*William Twisse stated his opinion in a famous letter (March 1635) to Joseph Mede, who suggested in reply that the New World might have been reserved instead for Gog and Magog. Mede's conjecture rankled the American Puritans throughout the century because (among other more obvious reasons) it seemed to echo their opponents' analogy between the New Englanders and the "unprofitable servant" whom Christ condemned to "outer darkness" (Matthew 25:30). In general, the settlers countered with a barrage of contrary images: "Zion the outcast," "light in darkness," the woman of Revelation 12, the exiled patriarchs and prophets. Indeed, they seem to have invoked Mede's conjecture precisely in order to refute it by way of Twisse, as Cotton Mather does, for instance, in *The Present State of New England* (Boston, 1690), p. 35, and *The Way to Prosperity* (Boston, 1690), p. 20. Nicholas Noyes (*New-Englands Duty* [Boston, 1698], pp. 44 ff.) and Samuel Sewall (*Phaenomena quaedam Apocalyptica* [Boston, 1697], pp. 39–40) similarly note the "Antick Fancy of *America's* being Hell" to preface their "Demonstration" of how "it should be the New Jerusalem" — Sewall adding for the consolation of the English saints that Boston was no further from London than from Jerusalem. No American Puritan remembered to say that Twisse was eventually persuaded by Mede about the dismal prospects in store for America.

like vision of Israel into the ambiguous two-handled engine of literal-prophetic history.

The transformation involved still another aspect of the Puritan concept of Israel: the doctrine of the National Conversion of the Jews. I spoke earlier of the Christian view of Israel's decline and fall; but for many Christians, from the Church Fathers through the Reformation, the story did not end there. Eventually, it was thought, God would restore Israel to its former glory. Directly before the Second Coming, His anger toward the Jews would abate, and He would reclaim them, literally and *in toto*, as His people once again. So their apostasy did not signify a broken national covenant after all. It was only a surface lesion in a "special branch of the Covenant of Grace,"* a sort of unhappy horological interlude between two divine acts — their call through Abraham at the start of Jewish history and their salvation through Christ at the close of the history of mankind.

The idea was a controversial one,† but it gained authority from rabbinical and cabalistic tradition. From Akiba through Rashi and

---

*Peter Bulkeley, *The Gospel-Covenant* (London, 1651), pp. 9–10; characteristically, Bulkeley's interpretation centers on the *figura* of the Babylonian captivity: "As their captivities in *Babel* resembled their captive condition now, so their deliverance out of *Babel* then, typed out their deliverance *by the bloud of the Covenant* [i.e., by grace]. *The Jewes though for the present they be as prisoners in the Pit, yet they shall be againe delivered out of it, by vertue of the Covenant made with their Fathers*. This is foretold in that place of *Jeremie* [where he] tells us, that *the City* (Jerusalem) *shall be builded* and *Israel* called upon to returne. And from all this concludes, *that all Israel shall come in and be saved*" (pp. 18–20, ellipses deleted; see also pp. 13–16).

†Calvin himself sharply disagreed, and a number of influential divines sustained his opinion, notably William Prynne. Others, like Hanserd Knollys, urged that the Jews' Conversion not only was clearly prophesied but had already begun. Still others, like Joseph Mede, wavered between the two possibilities, speculating that particular Jews might be redeemed but not all. Closest perhaps to the colonists' position was Nicholas Byfield, who argued that virtually all but the last of the end-time prophecies had been fulfilled, and Johan Alsted, the Ramist millenarian, whose commentaries on Revelation 20 emphasized the Conversion of the Jews. Whatever the precise influences were upon the New England clergy, it seems safe to say that their enthusiasm in this regard continued unabated through the century. Interestingly, this seems to have played some part even in the drama of Anne Hutchinson, whose followers regarded her, according to Winthrop, "as a Prophetesse, raised up of God for some kind of greate worke now at hand, as the calling of the Jewes" (*The Antinomian Controversy, 1636–1638: A Documentary History*, ed. David D. Hall [Middletown, Conn., 1968], p. 308).

Maimonides to Menasseh ben Israel (who helped secure the immigration of Jews to Cromwell's England as "a condition precedent to their Redemption"), Jewish theologians emphasized the prophecies of Israel's restoration. In the decades before and after the planting of Massachusetts, their exegeses provoked a widespread messianic Zionism. The rabbis were particularly affected by the Reformation, in which many of them saw proof of the hastening fulfillment of scriptural promises, and, following the calculations of the Zohar, the Hebrew "Book of Mysteries," they fixed upon the year 1648 as the *annus mirabilis*.[11]

Their apocalyptic fervor had a decided impact in turn upon the leading Reformers. Through the influence of continental and English scholars — Reuchlin, Pico, Scaliger, the Buxtorfs, William Gill, Henry More, and others — the study of Hebrew, along with the circulation of Hebrew literature in translation, facilitated an excited exchange of millennial speculations among Jewish and Christian scholars. It issued in the expectation of a mass conversion of Jewry, in the Protestants' adoption of various tenets of Hebrew apocalypticism,* and above all in the belief that a momentous change was at hand, for the Jews first, and then mankind at large.

The New Englanders embraced the doctrine of National Conversion as a testament to their own genetics of salvation. Samuel Gorton complained in 1646 about the settlers' "looking after, and foretelling so much . . . the calling of the Jews," and Increase Mather could say in 1710 (the year after he published his popular *Essay upon the Jews Conversion and the Millennium*), that "the Conversion of the Jews . . . has ever been received as a Truth in the Churches of *New-England*." It was a truth celebrated throughout the American jeremiads as the marriage of Christ and His church — "the great Jubile" or "illustrious Epithalamium," set upon the "*Apocalyptical Stage*," whereby "the Earth shall be marvellously filled with *Heavenly Influences*." In his preface to Shepard's *Parable of the Ten Virgins* (1636–40), Jonathan Mitchel applied the parable "to the times about

---

*For example, the concept of the fifth monarchy, which according to rabbinical estimates would come upon the fall of Rome, and the importance assigned to the study of the Zohar. Directly or indirectly, the influence of the Zohar is felt throughout seventeenth-century colonial writings. In general, the rabbis' concern with Daniel and Jeremiah delighted the Puritans because of the parallels they discerned between these prophecies and those in Revelation.

the expected calling of the *Jews* (and if so, the substance of the work may be accounted to be . . . seasonable for these times)," and John Cotton noted soon after that since New England enjoyed "such fellowship as the Church of the Jewes had with Christ coming out of Romish Babylon," the colonists might well "expect a powerfull and glorious calling of the Jewes." Long after 1648 had come and passed, the ministers discussed and prayed for the event. At times they undertook themselves to convert the Jews; they shared in the excitement through the 1660s — the crest of Shabb'tai Zvi's career — at the "constant reports from sundry places and hands" about an influx of Jews to the Holy Land, "carried on with great signs and wonders"; and during the height of John Eliot's missionary work some of them seriously contemplated the possibility that the native Indians were descended from the ten lost tribes,* so that every conversion carried further assurance (according to Thomas Shepard's 1648 tract on the Indians) that that "brighter day" was dawning "wherein East & West shall sing the song of the Lamb."[12]

In all this the New England Puritans were doing no more than many other Protestant millennialists of their time. They departed from tradition, however, in what I suggested was their main use of the doctrine of National Conversion: their application of the doctrine, literally and historically, to their own venture. It was an application which violated a fundamental tenet of Protestant exegesis — that the relation between the old chosen people and the new was solely spiritual — and an application for which the Puritans' rhetoric and vision had amply prepared them. As Israel *redivivus* in the type, they could claim all the ancient prerogatives. And from that vantage

---

*This belief was far less prevalent in New England, however, than some scholars have assumed. First, it did not originate with the Puritans but with the Spaniard Joannes Frederico Lummius and various Jesuit missionaries; by 1605, Samuel Purchas had broadcast to the English-speaking world the possibility that the Indians were Jews. Second, the enthusiasm in this respect of John Eliot and Edward Winslow never really took hold in New England — partly, no doubt, because of the limited (and always precarious) success of the Indian missions, but more importantly, I think, because this concept of the Indians violated the Puritans' concept of themselves, their fundamental distinction between Christ's Army and its Satanic enemies. In any case, by the time King Philip's War broke out the Indians were unequivocally identified with the doomed "dark brothers" of Scripture — Cain, Ishmael, Esau, and above all the heathen natives of the promised land, who were to be dispossessed by divine decree of what really belonged to God's chosen.

point, they could bring the type to bear directly upon their most pressing dilemma. Were not the "People of Israel," they reasoned, "like us, the poor People of *New England* brought into sad circumstances"? Clearly, the fact that "the unbelieving Nation of the *Jews* shall be converted and saved" carries a lesson for our unconverted-but-baptized offspring: "They who make nothing of the Covenant of God with faithful Ancestors, will see their error if ever they see the *Jews* converted." And therefore,

> such parents as have entered into a Covenant with the Lord may be assured, that the vertue, the blessing, the efficacy of the Covenant shall never be disannuled, but it shall go on to your children forever; by your Covenant, you have such hold of God, that you may be assured, he will be a God, not to you onely, but your seed [also] shall stand before the Lord, to serve him for ever. This you see fulfilled in the people of the Jewes, [and] what mercy *Abrahams* seed have belonging to them, the same doth belong to yours also; therefore this your Covenant shall draw in your children to partake of blessing and grace with you, never to be broken off.

If the figural parallel with Israel shaped the Puritan concept of errand, the doctrine of National Conversion certified the errand's progress. It served not only to validate the Halfway Covenant, but through that validation to explain away the dangers of declension once and for all. Even as they defended God's untoward judgments, the clergy maintained that God was about to pour His blessings upon the backsliding children, just as He would upon the house of Israel. For like the Jews, the colonists had "grown a little too secure and careless . . . neglecting of His Ordinances for the sake of their own Secular Accomodations." Like the Jews, they "that were the *only people of God in the world*, [became] involved in the most Awakening and Horrible Calamities; and [were shown the] . . . prospect of . . . a Speedy . . . *Ruine* before their Eyes." And like the Jews, the colonists might now, "in the days of the Messiah," expect that "God will remember his Covenant with their Ancestors." Accordingly, it was no longer only a question of trial. Primarily, it was a matter of patience and faith.[13]

This total identification — literal, spiritual, and figural — of Old Israel and New is a distinguishing trait of the jeremiads in the last decades of the seventeenth century. In his mocking rhymes of 1676

(*A Looking Glass for the Times*), Peter Folger, the Rhode Island eccentric and grandfather of Benjamin Franklin, describes the settlers looking for assurance to "the Prophet *Jeremy*" in the conviction that "*New
England* they are like the *Jews* / as like as like can be.*"* But his satire
gives only half the story. Increasingly during the last quarter of the
century, the clergy believed that New Englanders were like the Jews
as the Jews *would be*, when God would once again, miraculously,
make them His chosen people. Increase Mather's *Mystery of Israel's
Salvation* (1669) reports the Jews' current exodus to Palestine as an
incentive to New England's errand. Some three decades later,
Samuel Willard's *The Fountain Opened; or, The Admirable Blessing Plentifully to Be Dispensed at the National Conversion of the Jews* speaks of
National Conversion as a solution for New England's ills. Taking as
his main text Jeremiah's image of "Zion the outcast healed of her
wounds" (Jeremiah 30, 31) — a passage that since Augustine had
been applied to the elect, since the Reformation to the Jews, and
since 1630 by the colonial clergy to their church-state — Willard
links all three levels of meaning. His rendering submits all to God
and leaves virtually nothing to man, except the capacity to receive
mercies to be dispensed. Willard's treatise went through three editions by 1700, when it was appended to Samuel Sewall's *Phaenomena
quaedam Apocalyptica; or, The New Heavens as It Makes to Those Who
Stand upon the New Earth*.[14]
    The combination of texts was not accidental. During the first
decades of settlement, the Puritans had fused human initiative and
divine calling; the second generation had added to that the parallel
between antiquarianism and apocalypse, the appeal to group origins
and the summons to the future. Now, in the last years of the century, the orthodoxy took advantage of the rhetoric they inherited to
convey their lament through the promise of National Conversion.*

---

*This is not to say that the ministers began to look passively or smugly upon their
flocks' errant ways. Their lament persisted, along with their threats and pleas for
reformation. They warned as before that "the eyes of God and of his holy *Angels* are
upon you to see . . . how you Manage . . . this Trust" (Samuel Torrey, *Man's
Extemity, God's Opportunity* [Cambridge, Mass., 1695], pp. 55–56), and they even
lectured, at least once or twice, *against* presuming "upon Sovereign Grace, which we
are apt and (I fear we begin) to doe" (Jonathan Mitchel, *Nehemiah upon the Wall*
[Cambridge, Mass., 1671], p. 19). The growing emphasis upon the Jews' Conversion
merely brings to the fore the rhetorical strategy that underlies the American jeremiad

Perhaps the fullest definition of their method comes in Cotton Mather's election-day address of 1700, *A Pillar of Gratitude*. "A people there has been," Mather begins playfully, "of whom that Account may be given, *O Lord, Thou has brought a Vine, thou has cast out the Heathen, and planted it: Thou didst cause it to take deep Root, and it filled the Land.* . . . My Hearers all this while know not, whether I am giving an Account of *old Israel*, or of *New-England*: So Surprising has been the Parallel!" But his hearers did know. As Mather goes on to say, their leaders had long since clarified the matter. Spiritually *or* literally considered, the parallel between Old Israel and New England was a misleading one. In its spiritual sense, the flourishing vine emblemized not just New England but the entire church of the elect, for every believer was by definition implanted in Christ. In its secular sense, the vine of Israel pertained only superficially to New England history, for it betokened God's "voluntary Presence" with a people, His "*common* love" which alters as He finds alteration among men. As such it was above all "a Sign and an Example of Vengeance," teaching the immemorial lessons of mutability — "cracking and sinking," "blinding, hardening, ruining," turning from "a noble vine . . . to a degenerate vine, *Exod*. 32, 7, 8," and then festering till it stank worse than weeds.[15]

Spiritually *or* literally, then, the meaning of *Israel* was archetypal, and the two archetypes — Israel as the mirror of election and Israel as the model of secular history — were mutually exclusive. But figurally, as the New England clergy applied the types of Scripture, it took on the cumulative ambiguities of the errand. Looking to past and future, the orthodoxy posited a dual identification between Old Israel and New. One was retrospective: the progress from Canaan to America, according to biblical prophecy. The other was proleptic: as Israel would in time receive the blessings of National Conversion, so the New England Way would one day extend into the Theopolis

---

from the start. Perry Miller noted that the jeremiads served "as a cleansing ritual unconnected with any real belief that New England was in fact decaying, and as a factual declaration, deeply pessimistic" about human initiative (*The New England Mind: From Colony to Province* [1953; rpt. Boston, 1961], p. 51). He meant by this to point to the contradictory impulses in the genre, but we would do better, I think, to see in this paradoxical dual impulse the dynamics of Puritan ambiguity.

Americana. In the first case, the clergy "would *not* be understood, as if the Dispensations of God now did exactly quadrate with his Dispensation to the Jews." In the second case, they *would* be so understood: "Jerusalem was, New England is, they were, you are, . . . it is [all] so much the same that . . . [we may] put . . . in New Englands name instead of Jerusalem." What elsewhere was sheer contradiction became here the proof text of a unique, harmonious design. The proof was argued most fully in the political sermons, but its impact may best be gauged in certain nonclerical utterances: in the impassioned tracts of the 1690s, for example, by Judge Samuel Sewall and the merchant Joshua Scottow, or in the celebration of the errand, over twenty years before the Halfway Covenant and a half century before Cotton Mather's *Pillar of Gratitude*, by Captain Edward Johnson:

> As it was necessary that there should be a Moses and Aaron, before the Lord would deliver his people and destroy Pharaoh lest they should be wildered indeed in the Wilderness; so now it was needfull, that the Churches of Christ should first obtain their purity, and the civill government its power to defend them, before Antichrist comes to his finall ruine: and because you shall be sure the day is come indeed, behold the Lord Christ marshalling these N[ew] E[ngland] people. What the issue will be is assuredly known in the generall already. Babylon is fallen, is fallen. The poor remnant of Gods people [in America] have heard the noyse of the great fall.
> The noble Acts Jehova wrought his Israel to redeem,
> Surely this second work of his shall far more glorious seem.
> And now you antient people of Israel look out of your Prison grates, let these Armies of the Lord Christ [in America] provoke you to acknowledge he is certainly come, to put life into your dry bones.[16]

So conceived, the relation of the Hebrew exodus to the Great Migration meant simultaneously parallel and fulfillment, and in either case it was prophetic, interweaving the legend of New England's fathers with the promise of paradise to be. One way or the other, that is, the community's true meaning lay not in the present, but despite the present in its future salvation. Did not Isaiah predict, directly after reminding the Israelites to "Look unto Abraham your father," that "the Lord . . . will make [the] wilderness like Eden, and [the] desert like the Garden of the Lord"? And did not that prediction pertain directly to America itself, which "hath been desolate and unmarried for numerous ages" only to receive, in these latter days, "a greater salvation than that out of *Egypt* was"? Because, therefore, the ministers saw signs of Israel's salvation, they felt more confident of their own prospects; and because they felt confident, they looked more closely for signs of the Conversion of the Jews. In the case of both Old Israel and New, they explained, "the covenanted nation was like the ripe, unreaped field . . . waiting for the sickle of grace," or else like a field "much run to ruine . . . and gone beyond man," so that "it must be . . . God alone in some more than ordinary way of working that can retrieve" it. Putting the theocracy's name where Jeremiah had written that of Israel, they cried to the mocking "Ishmaelites of the world" — "the banterers and scoffers who jeered at New England as the self-styled New Jerusalem" — that "AMERICA is legible in these Promises." And for the encouragement of their local audiences they raised the prophetic call of Isaiah 52 (a text traditionally associated with the Bride in Jeremiah 31 and the Wife of the Lamb in Revelation 19): "Awake, Awake . . . O New-English *Zion*, and put on thy *Beautiful Garments*, O American *Jerusalem*."[17]

The argument may seem chimerical to us now, and probably it appeared so to a number of New Englanders then. But in fact it was closely related to the growth of the colony. It served to establish a distinctive regional tradition for the emigrants and their children, and it provided them with a sense of purpose, direction, and continuity, a mode of social discipline and self-criticism, and an assurance about the future during a troubled period of transition. In these and other ways, the development of the rhetoric was integral to the development of New England at large. The Halfway Covenant is a major mid-century example of this interaction. A major example in the last quarter of the century is what the Puritans named King Philip's War.

The immediate causes of war remain problematic. Whatever the case, in 1674 the Indian "King Philip" (Metacom, sachem of the Wampanoags) united most of the tribes in the area against the Bay settlers, and in the next two years — in what he correctly felt was a decisive conflict between the expanding colonies and the native inhabitants — he directed a series of attacks that threatened the entire settlement with annihilation. From the security of a later decade, the ministers gloried in "the Evident Hand of Heaven" that "Extinguished whole Nations of Salvages" as once God had laid waste the Massachusetts Bay tribes to make room for the first emigrants. But during the war itself the terror they shared with all other New Englanders expressed itself in a shift of rhetorical strategy. The shift may be discerned in the very titles of their discourses. In place of the earlier exhortations to duty and mission, we have discourses on *Righteousness Rained from Heaven*, *Man's Extremity, God's Opportunity*, *The Times of Man Are in the Hand of God*, and *The Necessity of the Pouring Out of the Spirit from on High*. More powerfully still, the shift in rhetoric appears in the covenant-renewal ceremonies which the clergy instituted at the height of the war, in March, 1675. The ceremonies called the settlers to reaffirm their commitment to the God of their fathers almost as a token gesture — a sign of grateful acquiescence to what was "graciously and gloriously" already well on its way. Since the "people of *New-England* are (if any under heaven are so) a *Covenant-People*," the Lord certainly intended to grant them victory. All He demanded from them was their sincere acceptance of His once and future aid, their "*solemn profession that we* [again] *fly for refuge to the . . . grace and mercy that is set before us*."[18]

The clergy liked to point out that such rededication was "*mystical* as well as *historical*." Historically, the Israelites had first used the ritual in the wilderness under Moses, before they went into battle against their enemies; they had done so later, with equal success, in Jerusalem under Nehemiah. Spiritually, rededication was an act incumbent on the elect who "had *as it were* lost the work or effect of former Conversion." The preachers reminded their audiences in this regard that covenant renewal pertained not to works but to that absolute "Covenant wherein men profess themselves *unable* to doe any thing of *themselves*," for precisely such men must periodically rededicate themselves. Although the new birth occurs once only, the experience of saints showed that the effects of grace might "so decay as to need to be done over again." These twin reasons for covenant renewal, historical and mystical, made it the duty of every believer to join in "open profession" with the community in time of distress. They also served dramatically to strengthen the bond between the personal and the social covenant. Beginning with this period, Jeremiah 31:33 and 50:5 (the texts which half a century before had separated private from public calling) became virtually interchangeable.* As the ministers explained it, the ceremony followed from the "Engagement made by God in the Covenant of Grace, *Jer.* 31.33," and by that token it demonstrated, as a New England community ritual, that "the generality of them" were "walking in the way to Zion with their faces hitherward, *Jer.* 50.4,5," certain "to be a *great* People, yea the greatest upon the Face of the Earth." [19] So understood, the ceremony itself, as it were, ensured the issue of the war.

Perhaps the most striking feature of the covenant renewals in this respect is their urgent, proto-revivalist call for prayer. The ministers had always insisted on prayer, of course; but during the war they began increasingly to stress that prayer *presupposed* success. In New Israel, they contended, prayer was not simply a response to passing events; above all it expressed the people's commitment to God's plan. When the clergy prayed for His intercession against King Philip, they did it so that what was predetermined might come to pass. Our pleading depends upon God's pledges, they argued, and He makes good His pledges upon our pleading. "*As the Lord hath made promises of great Blessings to his People; so he will be enquired of them . . . in the way of Prayer and Supplication in order to the performance of that which he hath promised, that he may do it for them.*" Through such tautologies (a natural consequence of their rhetoric of ambiguity), the ministers made covenant renewal an occasion for reaffirming all the tenets of their errand — especially, perhaps, their genetics of salvation. Let us rededicate ourselves, they intoned, by recalling

---

*Participation in covenant renewal, explained the ministers, meant that the colonist formerly "in the way to Hell . . . is [now] in the way to Heaven"; it meant, at the same time, that God's American people, relying on "the Aids of Grace," were being "helped unto the performance" of their mission by "their saving *Conversion* to God" (Increase Mather, *Returning unto God* [Boston, 1680], p. 7). From this perspective, the covenant renewals highlight various aspects of the rhetoric: the union of material and spiritual blessings, the efficacy of trial, and the mobilization of preparation into the service of a social errand. Covenant renewal does not add anything new to the tradition of the American jeremiad but, as a logical consequence of New England's genetics of salvation, serves to fulfill it.

God's decree to His chosen seed. "Plead in prayer for your children
. . . that God would fulfill his own promise." And to substantiate
their claim, they weighted their exhortations with entreaties for the
National Conversion of Israel. "Pray for . . . *The Calling of the
Jews;*" cry "with earnest Expectation, Oh that the Jewish Nation
were Converted!"[20] Such displays of concern, they explained, were
twice blessed. They blessed those who pleaded and those who were
pleaded for. They served as midwife at once to the birth of prophecies, to the new birth of unconverted children, and to the rebirth of
the Jews. What better guaranteed the joyous issue of their prayers
than this common cause of Old Israel and New in the work of redemption?*

The call for prayer in the American jeremiad extends beyond
King Philip's War into the eighteenth century. Combining as it does
the doctrines of covenant renewal and National Conversion, it marks
a high point in the process by which the New England clergy tried
(rhetorically) to meet the challenges of history. Let me illustrate this
by contrasting some key sermons delivered before and after King
Philip's War. I begin with the two most optimistic (and perhaps
most influential) jeremiads of the earlier period, by two leading supporters of the Halfway Covenant. The first is the election-day address of 1661 by John Norton:

Jeremiah looking at his sufferings, he will speak no more; but looking at

*In the 1680s, when such mass pleading had established itself as an institution of
the colonial Way, Increase Mather admitted that some Calvinists abroad regarded the
procedure — rededication, conversion, supplication, and all — with "evil surmisings,
and censures" (*The Duty of Parents* [Boston, 1703], p. 20). But they mistook its motive:
neither he nor any member of the orthodoxy ever questioned the insufficiency of
means, and all of them punctuated their directions with reminders that God "will be
gracious to whom he will be gracious, and will have Mercy upon whom he will have
Mercy." What they meant was that those now asking for mercy were also those who,
like the Jewish people, "he *will* in favour and mercy look to" (Increase Mather, *The
Divine Right* [Boston, 1680], p. 8; William Adams, *Gods Eye on the Contrite* [Cambridge,
Mass., 1685], p. 5). Or as Samuel Torrey put it ten years later: "If *Restoration* depended upon *Reformation*, it would be long enough before either would come to pass.
But God having foretold & promised both, we should *hope for much*, though there be
no sign of *Reformation*" (*Man's Extremity, God's Opportunity* [Cambridge, Mass., 1695],
pp. 57–58; ellipses deleted).

Gods promise, and it is as fire in his bones, he cannot but speak. If we look at Sion in the glass of the Promise, this Out-cast is both Marah [bitter], and Hephzibah [joyful], both a Widow, and Beulah [married]. Gods touching an impenitent Out-cast with repentance, is a signal of Gods having mercy thereon. Sions recovery by repentance from her backsliding is an effect of grace, and a fore-runner of the set time of Sion's mercy. [Thus] we must accept of Gods plaister [so that] the set time of mercy will come.

My second example comes from the great election-day address I discussed in chapter 1, Samuel Danforth's *Brief Recognition of New England's Errand into the Wilderness* (1670):

Now that the Lord hath smitten us, it is high time for us to *remember whence we are fallen, and repent.* [It is true,] *we are feeble and impotent.* [Yet] Remember the man that had a withered hand: Christ saith unto him, *Stretch forth thy hand, and it was restored whole.* How could he stretch forth his hand when it was shrunk up? The Almighty Power of Christ accompanying his Command enabled the man. [So, too, in our present circumstances] Jesus, the Great Physician of Israel hath undertaken the Cure, *I will restore health unto thee, and I will heal thee of thy wounds, saith the Lord,* Jer. 30.17.[21]

Both speakers use the *figura* of Zion to promise eventual triumph for the colony, on the premise that the colonists will cooperate. They invoke the chronometer, we might say, in order to persuade their listeners to readjust their sense of time. Both of them, of course, also intimate that God *will* heal the patient (Danforth, significantly, in more forceful terms than Norton). The "riddle of grace" they advance is that the physician will cure the "incurable." But they place due emphasis on acceptance, on man's probationary participation in his recovery.

The jeremiads after 1675 are at once more pessimistic of reformation and far more assured of salvation. Their characteristic tone is Samuel Torrey's in his long and fervent *Exhortation* of 1683. "*Nothing,*" he moans, "*is like to do us good, unless God will pour out his Spirit on us.* We have had experience of the *inefficacy* of means upon us to bring us into order and to a good frame. . . . *Judgements* have not done it. . . . *Deliverances* did not do it. . . . *Renewal of stroaks hath not done it.* . . . All ordinary means . . . have been altogether ineffectual."[22]

Unless God will pour out His spirit on us: the qualification, repeated over and again, directly and indirectly, grows in volume as the jeremiads proceed into the eighteenth century: *"When God hath once set a People under dispensation . . . their miseryes will be like to proceed, till there be the pouring out of the Spirit from on high."* The image of a helplessly degenerate saint awaiting regeneration resembles that of the castigated or forsaken saint but goes well beyond it. New England's success, Torrey insinuates, will be not only unmerited but involuntary. His main text, "Man's extremity, God's opportunity," submits all to God. As he interprets it, *extremity* means helplessness in the face of trial, and *opportunity*, a reliance on promises to be performed. Year after year, between 1680 and 1700, the colonial Jeremiahs repeated the lesson: "it is God's prerogative to help in this case"; "untill infinite power set a work by free grace . . . it will not be done"; "the vine shall revive" only "when the Lord is pleased to pour out of his Spirit." And in the same instant they recalled that other vine to which New England was ingrafted. Just when the Lord resolved to cast off Israel, "a very *Sinful, Backsliding People*," at that very moment "God, in his Sovereign Grace, makes a sure Promise of Mercy" — a pledge of National Conversion — "and ingageth himself to perform it," in an "extraordinary way of working by himself."[23]

The application seemed inescapable. Even "if it should come to pass that *New England* should yet *be more sinful & more miserable* than now it is . . . yet there is Scripture ground to hope, that after God had vindicated his Holiness by sore punishment on us, God would again *restore, reform* and *bless New England*." More than hope, there was precedent and prefiguration. God had withdrawn Himself from the Jews, yet He would deliver them, as He would New England, "out of the depth of apostasy and calamity." In both cases, He would elicit and empower their "stretched forth hands" (to recall Danforth's phrase) and "suffer himself to be overcome at last, and *quasi*, commanded by [His people's] prayers, . . . yield to their importunity." Now Jeremiah was speaking through New England's clergy not in the mixed tones of thunder and consolation, as he had to the first emigrants, but in tones of consolation which mixed a glory that was past and a greater glory to come. Recalling the fathers' "garden of pleasure" and all it promised for the future, they instructed the children (in the words of Nicholas Noyes, in May 1697), to "Expect that God will save *New-England* by Sovereign Grace. We have not only hope, but *a sure Foundation of Faith & Confidence in God for Salvation*. He will magnifie New England before the World. God will Save us from our sins & apostasy, by the power of his Spirit, and when this comes that great promise to the Church will be fulfilled."[24]

The apocalyptic intensity at the turn of the eighteenth century is best understood in terms of this development.* Increasingly after 1675 the ministers turned from the problems of the present toward memory and anticipation. Their paeans to the chiliad — itself a paradigmatic fusion of past and future (as well as of heaven and earth) — were above all a means of vindicating the theocracy. And their commitment to the theocracy, in turn, led them constantly to inquire into the exact time of Christ's return. They inherited the task from their predecessors — among others, Thomas Parker and Ephraim Huit had set the date for 1650, John Cotton for 1655, and William Aspinwall for 1673 — but they dwelt upon it almost to the point of obsession. For example, it forms both background and texture of Cotton Mather's *Magnalia Christi Americana*. Just before he began the Church History, Mather learned by special providence that he had been appointed "Herald of the Lord's Kingdome now approaching," and he rushed to the election stand to explain his calculations in detail. Through the "Figures variously *Embossed*" in the Bible's "*Prophetical* as well as . . . Historical *Calendar*," he had

---

*Perry Miller noted the millenarianism of Increase and Cotton Mather, but could not quite account for it; and so he called it a theological aberration — something that was not only unorthodox but diametrically opposed to the outlook of the early emigrants. In fact, expectations of the Second Coming pervade the entire period. They underlie Thomas Hooker's *Survey of the Summe of Churche-Discipline* (London, 1648); John Cotton's sermons on the apocalypse ("many of you may live to see it," he told his Boston congregation in *The Churches Resurrection* [London, 1642], p. 30); John Eliot's missionary *Tears of Repentance* (London, 1653); Peter Bulkeley's authoritative *The Gospel-Covenant* (London, 1651); even some of the poetry of Anne Bradstreet, who took a militant's pride in the approaching Armageddon — in her 1642 "Dialogue between Old England and New," it is "*New* England," significantly, that announces the calling of the Jews and Resurrection Day (*Works*, ed. Jeannine Hensley [Cambridge, Mass., 1967], pp. 185–87). The parade of prominent names includes William Aspinwall, John Davenport, Robert Holyoke, William Hooke, Ephraim Huit, John Nowell, Samuel Sewall, Thomas Shepard, Edward Taylor, John Wilson, and others.

measured "the *Last Hours* of Time" and could assure the assembly that the "Sabbatism . . . seems just going to lay its Arrest *upon us*." In 1698, the year he finished his history, he took the election stand to announce *"Good Tidings of Great Joy"* (like the angel heralding the Incarnation) in "a Message from Heaven": "O People of God, . . . *there is a* REVOLUTION *and a* REFORMATION *at the very Door* . . . [and] the bigger part of this Assembly, may in the course of Nature, live to see it: There stand those within these Walls this Day, That shall see . . . when the *Vail* that has been upon the Hearts of the *Jewish Nation*, shall be taken off." The phrases reappear throughout the *Magnalia* itself — "an history," the author tells us, "to anticipate the state of the New Jerusalem" — in which "the mighty deeds of Christ" elevate the pristine New England venture to its highest epic and mythical proportions.* Acclaiming the errand as the "last conflict with anti-christ" in *"the utmost parts of the earth,"* Mather links it at the end of his work to the impending millennium.[25]

In this respect, the *Magnalia* is the epitome of the seventeenth-century jeremiad. Its sevenfold division not only images the Sabbatism — which through "the successes . . . of his chosen people in the Wilderness" was becoming "within the last few sevens of years

---

*Mather's millennialism at this time is worth special emphasis because the *Magnalia* has so often been read as a cry of despair. Thus Peter Gay claims that when Mather says *"De Tristibus* . . . may be a proper title for the book I am now writing" he is referring to the history as a whole (*A Loss of Mastery: Puritan Historians in Colonial America* [Berkeley, 1966], p. 69). In fact, Mather here refers only to the seventh book, whose purpose is to relate "the Afflictive Disturbances . . . Suffered From . . . Various Adversaries: And the Wonderful Methods and Mercies Whereby the Churches [of New England] have been Delivered out of their Difficulties" (II, 487). The significance of those deliverances are indicated by the title of the last section of this last Book, "Arma Virosque Cano," a title that recalls the Virgilian invocation with which Mather opens the History (as well as the numerous echoes from the *Aeneid* thereafter), and so suggests the epic proportions of his narrative. For Mather, of course, New England's story not only parallels but supersedes that of the founding of Rome, as his literary "assistance" from Christ excels the inspiration of Virgil's muse, as the "exemplary heroes" he celebrates resemble but outshine the men of Aeneas' band — not only as Christians but as seafarers and conquerors of hostile pagan tribes — and, most spectacularly, as the millennium toward which the Reformation is moving provides the far more glorious antitype of the Augustan *Pax Romana*. Undoubtedly, the proper title for Mather's work is the exultant one he gave it: *Magnalia Christi Americana*, "The Great Acts of Christ in America."

nearer to accomplishment" — but holds aloft the "seven golden candlesticks" of the Old-New Jerusalem and sounds the seven trumpet blasts that bring down the walls of Jericho, Satan's figural stronghold. The *Magnalia* epitomizes the American jeremiad in another respect as well: in the self-conscious isolation of the author from his audience. The ministers' sharpening sense of alienation, I have suggested, emerges through the very vehemence of their commitment: the more tenaciously they uphold the ideal, the more they seem to be talking to themselves (and for themselves). The entire process may be traced directly through their changing views of their role as "watchmen." To the first-generation clergy, the role carried the high responsibilities of being the architect and guardian of society, a man by whose "watch . . . you may be made conquerors." During the 1660s, the concept of watchman took on the sterner implications of a *"watchfull shepherd,"* warning his flock away from temptations. In the early 1670s the orthodoxy came to see itself as a beleaguered watchman for God, a "gap-man" holding back the floodwaters of apostasy and berated by those he seeks to protect.[26] After 1675, and particularly during the early 1690s (with the witchcraft trials and the failure of the charter negotiations), the Old Guard ministers retreated further and further into their vision. Like the prophets who foretold their errand, they set themselves to search out the future as exiled watchers for the Second Coming.*

This sense of alienation is another major aspect of the *Magnalia*,

---

*This fourfold pattern is somewhat overschematic (it neglects a number of foreshadowings and overlappings), but it is accurate, I believe, in general terms. Following are representative testimonies in the clergy's developing definition of its role: (1) *to 1660:* "The Lord gives us to conclude that the future harvest is great, when he sends forth already so many [ministers as] labourers" (Charles Chauncey, *Gods Mercy* [Cambridge, Mass., 1655], pp. 11–12); (2) *1660–70:* "the Word of God is likened to *fire*, and to a *hammer*, Jer. 23.29. in its efficacy" (John Davenport, *Gods Call* [Cambridge, Mass., 1669], pp. 6–8); (3) *1670–75:* "Time was, when the Messengers of Christ were precious and welcome (even when they *came with a Rod*). . . . But now they are become the Enemies" (Urian Oakes, *New-England Pleaded With* [Cambridge, Mass., 1673], p. 26); (4) *1680–1700:* the minister must proclaim that "the Day is at hand," like "the Baptist, *who was the voice of one crying in the wilderness*" (Cotton Mather, *Midnight Cry* [Boston, 1692], p. 7). This last stage in a sense returns us to the first, for in both the minister stands as harbinger of a new era. The difference, however, in the image of the "labourers" preparing the community for the harvest and that of the prophet in the wilderness suggests, in its increasing reliance upon forms of the imagination, the development I have been describing.

inextricably bound up with its imaginative intensity. Mather felt
by the mid-1690s that the colony had strayed beyond recall, that
"hardly any but my Father, and myself," as he confided to his diary
in 1700, "appear in Defence of our invaded *Churches*," and that the
Church History itself would elicit widespread abuse. But as prophet
of the "true" New England he could secure the errand despite *their*
invasion. John Norton in 1661 acclaimed the great pattern "that
sheweth what *New-England* is"; seven years later William Stoughton
feared that "New England [is] in danger this day to be lost even in
New England; by 1683, the orthodoxy acknowledged "that *N*[ew]-
England is not to be found in *N*[ew]-*England*." Mather accepts the
legacy with pride. In his General Introduction to the *Magnalia* (the
most animated apologia on record for the Puritan errand), he declares that with the "stones they throw at this book . . . I will
build my self a monument. . . . Whether New-England may
live [horologically] any where else or no, it must *live* [chronomet-
rically] in our History!"[27] His defiant and solitary vision caps the
last stage in the growth of the American Puritan jeremiad. The
century-long effort to unite two disparate levels of thought — the
rhetoric that bent history, theology, and sociology to that single purpose — is ultimately forced back into the "monument" of the individual mind and will, and creates its most pronounced success out of
apparent failure.

All this is to see the *Magnalia* from Mather's point of view. It is a
partial perspective that has been surprisingly influential. On the one
hand, it has fed into Perry Miller's notion of colonial declension. On
the other hand, it has lent support to the contrast historians have
recently promulgated between "the articulate few" and the community at large. And we might add to this contrast the differences, in
the early eighteenth century, between Joseph Morgan's imaginary
History of the Kingdom of Basaruah and Thomas Prince's *Chronological
History of New England in the Form of Annals*. Morgan's work obviously derives from the seventeenth-century jeremiads.* The con-

---

*Joseph Morgan's *The History of the Kingdom of Basaruah* (Boston, 1715) has often
been compared to John Bunyan's *Holy War*, and there is some justice in the comparison: the two writers share what might be called the Puritan-allegorical mode. But by
far the most prominent and distinctive influence upon Morgan is that of the American
Puritan jeremiad. To select one of many specific links, see Cotton Mather's election-
day sermon of 1689, which discusses America's prospects through a parable of the
Fighting City and the Godly City (*Way to Prosperity*, pp. 31 ff.).

tinuities are transparent in his account of the "poor barren Country," in his denunciations of schism and backsliding (intermixed with prayers for the chiliad) and above all in his description of the kingdom of Basaruah, whose name images the union of flesh (*basar*) and spirit (*ruach*) and whose "true inhabitants," a community of visible saints charged with a world-redemptive mission, await the imminent descent of New Jerusalem. Prince's *Chronological Annals*, we are told, has the contrary spirit of the Yankee majority. Though it reflects Enlightenment ideas (and so is supposed to have opened a new epoch in American historiography), the work owes its interest for later readers to the sheer bulk of its information. "The *orderly Succession* of these Transactions and Events," Prince rightly remarks, were "too much neglected by our [earlier] Historians." What he offers, accordingly, is a "naked REGISTER" — "only *Facts* in a *Chronological Epitome*," stripped of "artificial Ornaments" and other devices the Puritans used "to raise the Imagination. . . . The meer Tables and Calculations I was forced to make," boasts the author, "would compose a Folio." In face of these overwhelming tabular facts the old rhetoric dissolves, Mather's millennial calculations vanish into thin air, and the giants of the cloud-capp'd *Arbella* migration deflate to a prosaic, hardworking people concerned with "*Number of . . . Offspring*," "*Changes of Government*," "*Maintenance of Trade*," and "Acres of Land to be allotted."[28]

Separately considered, Prince's account and Mather's would seem to sustain the familiar thesis of Puritan declension. But the separation is fundamentally a misleading one. Without entering into the problematics of declension itself, I should like to stress once again that the Puritan vision survived the collapse of the church-state, and that the central themes of our culture attest to its sustained *mass* impact. Indeed, the impact is felt even in Prince's writings — implicitly, in the *Chronological History*, where "*Seven* Great *Periods* of Time" precede the climactic entry of New England upon "the stage of History"; and explicitly, in his forceful election-day address of 1730, *The People of New England*. Interweaving the naked facts he assembled with interpretations of those facts drawn from a host of seventeenth-century jeremiads — by Higginson, Hubbard, Mitchel, Stoughton, and others — Prince portrays the Bay planters as "particular antitypes" of the "ancient Israelites," a holy remnant for

whom "the desert . . . blossoms as a rose" and upon whom "the
Spirit from on high is poured." "May we be Emmanuel's land," he
concludes; may all "nations see our righteousness and all kings our
glory." Throughout the discourse, Prince's parallels and proof texts
give voice to America's defunct first elite, yet far from being "artificial Ornaments" they express for orator and audience alike a fundamental cultural aspiration. They come down to us as testimony to
the popular, *historical* force of the Puritan vision — remind us that
the colonial Jeremiahs did not speak solely for themselves, not even
in the twilight of the orthodoxy when those watchmen-prophets felt
betrayed by a generation of vipers. Somehow, evidently, the prosaic, industrious eighteenth-century Yankees found it deeply fortify-
ing — expedient as well as elevating — to contemplate the once and
future city which their forefathers had set upon a hill "to bridge the
gap between God and man,"[29] and they were to respond en masse
when evangelicals (like Jonathan Edwards, Thomas Prince, and
Thomas Prince, Jr.), Liberals (like Edwards's chief antagonist,
Charles Chauncy), and Libertarians (from Jonathan Mayhew to Sam
Adams) would summon them once more, in 1740, 1745, and 1776,
toward the long-prefigured New Canaan in America.

For the Old Guard's sense of alienation, let me repeat, represents
only *their* view of things.* To accept it uncritically is to shut out
perhaps the most vital aspect of the transition from Puritan to Yankee New England, if not the major irony of colonial history. For the
emigrant leaders, the jeremiad was a means of social control, but the
society they established rapidly proved inadequate to New England's "wilderness-condition." Primarily, to be sure, they based
their authority on an agency superior to human failings, the prophet-

---

*It also represents a self-conscious cultural role. Significantly, many of them ad-
justed very well to the new era. We know, for example, that despite his complaints
Cotton Mather remained deeply engaged in colonial affairs. The self-declared failure
also was a central figure in the revolt against Governor Edmund Andros; the mentor
and close affiliate of Andros's replacement, William Phips; a tireless organizer of
"societies to do good;" a champion of Enlightenment ideas in the New World; and
(as his bibliographer has pointed out) a "matinée idol" of the Boston pulpit (Thomas J.
Holmes, "Cotton Mather and His Writings on Witchcraft," *Papers of the Bibliographical
Society of America*, 18 [1924], 41). Even those actions or addresses that tended most to
isolate him from his countrymen — during the witchcraft trials and, later, the inocu-
lation controversy — reveal his continuing involvement and influence.

ic types of Scripture; but they were too sanguine about their experiment to rely on prophecy altogether. They invested their dream in outmoded theocratic institutions, and accordingly their jeremiads constantly reveal the friction between promise and fact. In the last decades of the century, when it became clear that practical measures would no longer suffice, the Puritan orthodoxy found solace by withdrawing into the rhetoric itself. They understood the shift in strategy as an effort to establish a colossal dike against the flow of events, to raise a figural wall of fire that would make their New Israel impervious to time. In fact, they were being forced by history to enlarge their ideal of New Israel into a vision that was so broad in its implications, and so specifically American in its application, that it could survive the failure of theocracy. Hence the fruitful interaction between rhetoric and society in late seventeenth-century New England. Insisting that the theocracy was the American chronometer, the ministers drained it of its discrete theological and institutional content. Intent on preserving the past, they transformed it (as legend) into a malleable guide to the future. Seeking to defend the Good Old Way, they abstracted from its antiquated social forms the larger, vaguer, and more flexible forms of symbol and metaphor (*new chosen people, city on a hill, promised land, destined progress, New Eden, American Jerusalem*), and so facilitated the movement from visible saint to American patriot, sacred errand to manifest destiny, colony to republic to imperial power. In spite of themselves, as it were, the latter-day orthodoxy freed their rhetoric for the use and abuse of subsequent generations of Americans.

4

The Typology
of America's Mission

The Puritan jeremiad set out the sacred history of the New World; the eighteenth-century jeremiad established the typology of America's mission. That outlook, to be sure, had become almost explicit by the last decades of the seventeenth century. But the Puritans were careful to make Scripture the basis of their figuralism. They always rooted their exegeses (however strained) in biblical texts, and they appealed to (even as they departed from) a common tradition of Reformed hermeneutics. Because they believed the Reformation was reaching its fulfillment in America, and because they identified themselves primarily in religious terms, they found it necessary to include all the standard landmarks of Protestant historiography. Their Yankee heirs felt relatively free of such constraints. During the eighteenth century, the meaning of Protestant identity became increasingly vague; typology took on the hazy significance of metaphor, image, and symbol; what passed for the divine plan lost its strict grounding in Scripture; "providence" itself was shaken loose from its religious framework to become part of the belief in human progress. The Yankee Jeremiahs took advantage of this movement "from sacred to profane"[1] to shift the focus of figural authority. In effect, they incorporated Bible history into the American experience — they substituted a regional for a biblical past, consecrated the American present as a movement from promise to fulfillment, and translated

93

fulfillment from its meaning within the closed system of sacred history into a metaphor for limitless secular improvement.

All this was a matter of extension and adaptation, not of transformation. The Puritan clergy had set out to blur traditional distinctions between the world and the kingdom. Their rhetoric issued in a unique mode of ambiguity that precluded the conflict of heaven's time and man's. "Canaan" was a spiritual state for them, as it was for other Christians; but it was also (in another, but not conflicting sense) their country. They spoke of the mutuality (rather than the coexistence) of fact and ideal. By "church-state" they meant a separation of powers in the belief that in the American Canaan, and there only, the ecclesiastical and the civic order were not really distinct. *By their very contradictions they were made to correspond.* And in the course of time the correspondence yielded the secular basis of multidenominational religion and the sacral view of free-enterprise economics. Both these developments were rooted in the heterodox tenets established a century before: the moral distinction between the Old World and the New (as between Egypt and Canaan), the interrelation of material and spiritual blessings, the concept of a new chosen people whose special calling entailed special trials, and above all a mythic view of history that extended New England's past into an apocalypse which stood "near, even at the door," requiring one last great act, one more climactic pouring out of the spirit, in order to realize itself.

Recent scholars have recognized the importance of millennialism in our religious and social history. But by and large they have begun their account not with the Puritans but with the Edwardsian revivals. Their dating is based on what they have assumed to be a fundamental theological shift. Technically speaking, the seventeenth-century colonists (like most Protestants of their time) were pre-millennialists. That is, they believed that the descent of New Jerusalem would be preceded and attended by a series of cataclysmic divine judgments and followed by a universal change in all things. Jonathan Edwards, on the contrary, was a post-millennialist; he posited a final golden age within history, and thereby freed humanity, so to speak, to participate in the revolutions of the apocalypse. Students of the Great Awakening have used this distinction to make Edwards out to

be a radically innovative historian, the first New World spokesman
for an optimistic view of human progress.

The distinction is a questionable one. Historians of religion have
long noted that pre- and post-millennialism are often present in the
same movement, sometimes in the same thinker. And even if we
accept a significant difference between the two approaches it is by no
means certain that Edwards is the first colonial post-millennialist.
David Smith, for one, has argued that that honor belongs to the
latter-day theocrats (like Samuel Sewall, Cotton Mather, and Joseph
Morgan), and if to them, then also, I would maintain, to the first-
and second-generation ministers who made the doctrine of the
chiliad "almost canonical" in their church-state.[2] For chiliasm, the
belief in an earthly paradise, recasts the apocalyptic hope into something like the Edwardsian idea of progress, especially when it is
accompanied, as it was in early New England, by a figural sense of
fulfillment. "The flourishing beauty of . . . heavenly grace," wrote
William Hubbard, "which did so strangely metamorphose the visage
of the face of things at first in the world . . . was the verdant lustre
. . . that turned [our] rough and barren wilderness . . . into a
fruitful Carmel or fragrant Sharon"; and New Jerusalem, in turn,
would bring that lustre to a "more brilliant glow."[3] The spiraling
process that Hubbard outlines (Creation to Eden to Canaan to New
Canaan to New Canaan in America to New Eden) is a commonplace
of the jeremiad. It calls attention to the special implications of the
Puritans' eschatology of errand — what we might call their version
of *American* millennialism.

For though Hubbard and his colleagues believed the millennium
would involve a drastic overturning, that overturning meant
"metamorphosis" to them: a change in this world, and most dramatically in their New World. Their errand led not from earth to heaven
(like the pilgrimage of the Plymouth settlers), but from lesser to
greater glories on the American strand. As they conceived it, New
Jerusalem would come not to abrogate their venture, but to fulfill it.
The apocalyptic wonders were for them part of the latter-day "magnalia Christi Americana," and the millennium itself, by extension,
part of the country's history. Whereas their European contemporaries expected the millennium to bring secular history to an end,

the New England Puritans spoke of the millennium as the motivating force of their errand. America, in their view (like Eden, Canaan, and New Jerusalem), was intrinsic to the progress of the work of redemption. They acknowledged, of course, that New Jerusalem was drastically different and all-too-distant from the New England church-state. But in the eye of prophecy, it was already present for them, as the harvest is implicit in the planting, the glorified in the justified saint, and the antitype in the *figura*. "Though there be in special one grand accomplishment of Scripture Prophecies," said William Adams on a fast day in 1678, "yet there hath been a glorious accomplishment of it already," albeit a "partile accomplishment . . . wherein those . . . promises are fulfilled in their measure and degree."[4]

Adams was not just speaking for the mid-century clergy; he was making explicit what the orthodox had believed from the start. In urging John Davenport to follow him to America, John Cotton wrote that the "order of the churches and the commonwealth [here] . . . brought into his mind the new heaven and the new earth"; and in general Cotton's "description of the millennium," as several scholars have recognized, "sounds very like the holy commonwealth already established in Massachusetts," a sort of "thousand-year extension of the New England Way." The second- and third-generation ministers simply drew out the implications. In transforming the American wilderness, God, they explained, was providing through their church-state "a type and Embleme of New Jerusalem," "a *First Fruits* of that which shall in due time be accomplished in the world throughout." As the theocracy foreshadowed New Jerusalem, so New Jerusalem would be the Good Old Way written large. Accordingly, their descriptions of the chiliad center largely upon comparatives. During the chiliad, Christ would bless them "in a *more* Glorious manner," awaken them to "a *more* Reformed State than ever," ensure "*more* wonderful . . . Deliverances," and make their land "*more* Glorious, *more* Heavenly, *more* Universal far away than what was in the former [times]." As the aged John Higginson put it in 1697,

> if we look on the *dark side*, the *humane side* of this work, there is much of humane weakness, and imperfection; [but] if we look on the *light side*, the *divine side* of this work, we may see, that God hath established His

covenant [to] be the God of his *people* and of their *seed* with them, and after them. And therefore *all that the Lord hath done for his people in* New England may stand as a *monument*, in relation to future times, of a fuller and better *reformation* than hath yet appeared, [even to] those times of greater light and holiness which are to come, when the Lord shall make Jerusalem a praise in the earth.[5]

In view of these parallels between Edwards and the Puritans, it seems to me significant that Edwards himself denied that he differed in any substantial way from his predecessors. We know that he was particularly influenced by Thomas Shepard's *Parable of the Ten Virgins* (1636), and in 1744 he made the legacy clear in complaining about the "slanderous" charges of Charles Chauncy, the leading spokesman for the Old Light orthodoxy. Chauncy had accused Edwards of having "often said that the millennium was already begun"; but the truth was, Edwards wrote, that he had seen the revivals as no more than "forerunners of those glorious times." Even at the peak of his enthusiasm, during the harvests of 1739–41, he had known (and stated in his *Thoughts on the Revival*) "that there would be many changes, revivings and intermissions, and returns of dark clouds and threatening circumstances, before . . . Christ's kingdom shall be everywhere established." Had not Thomas Shepard and all the "fathers" — John Davenport, John Cotton, Richard Mather, and others — spoken in much the same terms about the prospects in store for New England?[6] No doubt such assertions of filiopietism were a source of Edwards's appeal. The New Lights revolted not (as some have said) against paternal authority, but against an older generation that they thought had betrayed the founding fathers. No doubt, too, Edwards exaggerated his bonds with the past, much as the latter-day Puritans had exaggerated theirs with the theocracy, and as nineteenth-century evangelicals were to exaggerate their loyalty to Edwards. But the sense of continuity was itself part of the myth; the very discrepancy between assertion and fact attests to the persistence of Puritan rhetoric. This does not explain away the discrepancy, of course. As I noted earlier, revivalist rhetoric involved an important extension of Puritan views, and I will return to this later in the chapter. But for the moment it seems worthwhile, in view of current scholarship, to trace the connections that Edwards suggests.

Certain rather minor aspects of Edwards's thought deserve attention in this regard: his use of the doctrine of the National Conversion; his millennial interpretations of current events, at home and
abroad; his "keys" to certain prophetic passages, such as Jeremiah
31:31–33 and 50:5; even a parallel so commonplace, by 1740, as his
view of John the Baptist as *figura* of New England's errand. I mention these details because they are symptomatic of what I consider to
be the crucial connection between Puritans and Edwardsians: their
common emphasis on process. In contrast to European chiliasts,
both groups concerned themselves far less with the final event than
with the design of gradual fulfillment. For both the time was always
at hand, but somehow that was of secondary interest. The real issue
was the *figural* meaning of the present. Both groups raised the midnight cry of the watchers for New Jerusalem — "we are come near
it," we "cannot be very far" — in order to assess the unfolding
process. And for both the assessment was a question of horologicals
and chronometricals. The entire work of redemption, Edwards explained, "was virtually done and finished" (conceived, formed, and
consummated) before Creation itself, "but not actually." *Virtually*, in
the eye of eternity, every act merges with all others: the "events of
providence are . . . all one work." *Actually*, on the human level,
God's plan opens into a series of "distinct, independent works" —
and yet, Edwards continues, these works are so bound together,
"wheel within wheel," as to constitute a single harmonious design.
As with the Puritans, then, conditional and absolute coalesce. History becomes a function of prophecy. And with the Puritans, further, Edwards applies the correspondence especially to "these latter
days" (as the Cambridge Platform put it) wherein we may "expect
[to] . . . enjoy in this world a . . . *more* glorious condition."[7]

What distinguishes Edwards's application is the greater consist-
ency of its logic. His forebears' concept of errand, for all its internal
coherence, is marred (from the standpoint of the *actual*) by its pre-
millennialism. The process of fulfillment they posited, leading step
by inevitable step from Eden to New Canaan, is blurred (if not
undermined) by its reliance on an entirely extraterrestrial agency —
in C. C. Goen's phrase, a superhuman "shattering of the order of
nature." Edwards, by changing the scenario for this last act of the
errand, welded the whole progression into an organic human-divine
(and natural-divine) whole. That was his contribution. In cultural

terms, it had enormous import for the course of American millennialism. But as a view of history, it simply drew out the implications
of the outlook developed a century before. "Though there has been a
glorious fulfillment of . . . prophecies already," Edwards wrote in
1740, describing the chiliad in phrases that make the legacy unmistakable, "other times are only forerunners and preparatories to this,"
as the exodus of Israel from Babylon "typified" the Reformation and
the Great Migration. And what the Great Migration meant now
seemed to him "gloriously visible." Christ, he announced, will have
"the heathen for his inheritance, and the uttermost parts of the earth
for his possession, . . . [a] nation shall be born in a day, . . . the
Jews shall be called in," and Protestant America, climactically, will
become another, greater Mountain of Holiness, "Beautiful as *Tirzah*,
comely as *Jerusalem*, and terrible as an Army with Banners" — "*Put
on thy beautiful garments*, O America, *the holy* city!"[8]

Edwards's conviction that sacred history was reaching its apex in
the New World seals his indebtedness to the Puritans. Without
forgetting his very considerable borrowings from European thinkers
— without forgetting either that his millennialism both antedates
and postdates his hopes for the Awakening (and that eventually he
may have lost faith in America's mission)* — it seems safe to say that,
at the height of his fervor, Edwards adopted wholesale the Puritan
vision of the New World. America was discovered, he writes, to
prepare "the way for the future, glorious times," so "that the new
and most glorious state of God's church on earth might commence
there." In other words, *discovery* was not, in this case, simply an
event in history, the opening of new territories to European Christians. It was the unveiling of some momentous truth, as an inspired
exegete unveils the meaning of an obscure passage in Scripture. In
this hermeneutic sense, Edwards *discovered* America in Scripture,

---

*This reversal is problematic and by no means definitive. Indeed, in view of the
parallels suggested above, and of Edwards's recently published "Notes on the
Apocalypse," it might be rewarding to extend the comparison between Edwards and
Cotton Mather to the last periods of their lives. I think here of Edwards's stubborn
optimism despite his growing sense of alienation, and also, in this regard, of his avid
transatlantic correspondence, his interest in German Pietism, and his affinities with
Scottish divines. Especially relevant is Edwards's obsessive speculation about current
events, centering on the Protestant-Catholic conflicts in Europe and especially in
America.

specifically in the apocalyptic passage, Isaiah 66:19.* And like the Puritan Jeremiahs before him, he proceeded to celebrate the "golden age" of the first planters as "the dawn of that glorious day." For "if we consider the circumstances of the settlement of New England," he felt sure, "it must needs appear . . . to be the place whence this work [the arrival of "the *new heavens* and the *new earth*"] shall principally take its rise." In any case, "we can't reasonably think otherwise, than that this great work of God . . . will begin in America."[9]

Given these premises, Edwards's view of the Awakening was a foregone conclusion. English millennialists like Moses Lowman helped him decide on particular apocalyptic dates; German Pietists like August Hermann Francke and English evangelists like George Whitefield heightened his sense of expectancy. But in the main his concept of the Northampton Millennium derived from Puritan New England. And appropriately he described the Awakening (by con-

*And I wil set a signe among them, & wil send those that escape of them, unto the . . . yles afarre of, that have not heard my fame, nether have sene my glorie, & thei shal declare my glorie among the Gentiles.

And they shal bring all your brethren for an offring unto the Lord out of all nations . . . to Jerusalem mine holie Mountaine. . . .

For as ye newe heavens, & the newe earth which I wil make, shal remaine before me, saith the Lord, so shal your sede and your name continue. (Isaiah 66:19–20, 22)

Edwards was surely also thinking of the prophecy from Isaiah 59:19 ("So shal they feare the Name of the Lord from the West, and his glorie from the rising of the sunne") when he announced that the American sun would rise from the west "contrary to the course of the world" (*Images or Shadows of Divine Things*, ed. Perry Miller [New Haven, 1949], p. 116); the same text was used in this connection by Edward Johnson and Cotton Mather in the seventeenth century, and in 1781 by Edwards's grandson, Timothy Dwight, who noted that the text "really refers to the Millennium, and the times immediately preceding," and made it the subject of his address on the defeat of Cornwallis (*A Sermon Preached at Northampton* [New Haven, 1781], pp. 3 ff.). Cotton Mather's favorite example of the biblical prophecy of America came from the Psalms (see his *Psalterium Americanum* [Boston, 1718], p. 40):

Thou hast delivered me from the contentions of the people: thou hast made me the head of the heathen: a people, *whome* I have not knowen, shal serve me.

As sone as thei heare, thei shal obey me: the strangers shal be in subjection to me.

Therefore I wil praise thee, O Lord, among the nations, and wil sing unto thy Name.

Great deliverances giveth he . . . & sheweth mercie to his anointed . . . and to his sede for ever. (Psalms 18:43, 44, 49, 50)

trast with a corrupt Old World) as a union of the Great Migration and the theocratic garden of God:

> a great and wonderful event . . . [was] suddenly brought to pass . . . such as . . . scarce [had] ever been heard of in any land. Who . . . would have thought that in so little time there would be such a change? . . . The New Jerusalem in this respect has begun to come down from heaven, and perhaps never were more of the prelibations of heaven's glory given upon earth. . . . [Multitudes all at once] resort to him when he orders his banner to be displayed . . . [and like] an army . . . obey the sound of [His] trumpet. . . . Christ in an extraordinary manner . . . appears in his visible church in . . . the prelude to that glorious work of God, so often foretold in Scripture, which in the progress and issue of it shall renew the world of mankind.

Edwards's passage reverberates with echoes from seventeenth-century writings: Edward Johnson's rendering in 1654 of the emigrants' call to America, Increase Mather's record of covenant renewals, Joshua Scottow's memories of the founders' achievements. The list of correspondences could easily be extended; and it includes not only Edwards's account of things past and present, but also his forecasts of things to come. In most respects, his description of the millennium sounds very much like the one offered by seventeenth-century colonial divines. Like them, Edwards posited vast increases in population, ecumenism in faith, great piety, "true liberty," general prosperity, and an expansion of scientific, moral, and religious knowledge.[10]

Especially revealing, in this context, is Edwards's emphasis on trial. Scholars have contrasted the Puritans' "cosmic despair" with the revivalists' "high cosmic optimism," and some have gone so far as to suggest that "Edwards's most impressive achievement was to purge Calvinist millenarianism of all those [pessimistic] seventeenth-century elements." This is to simplify both sides of the contrast.* As the Puritan Jeremiahs found a way out of despair so, conversely, the eighteenth-century Calvinists found ample opportu-

---

*For example, Heimert distinguishes between the Puritan fear of apocalyptic earthquakes and the optimistic Calvinist view which "interpreted the tremors as . . . a harbinger of the millennium" (*Religion*, p. 75). But the Calvinists also spoke of those earthquakes with fear and trembling, and on their part Puritans throughout the seventeenth century hopefully anticipated the earthquakes "which shall shake . . . the *Papal Empire* to pieces" (Cotton Mather, *The Serviceable Man* [Boston, 1690], pp. 52–53).

nity to remind their audiences of the dangers before them — the "cataclysms," the "ferment and struggle," the "mighty and violent opposition" that would precede the overthrow of Satan's kingdom. Darkness and affliction, they explained, were no more than what was to be expected. The Lord must "humble us ere [He] return with greater mercies." Fusing threat and promise, *"Sinai's* dreadful Thunder" and "the Jubilee Trumpet of the Gospel," the revivalists made probation their overriding metaphor for the times. If it seemed that God was about "to forsake this land, and to bring most awful judgments upon it" — if the "state of the nation . . . never looked so threatening" — then there was cause to rejoice. It was precisely through such a "time of testing" that Christ's American soldiers could prove their sainthood and as it were assert their right to "make New England a . . . heaven upon earth."[11]

Insofar as the revivalist strategy here may be said to vary from that of the Puritan jeremiad, it does so in being more direct. Edwards seems at times to discard horologicals even as a rhetorical alternative. When he descries dark times ahead, he at once brings forward the "great reason we have assuredly to expect the fulfillment" of heaven's promise. His view of probation, that is, tends to eliminate the complexities of the early political sermons, with their Janus-faced image of Jeremiah. What matters is not so much the past as the future. Not He who cast off the chosen people is New England's Judge, but He who would in due time restore them: the God of National Salvation, pining "to be gracious to us, as though he chose to make us monuments of his grace, . . . and wait[ing] only to have us open our mouths wide, that he may fill them." In such circumstances the options presented to the colonist no longer entailed the prospect of failure. Instead, as in the latter-day Puritan jeremiad, the substance of trial devolved upon acceptance. The problem was simply, comprehensively, to "acknowledge God in his work." Like the preachers of half a century before, Edwards warns "how dangerous it will be" for the man who will "forbear to do so," and how blessed is he who complies. And to drive home the point, he turns to the familiar Puritan parallel with Nehemiah:

> When God redeemed his people from their Babylonish captivity, and they rebuilt Jerusalem, it was . . . a remarkable type of the great deliverance of the Christian church . . . in the latter days. . . . But

we read of some that opposed the Jews in that affair, and ridiculed
God's people . . . and despised their hope . . . and so brought
Nehemiah's imprecation upon [them]. . . . But for persons to
arise . . . in such a work . . . will be to put themselves very much
in the way of divine blessing. . . . [All this, which] may be argued
from . . . those that helped in rebuilding the wall of Jerusalem . . .
[is eminently applicable to] such a time as this, when God is setting up
his kingdom on his holy hill.[12]

The similarities between such passages and those in the Puritan
jeremiads involve not only the concept but the very terms of trial.
For Edwards as for the seventeenth-century clergy, personal salvation was linked to public success and both flowed into the process of
the work of redemption. This fusion of images is part of Christian
tradition, of course; but we have seen that the Puritans used it in
their covenant-renewal ceremonies with special force and to a special
end: to equate conversion, socialization, and the triumph of the
church with a unique American enterprise. This was also a central aspect of the Edwardsian concerts of prayer. For the revivalist dilemma, like the Puritan, was that in the long run good works
were not good enough. Inevitably, it would seem, the form took
priority over the content. When the ministers of the Awakening
looked about them, they had to admit that the visible saints (no less
frequently now than a century before) were more concerned with
pietism than with piety. Inquiring only *"What strict Duty requires of
them,"* their flocks displayed "but little inward heart conformity to
[Christ]." Like the old orthodoxy, the New Light ministers concluded that the true religion "practised in the first, and . . . best
times of New England, [had] grown . . . out of credit!" And again
they found consolation in the principle of man's helplessness. "The
insufficiency of human beings," said Edwards, "to bring to pass any
such happy change in the world as is foretold . . . does now remarkably appear." The one "effectual remedy" for God's straying
and afflicted people was to raise "their cries . . . for a general out-
pouring of his Spirit," to unite in *"Extraordinary Prayer, for the . . .
Advancement of Christ's Kingdom on Earth, Pursuant to Scripture Promises
and Prophecies Concerning the Last Time."*[13]

The differences between covenant renewal and concert of prayer,
important though these are, should not be allowed to obscure the
parallels between the two rituals. Like the Mathers, Edwards based

his assurance in prayer on the figural precedents of the Israelites' covenant renewals under Joshua and Nehemiah. Then, God led His people from captivity to Canaan; now, when the "work of his grace has been begun . . . in New England," God was calling upon His people to a "solemn, public renewing of their covenant." Had He not told His prophets that the remnant would be restored by miracle rather than human stratagem? It was their duty to plead for restoration because, according to the old tautology, the prophecies foretold it. Our very "spirit of prayer," said Edwards, was long ago predicted as an event "preceding and introducing that glorious day." If any sense of doubt remained — any possibility of reversal in mankind's journey from Canaan through Boston and Northampton to New Jerusalem — it was on the level of rhetorical ambiguity: of the "present miserable foresaken condition of the Jews," or of the suffering saint.* Both these figures, we recall, were commonplace in the seventeenth-century jeremiads; so too was the moral that Edwards drew from them: "With what confidence may we go before God, and pray for that, of which we have so many exceeding precious and glorious promises to plead!"[14]

According to the *Magnalia*'s General Introduction, those promises had been "opened" in the ends of the earth by the Puritan Ark of Christ "victoriously sailing round the *globe*," changing geography into "*Christiano-graphy*." Exactly a century later David Austin, speaking in his "Advertisement" to Edwards's *History of the Work of Redemption* of the Revolutionary trial then underway in the United States, reiterated the promise through his eulogy to Edwards: "Though to the eye of unbelief, the Ark may seem, *now*, to be involved in tempestuous weather, and soon to be foundered through the probable failure of borrowed strength; yet, to the joy of the passengers there are those, who, looking through the mists of human or infernal jars, do hail the approach of MILLENNIAL DAY! On the Ocean of the Millennium [our] . . . Ark shall safely and uninterruptedly sail."[15]†

---

*One of Edwards's typical examples in this regard (and a favorite as well of the seventeenth-century New England jeremiad) was Samson, who "received the strength to pull down Dagon's temple, through prayer . . . [as] the people of God, in the latter days, will . . . aid in pulling down the kingdom of Satan" (*Works* [New York, 1830], I, 482).

† In both cases the use of ark for ship of state emblemizes the union of secular and

Austin was speaking here directly to the fate of revivalism in the eighteenth century. His scorn for the skeptic's "unbelief" reminds us that since 1742 a growing number of the Enlightenment Liberals had been heaping contempt upon "enthusiasts" like himself, mocking their effort to mix history and prophecy, or (as the influential Unitarian William Ellery Channing wrote of Samuel Hopkins) to feed "on visions of a holiness" that issued from some deranged "region of imagination." Had not the times amply proved the folly of Edwards's notion that "the *Millennium* shall begin in AMERICA"? Charles Chauncy, Boston's leading rationalist theologian, repeatedly made that "vain Conceit" a lesson in horologicals, with due warning to all decent Christians to eschew that which *"it is not for us to know."* [16] But the lesson failed to persuade. Austin's optimism, his sense of the apocalyptic "joy" aboard the American ship of state, bespeaks the continuing vitality of Edwardsian revivalism. And revivalism remained vital to the culture, I would suggest, because Edwards neither broke with the Puritans nor aligned himself with them, but molded their myth to fit the needs of his own times. From the perspective I have been advancing, his contribution was to make revivalism a force toward independence by making it part of the evolving belief in America's mission. This is only a partial perspective on Edwards's achievement, of course. It reveals the provincialism of a brilliant mind, the capacity of a great religious philosopher to be misled by cultural afflatus into an astonishing arrogance, both on his own behalf and on behalf of his region and continent. Nonetheless, insofar as Edwards's arrogance reflects a set of widely shared beliefs, it seems to me to illuminate some salient implications of his thought.

It indicates, first of all, that Edwards drew out the proto-nationalistic tendencies of the New England Way. He inherited the concept of a new chosen people, and enlarged its constituency from saintly New England theocrats to newborn American saints. In fact, if not in theory, theocracy had meant tribalism, the literal and exclusive continuity from elect father to (presumably) elect son. Revivalist

sacred history, through its figural association of Noah, the ark of Israel, the church, and the errand. And in both cases the image is remarkable for the rhetorical continuities it suggests: e.g., from Joshua Scottow's *Narrative of Massachusetts* (1694) through Joseph Warren's oration on the Boston Massacre (1775), Melville's *White-Jacket*, and W. E. Arthur's July Fourth speech of 1850.

conversion opened the ranks of the American army of Christ to every white Protestant believer. Whereas the Puritan covenant renewals called the children of New England to their filial obligations, the Edwardsian concerts of prayer sought to awaken all prospective American saints, north and south, to the state of their souls, the shortcomings of their society, and the destiny of their New World Canaan.

In effect, Edwards expanded the Puritans' genetics of salvation into a genealogy of the latter-day American church. He rendered the legend of the founding fathers the common property of all New World evangelicals, and thus opened the prospect for expanding the Puritan past into a *figura* of the American Way. This accounts for the high optimism I noted in the revivalist jeremiad. The Puritans also described their mission in terms of "Christ's mighty deeds in America." But they were committed to a regionally defined, doctrinally exclusive way of life; and for all their self-assurance they never quite managed to reconcile the restrictive and expansive tendencies of their thought. Edwards had no such conflicts. He could afford to adopt a post-millennial view because he required no supernatural event to bridge the gap between an "enclosed garden" and the country at large, or between an outmoded past and a world-redemptive future. By freeing the jeremiad from the confines of theocracy, he harnessed the Puritan vision to the conditions of a new age. The New England Way, as he explained it, was above all a shadow or type of the "blessed union of love" that would knit together, as one city on a hill, all of Protestant America.

For if Edwards abandoned the Puritan belief in theocracy, he nonetheless retained (in substance) the Puritan vision of personal/ communal exceptionalism. As Alan Heimert notes, he differed from English revivalists, including Whitefield, by his emphasis on corporate mission. Edwards attacked the Separates for their spiritual pride, and the colonial establishment for its lax method of church admission. The "middle way" he espoused was, like Cotton's, an ambiguous union of extremes: it aspired simultaneously to absolute purity and to a full involvement in this world. In America, Edwards insisted, "the holy community must serve as a type of New Jerusalem" and hence as an earthly "instrument for bringing it into being." The Separates argued (as Williams had against Cotton) that typologically there was a "plain Difference between the World and the Church." Edwards replied (as Cotton had to Williams) that the story of America was intrinsic to sacred history. The aim of the American church, therefore, as "a type of New Jerusalem," was not merely "the salvation of individuals, but of society," since the society, in this case, was by definition engaged in "the forwarding of the Work of Redemption."[17]*

I invoke the parallel now to stress the change from 1640 to 1740. We have often been told that Edwards's position in the culture was a transitional one. Undoubtedly it was, if we add that the transition marked not the passing of an old order but the unfolding of a new stage of growth in colonial society. According to Perry Miller, Edwards was a modernist in spite of himself — the first American to recast Puritanism into "the idiom of empirical psychology" — and thus a central figure in the movement toward the values of liberal free enterprise and "possessive individualism."† There is a good deal

---

*Various nineteenth-century writers suggest something in this respect of Edwards's place in culture. Among Edwardsians, see for example E. C. Smyth's tribute, in the special Edwards Centennial volume of *The Congregationalist*, to Edwards's "great appreciation of America's place and part in the progress and universal establishment of the Kingdom of Redemption — a vision of America for Christ" (38 [1903], 458). Among anti-Edwardsians, the most articulate assessment is that of Harriet Beecher Stowe in *Oldtown Folks* (1869). Perhaps the broadest such interpretation of Edwards during this period comes from George Bancroft, in his *History of the United States* (see also his brief biography of Edwards in *The New American Encyclopaedia* [New York, 1859], Vol. VII). These and other nineteenth-century views of Edwards are discussed in Donald Weber, "The Image of Jonathan Edwards in American Culture," Diss. Columbia 1977.

† This term is taken from C. B. Macpherson, who argues that Locke's empiricism tended to draw out of Puritan thought the tenets of "possessive individualism," a moral justification for capitalism based on the theory that "society is a human contrivance for the protection of the individual's property in his person and goods, and (therefore) for the maintenance of orderly relations of exchange between individuals regarded as proprietors of themselves" (*The Political Theory of Possessive Individualism: Hobbes to Locke* [Oxford, 1962], pp. 264, 221). Like Miller's study of Edwards, this "presentist" analysis requires broad qualifications, but offers important clues nonetheless to the *implications* of certain ideas and movements — in this case, to the implicit link between Edwards and other evangelicals of his time in the evolution of the laissez-faire state (cf. E. P. Thompson, *The Makings of the English Working Class* [New York, 1966], pp. 26–76). My argument, let me emphasize, is not that Edwards was *the* agent of continuity, but a main representative of a general cultural movement.

of evidence for this view; but even more to support the case for Edwards the traditionalist — the orthodox Calvinist who sought passionately to curb the threat of modernism by all means at his disposal, including the ideal of christic selfhood. In direct opposition to Locke, he maintained that true individuation was not a self-contained, empirical process but a public and spiritual commitment. Regeneration for him depended on conformity through grace to "a principle of oneness that is manifested . . . as identical multiple units of generic consciousness." What brings together these two sides of Edwards's thought, at least during the period of the Awakening, was his effort to link regeneration to the destiny of the New World. American Protestants, after all, had a special role to play in God's plan. For them, above all other peoples, conversion, rebirth, and "generic consciousness" were manifested typologically, through the correspondence (which Edwards never tired of explaining) between personal fulfillment and social harmony. The result, however unintended, was that he went further than his predecessors in adjusting the Puritan chronometer to the "virtuous expediencies" of his age. Recent historians of religion have observed that Edwards's "ethics were prudent and flexible applications of the early Puritan tradition to the settled life of mid-eighteenth-century Massachusetts," that his chief followers "tended to espouse a . . . radically egalitarian, libertarian, and fraternal view of . . . social and political life," and that his theology proved flexible enough for them to "empower the theory of a nation."[18] Edwards should not be burdened with all the sins of his disciples, of course; but in this case we cannot entirely dissociate his thought from theirs. By implication, it seems clear, his long labor to wed Calvin and Locke issued in the union of eschatology and self-interest under the canopy of American progress.

From this perspective, Edwards's post-millennialism is indeed a major contribution to the vision of the American jeremiad. By opening the future to human control, he adapted the Puritan concept of process to the needs of an enterprise that had grown beyond the limits of a particular region or religious sect. The Bay theocrats had joined secular to sacred history, and posited a continual increase of material/spiritual blessings. Edwards made the spiral of redemption synonymous with the advance of mankind. In doing so, as Cushing Strout has shown, he "provided an exit from the harsh confines of

the Calvinism [he] expounded and paved the way for . . . new Arminian theologies of belief in the free will and moral strivings." The
historical ironies this involved may be more strongly stated. Edwards sanctified a worldliness he would have despised, and lent
support to new ideologies that linked American striving with Scripture prophecy, economic reform with the work of the spirit, and
libertarian ideals with the approach of New Jerusalem. Thus his use
of commercial imagery ("to live unto God . . . is the business and
. . . the trade of a Christian") became a mainstay of Yankee
pietism.* Thus his figural view of economics (the increase in colonial
trade "is a type and forerunner" of the time when the whole world
"shall be supplied with spiritual treasures from America") reappears
in countless promotional tracts.[19] And thus the Awakening he inspired, as Richard Bushman has shown, encouraged "worldly
ambition and resistance to [conservative forms of] social authority"
— a middle-class upsurgence that resulted in territorial expansion,
"increased economic opportunities," a "multitude of new traders
who called for currency issues," and a rising demand for democratic
self-government, all of this sustained and augmented by the sense
that it reflected some grand providential design.[20]†

---

*The horological counterpart to Edwards's vision is best expressed (appropriately)
by Charles Chauncy, the leading opponent of the Great Awakening. When Edwards
speaks of "business" or "trade" his focus is entirely on the *figura*. Chauncy justifies the
economic values of his society by finding correspondences between industry,
property, self-help, free-enterprise expediency, and "the Christian Law" (see for
example his *Idle-Poor* [Boston, 1752], pp. 7, 22, 24, and *Seasonable Thoughts* [Boston,
1743], pp. 63–64). Amy Lang traces the line of thought connecting both Edwards
and Chauncy in this respect back to the seventeenth-century Puritans and forward to
the Transcendentalists ("The Antinomian Strain in American Culture," Diss.
Columbia 1979).

†All this (to repeat) is to speak of effect, not intent, and I do not mean to ignore
the differences between the two. I would agree, for example, with Nathan O. Hatch's
contrast between the Edwardsian "praying bands of pious saints" and Revolutionary
Calvinists "like Abraham Keteltas . . . [who] welcomed to the cause of God anyone
who would take up the sword against the anti-christ of British tyranny . . . [and
who saw secular] American society as the model upon which the millennial kingdom
would be based" ("The Origins of Civil Millennialism in America: New England
Clergymen, War with France, and the Revolution," *William and Mary Quarterly*, 31

Edwardsian revivalism, I need hardly say, was only one of several factors in this development. Other movements and ideas played important roles in harnessing the Puritan vision to the conditions of eighteenth-century life. I might mention the "organic" theory of the growth of civilization, the abiding force of libertarianism, the resurgence of the classical concepts of *translatio studii* and *translatio imperii* ("the Westward course of empire") and the belief in natural or "Adamic" man. All of these, and others, contributed: some to redefine the city on a hill as a model of middle-class economy, others to translate the wonders of the chiliad into the virtues of democratic capitalism (legal equality, open opportunity, self-help). In virtually every case, the idea, or set of ideas, underwent the same transmutation in its Atlantic crossing as had the rhetoric of the jeremiad. In Enlightenment Europe, for example, the return to nature meant a static condition (whether pastoral or utopian); whereas the "Westward course of empire" implied a cyclical view of history.* In En-

---

[1974], 409). The distinction is perfectly sound, and it applies as well to the economic, ideological, and social issues that led to Revolution. Of course the revivalists were addressing converts, or potential converts, whereas the radical Whigs were mobilizing citizens. Of course the Revolutionaries had political ends whereas the revivalists were trying to "drive back the forces of darkness." What is significant is that, despite these predictable differences, a common pattern may be discerned. The striking cultural fact is that civic oppression should take the form of Antichrist, while "promoting the kingdom" should assume such specifically *American* implications that ministers like Keteltas could vaunt republicanism as "the cause of . . . heaven against hell — of the kind Parent of the universe, against the prince of darkness" (*God Arising* [Newburyport, Mass., 1777], p. 30). Roland Delattre is right to speak of the "skewing" of Edwards's political thought by men like Isaac Backus and Samuel Hopkins ("Beauty and Politics: A Problematic Legacy of Jonathan Edwards," in *American Philosophy from Edwards to Quine*, ed. R. W. Shahan and K. R. Merrill [Norman, Okla., 1977], pp. 21–22), but Delattre also notes here that in a broad cultural view the "Great Awakening helped prepare the ground for the Revolution," and in this view it is entirely fitting that Edwards's chief followers should have revised his timetable to make the Revolution *the* apocalyptic event, and called for revivals as a continuation of the millennial reign, rather than (like Edwards) as harbingers of the millennium.

*. . . *Empires* carry in them their own Bane,
And in a fatal Circle ever run
From virtuous *Industry* and *Valor*, first
To *Wealth* and *Conquest*, next to *Luxury*;

lightenment America, these conflicting views were absorbed into a progressive figural outlook, and transformed into alternative modes of cultural affirmation.

Significantly, historians who have failed to take Puritan continuities into account have also failed to account for that transformation. When colonial writers sang "Paradise a new" they were not thinking of Adam's garden. They envisioned the new end-time Eden, where a gathering of new Adams would "build the *finish'd* bliss." Far from being nostalgic or primitivistic, their paradise was to be the result of a series of reformations in history, and therefore a fulfillment of social as well as spiritual norms. And if those were now the norms of a secular era — if they posited a "reasonable paradise," a host of peaceable kingdoms blossoming in enlightened self-interest "under the . . . hand of *industry*" — they nonetheless reflected the old figural outlook. Liberty, equality, and property were not merely civic ideals. They were part of God's plan. America, as the home of libertarian principles, was the lasting "habitation of justice and mountain of holiness," awaiting the "awful commination of God," as John Barnard said in 1734, quoting Jeremiah 31. In the words of Jonathan Mayhew and Ebenezer Thayer, America's liberal "civil polity" had made what was "once desert . . . blossom as a rose, [with] the glory of Lebanon, . . . [and] the excellency of Carmel and Sharon"; if the colonies persisted in their present political and economic course, "God will . . . give us to see the good of his chosen," and "cause the Righteousness of our Jerusalem to go forth as brightness, and the Salvation thereof as a Lamp that burneth: Yea in every respect it [will] be said of us, . . . Happy art thou, O Israel: who is like unto thee, O People favored by the Lord!"[21]

Rhetorically considered, the continuity of vision is so pronounced that it seems at times the writers were intent upon bolstering the Puritan concepts. It is as though they were trying to justify the

---

And then to foul *Corruption*, bloted *Morals*,
Faction and *Anarchy*, a horrid Train!

(William Smith of New York, 1752, cited in Michael McGiffert, *The Question of* '76 [Williamsburg, Va., 1977], p. 10)

In the aftermath of the Revolution certain disillusioned Americans would invoke this European concept of the *translatio imperii* to protest what they considered the degeneration of American democracy. But it seems safe to say that for the most part their countrymen kept the faith.

Good Old Way by bringing it up to date. They revealed "not a new purpose," as Heimert has observed, "but only new instruments." By the old instruments, the future was to be a heavenly version of the church-state; by the new ones, "a mercantile version of the philosopher's heavenly city." In both cases the intention was to display, for the colonists' encouragement and the world's admiration, America's ordained destiny. Still, there is an important distinction to be made. In this philosopher's heavenly city, Scripture was only one of many sources of authority, and figuralism involved a secular mode of identity. When the influential rationalist William Smith asked his countrymen to "Look back, with reverence back . . . to the mighty purpose which [their] fathers had in view" — and then to look about them and "Behold . . . the garden of the Lord!" — the "chosen seat of Freedom, Arts, and Heavenly Knowledge" — he was not speaking as a scriptural exegete, nor was the "mighty purpose" he referred to wholly a religious one.[22] *Heavenly* was a metaphor for him, as *mountain of holiness* was for Barnard, and *Jerusalem* for Mayhew and Thayer.

And yet obviously he did have a religious meaning in mind. That meaning violated religious tradition, to be sure, but it had gained such wide acceptance as to merit the term traditional in its own right. Smith's use of Scripture was purposeful in that it imposed a sacred scheme on local events. *Garden of the Lord* was not just a figure of speech, but a key to the progress of the country. The *fathers* he reverently invoked were "particular antitypes" of "the ancient Israelites" in the sense that what they had begun would eventuate in an "earthly paradise." And if by other standards *antitype* and *paradise*, as Smith used these terms, were secular designations, by the standards of his own audience — and that of Barnard, Mayhew, and Thayer — they served as reminders that here, as nowhere else, the secular was infused with special significance. To this end, in a centennial speech on the Great Migration, Thomas Foxcroft predicted an expansion of political rights on the basis of divine promises fulfilled ("Glorious Things have been spoken of thee, O City of God . . . as of Jerusalem of old"). To this end, too, twenty-seven years later, Thomas Frink envisioned unlimited growth for the New World *"Tribes of the Lord."* Nehemiah's Jerusalem, he declared, "does most graphically set forth in Figure this wonderful Reformation of the World in these latter Days"; our New Israel is the type of *this blessed Millennium* expressed by the *new Heavens* and a *new Earth.*"[23]

New Israel, New World, new heavens and new earth: it was the common vision of the time, and it derived, unmistakably, from Puritan New England. For while Europeans continued to use the "Westward course of empire" as an example of the vanity of human wishes — prosperity leading to corruption and decay — the colonial Jeremiahs recast this into a variation on Daniel's apocalyptic scheme of the "four empires" (or "monarchies").* By and large, it was the latter version that the eighteenth-century colonists adopted, dispensing as they did so with the scriptural proof. Or rather, they transferred their proof text from the Scriptures to the story of America. The "star of empire" meant far more for them than the movement of civilization from the Old World to the New. It signaled the "complete fulfillment" of "the various ancient prophecies." It was the morning star heralding the triumphant sun/Son that (in Edwards's

---

*A brief illustration must suffice. A favorite poem among the New England Puritans was George Herbert's "The Church Militant," which uses the *translatio* theme in its traditional form. Religion, writes Herbert, has always moved from East to West, once from Asia to Europe, now from Europe to America — "Yet as the Church shall thither westward flie, / So Sinne shall trace and dog her instantly" (*Works*, ed. F. E. Hutchinson [Oxford, 1941], pp. 216–18). In short, New England's errand is just another exemplum of the vanity of human wishes. The American Puritans managed to quote the poem in a way that precisely inverted its meaning — i.e., in a way that accommodated it to their version of the jeremiad. Consider, for example, Joshua Scottow's "application" of Herbert's text to the Great Migration: "That this Design was Super-humane, will be evidenced by the *Primum Mobile*, or grand Wheel thereof. The Setting up of Christ's Kingdom was the main spring of motion, and at such a time *Herbert* Prophetically sang '*Religion Stands on Tiptoe in Our Land, / Ready to pass to the* AMERICAN *Strand.*' Infinite Wisdom directed this [enterprise]. Divine Courage and Resolution managed it, Super-humane Sedulity attended it, And Angelical Swiftness finished it, according to predeterminate Design" (*A Narrative of the Planting* [Boston, 1694], pp. 287–88, 292; ellipses deleted).

In 1726, Americans found a more compatible English text for their purpose: Bishop Berkeley's "America or the Muse's Refuge, A Prophecy," which made the westward course of empire a variation on the Danielic apocalypse. Berkeley's lines are cited by American writers throughout the century, as in Hugh Henry Brackenridge's "Poem on the Divine Revelation" (1774). Later on, patriots like Franklin and Joel Barlow found support for this view in Richard Price's millennial vision of the American Revolution and in Condorcet's theory of progress.

words) would "rise in the West, contrary to the course of . . . the world." And this holds true for everything that *empire*, *West*, and *fulfillment* evoked in eighteenth-century America. Libertarianism was not just a better way of life, but "the long-promised glory," its "Light spread[ing] from the day-spring in the west . . . until the perfect day."[24] When John Murray and Ebenezer Baldwin considered the prospects of free trade and open competition, what came to mind was "IMMANUEL'S LAND," the "Seat of that glorious Kingdom, which Christ shall erect upon Earth in the latter days." "If all the youth were educated, in the manner we recommend," wrote Charles Turner, "*The Kingdom of God* would appear." If we maintain our rate of westward expansion, said John Mellen, we will achieve that "which the scripture prophecies represent as constituting the glory of the latter days."[25]

It was not a matter of attaining innocence, more land and wealth, the benefits of civilization. These were the tangible proof of something greater. Elsewhere, such advances might make (temporarily) for a good society. In America, as an English traveler marveled at mid–century, the concept of *translatio* carried a new "idea, strange as it was visionary," that at some approaching "destined moment . . . America is to give law to the rest of the world." This was variously proclaimed as an "empire of liberty," "an empire of reason," "an empire of virtue," "an empire of love," "a great and mighty Empire; the largest the World ever saw." What unites these descriptions — what infuses them all with that single strange and visionary idea — is their equation of progress with biblical prophecy as *American* millennialism. Here alone, "*Industry* and *Valor*," "*Wealth* and *Conquest*," were not the harbingers of decay, but "striking traits of grandeur and magnificence, which the Divine Economist . . . reserved to crown the closing scene" of time — signs "that Heaven has great and gracious purposes towards this continent, which no human power or human device shall be able finally to frustrate" — for while "Earth's bloodstained empires . . . their gradual progress run,"

> Here the pure Church, descending from her God,
> Shall fix on earth her long and last abode;
> Zion arise, in radiant splendors dress'd.
> .   .   .   .
> O Land supremely blest! to thee tis given

To taste the choicest joys of bounteous heaven;
Thy rising Glory shall expand its rays,
And lands and times unknown rehearse thine endless praise.

.   .   .   .   .

No dangerous tree with deadly fruit shall grow,
No tempting serpent to allure the soul
From native innocence. — A *Canaan* here,
Another *Canaan* shall excel the old,
And from a fairer Pisgah's top be seen.[26]

The high optimism at mid-century — on the part of both the revivalists and the celebrants of Yankee America — reflected the material progress of the colonies. Despite a widening gap after 1730
between rich and poor, the poor were better off than their forebears
had been. An extraordinary increase in population led to an extraordinary proportion of young people, many of them sanguine about
their prospects for self-advancement. Not all of them succeeded, to
be sure, but by 1740 the general living standard seems to have
equaled or surpassed that of any European country. It may well
be that this spectacular economic growth nourished ambitions that
led into the French and Indian War. In any case, the war itself proved
to be a triumph equally for English foreign policy, for the colonies'
burgeoning free-enterprise institutions, and for the rhetoric of the
American jeremiad. Extending the old techniques to accommodate
commercial, military, and territorial aims — clothing imperialism as
holy war — the clergy summoned the colonists to an Anglo-Protes-
tant errand into the Catholic wilderness. The French were "the offspring of that *Scarlet Whore*," French Canada "the North American
Babylon," and the invasion itself a "grand decisive conflict between
the Lamb and beast," preview of Armageddon.* From the siege
of Louisbourg (1745) to the Peace of Paris (1763), all of New England, as Nathan Hatch has shown, was gripped in "millennial

---

*Significantly, the equation between French Canada and Babylon was not the
invention of the mid-eighteenth-century clergy. As John Seelye points out, it appears
in Cotton Mather's "Lecture" on John Williams's captivity experience, *The Redeemed
Captive*, in which Mather celebrates "the captive's return . . . with numerous quotations from Exodus and the Psalms testifying to God's protection of his Chosen
People" (*Prophetic Waters: The River in American Life and Literature, 1582–1730* [New
York, 1976], p. 250).

optimism." Hatch, noting the infusion of new concepts, claims that this "civil millennialism" marked a radical departure in colonial eschatology. His claim is no more valid, I believe, than that which has been made for Edwardsian post-millennialism; but he is surely right about the mood of the times. Liberals and Calvinists from Massachusetts to Virginia — including Edwards's old antagonist Charles Chauncy — joined in predicting that the downfall of French Canada would bring "a most signal revolution in the civil and religious state of things in this world." Even the elegant Mather Byles, Cotton Mather's wry and sophisticated grandnephew, could not constrain his enthusiasm. "What a scene of Wonder opens to our View!" he exclaimed after the British victory of Louisbourg. "Good God! What an astonishing Scene of Wonders!" Other ministers were more fervent still in their enthusiasm. Their sermon titles give praise to *God the Strength and Salvation of His people*; the sermons themselves announce the fall of Babylon and (with the signing of the peace treaty) "the accomplishment of the scripture-prophecies relative to the Millennial State."[27]

Significantly, Edwards adopted essentially the same view of the war. From his wilderness exile at Stockbridge he exulted in every hopeful scrap of news. His "Account of Events Probably Fulfilling the Sixth Vial" — fulfilling, that is, the last of the prophecies before those concerning the advent of New Jerusalem — includes reports culled from a host of local newspapers in Boston and New York. Nothing, it would seem, was too petty, too flagrantly secular or self-seeking, to contribute to his calculations. The capture of the *Duc de Chartres*, increases in New England's "trade and acquisitions," signs of commercial, military, and moral decline in France, political "distresses" in French Canada, the naval victory at Cape François, the (piratical) seizure of French stores of gold, provisions, merchandise, and armaments — every fact that touched upon the war was pregnant with prophetic meaning, as much an image or shadow of things to come as was any fact of Scripture. "The late wonderful works of God in America," Edwards wrote to a Scottish correspondent after the battle of Cape Breton, were hastening the completion of the divine plan. They bespoke "an extraordinary spirit of prayer given the people of God in New England, with respect to this undertaking, more than any public affair within my remembrance."

Clearly, "the Most High has made his hand manifest, in a most apparent and marvelous manner . . . it being perhaps a dispensation of providence, the most remarkable in its kind, that has been in many ages . . . and a great argument . . . that we live in an age, wherein divine wonders are to be expected."[28]

Edwards's enthusiasm about the French and Indian War is a striking testament to the continuities between revivalist and civil millennialism. But the war contributed in its own right toward broadening the scope of the jeremiad. The revivalists had enlarged the errand to include the visible saints not only of Massachusetts but of all the English colonies. The established clergy from 1745 to 1763 went further still. In mobilizing the "patriotic inhabitants of Protestant America," they associated "our Sion" with "our Colonies" in a wholly secular sense. The basis of their plea was not only religion but specifically the civic traditions of Anglo-America — not only evangelical Protestantism, that is, but English libertarianism. To some extent, this issued in a heightened sense of loyalty to "the mother country." Britain was the source of colonial liberties, and the writings of this decade continually celebrate that legacy. But as Paul Varg has observed, they also speak over and again of *America* and *Americans*, and increasingly they extol "the founding fathers, who left England . . . and labored in the expectation that the blessings of freedom would be the inheritance of their posterity." *The blessings of freedom!* This may seem a long way from theocracy, but the *freedom* being invoked was not merely a secular ideal. As both clerical and civic leaders stressed, it brought the blessings of time and eternity. Did not God Himself lay "His arm bare for the salvation of our fathers in this land," so that they might fashion a "New Canaan of Liberty"?[29]

These terms were to carry special force in the next two decades; but I call attention to them now to indicate the widening scope of the myth. The Puritans Jeremiahs had justified the errand by reference to the Israelite exodus. The eighteenth-century Jeremiahs justified both the Israelites and the Puritans by reference to their own progress. And having done so, they invoked the example of the Bay emigrants — "those heroes of virtue," as Jonathan Mayhew said in 1754, "smitten with a Love of Liberty" — in order to inspire their countrymen to still greater deeds. "Liberty was the noble errand of our fathers across the Atlantic"; they "set the seas and skies, Monsters and savages, Tyrants and Devils at Defyance, for the sake of liberty."[30] So adapted and revised, the legend of the Puritan founders belonged unequivocally to all white Protestant colonists.* As "the Children of *Israel* [were] led out of *Egypt*," cried Theodorus Frelinghuysen of New York in 1754, "So [were] our Ancestors brought over from Europe to this land." As "God Almighty [gave] them the Land of the Heathen," so now He intends to give French Canada to the forces of Protestant America.[31] And as He punished the Israelites and Puritans for their transgressions, so now He is afflicting us with the French Catholics and their Indian allies, "speak-[ing] to us, as he did against Israel, by warning Dispensations of his Providence." Let us therefore remember God's promises to Old Israel and New; let us "act as they did" and surely God's "Wrath will be appeased, his Judgments removed, . . . [and] we shall see his Salvation."[32]

The message was repeated steadily through the war years, in such jeremiads as Philip Reading's *The Protestant Danger* (Philadelphia, 1755), Nathaniel Potter's *Discourse on Jeremiah* (Boston, 1758), Ebenezer Prime's *Importance of the Divine Presence* (New York, 1759), Samuel Dunbar's *Presence of God* (Boston, 1760), and David Hall's *Israel's Triumph* (Boston, 1761). During the last, critical stage of the conflict, the ministers tended to mute their threats. But no sooner

---

*By 1765, this legend had become a staple of colonial rhetoric. The year of the Stamp Act brought *The History of New Jersey* by the Quaker Samuel Smith, with its eulogy to the Puritan mission of "religious and civil freedom" (Wesley Frank Craven, *The Legend of the Founding Fathers* [New York, 1956], p. 46); John Adams's magisterial "Dissertation on the Canon and Feudal Law," which argues that the Puritans were inspired by a love of "freedom of inquiry," that their government stood "in direct opposition to the canon and feudal systems," and that they transmitted that "government down to their posterity, with the means of securing and preserving it forever" (*Works*, ed. Charles Francis Adams [Boston, 1850–56], III, 464); and the famous letter of Sam Adams to the revivalist George Whitefield, where in effect Adams grounds the legal claims for independence on the charter granted to the *Arbella* emigrants (*Writings*, ed. Henry A. Cushing [New York, 1968], I. 26–33). During the same period Sam Adams defended the nation's "rights" under the pseudonym of "Cotton Mather," John Cleaveland attacked Governor Thomas Hutchinson under the pseudonym of "Johannes in Eremo" (taken from Cotton Mather's *Magnalia*), and William Gordon urged the General Court of Massachusetts to read Mather's *Magnalia* in order to ascertain the meaning of American liberties.

was peace declared than they resumed the lament in full force. The battles just past, they warned, did not resolve the crisis. Far from it: "the great season of our national probation" had only begun. Like the Jeremiahs of 1740, they saw evidence wherever they looked of degeneracy — "delicacies and luxuries" abounding, "unsubdued lusts permitted to range and riot at large among the tempting sweets of a fertile peaceful country" — an ungrateful people that gave every sign of seeking a captain to lead them back to Egypt. The thunder of their moral complaint continues into the Revolutionary era. Popery, corruption, and backsliding, self-love and self-interest, "dissipation, extravagance, gaming, idleness and intemperance" — all the "enormities" enumerated by the Synod of 1679 returned in the sermons of the 1760s and 1770s.[33] The cause now was independence, not British-American Protestantism; the social ideal a republic, not a theocracy or an enlightened monarchy. And of course the enemy assumed another, subtler, and more perfidious form. The English king, rather than the French, was now the instrument of the Scarlet Whore; England rather than French Canada was the modern Babylon; the danger within came from European fashions and royal agents rather than from Indians, Jesuits, or heretics.

And yet the rhetoric, while dramatically enlarged in its applications, has essentially the same structure. The shifts in subject and concept during this period show the flexibility of the form; the widespread use of the jeremiad to mobilize the country attests to its efficacy. Never did the voice of Jeremiah sound more loudly in the land than in the springtime of the republic. It may be the "Will of Heaven," wrote John Adams on the eve of independence, that "Americans shall suffer Calamities still more wasting and Distresses yet more dreadfull. . . . The Furnace of Affliction produces Refinement, in States as well as Individuals." That was July 3, 1776. Not long before, he had heard a minister predicting that God would "come with a vengeance" upon the land — and "the whole prophecy," Adams told his wife, "filled and swelled the bosom of every hearer." He knew that in saying this he was not instructing but confirming Abigail in her faith. She herself had comforted him often enough about the ambiguities of God's wrath with His chosen. Both of them realized that, by "the intention of Heaven," it was *through* "all the gloom," *by means of* "blood and treason," that the nation's "deliverance [would] be wrought out . . . as it was for the children of Israel." Declension, doubt, political and economic reversal — as they detailed the afflictions of God's Country, it all amounted once again to the "day of Israel's trials." Both of them could endorse the promise, emblazoned in rough print on a Vermont Thanksgiving broadside, that "God would yet make us glad, according to the Days wherein we have been afflicted, and the Time in which we have seen Evil."[34]

The Vermont broadside is characteristic of a host of civic as well as clerical writings — treatises, orations, pamphlets — which, having detailed "every iniquity, every moral evil, [that] has abounded among us," sound an urgent summons for covenant renewal and concert of prayer. In Cushing Strout's fine summary, "it was not only bliss to be alive in such a revolutionary dawn; it was also agony, for the guilt of backsliding was much greater precisely because of the great things God had done for the American people. Like Samuel West, all American ministers knew the relevant passage in Amos [3:2]: 'You only have I known of all the families of the earth; therefore will I punish you for all your iniquities.' Chosen in glory, America was chosen in woe."[35]

West's approach had proved itself often enough in the past. Its crucial function in the Revolution may be seen in the assessments of two recent historians of the period. According to Edmund Morgan,

> Parliamentary taxation offered Americans the prospect of poverty and adversity, and, as of old, adversity provided a spur to virtue. . . . As their Puritan forefathers had met providential disasters with a renewal of the virtue that would restore God's favor, the Revolutionary generation met taxation with a self-denial and industry that would hopefully restore their accustomed freedom and simultaneously enable them to identify with their virtuous ancestors. . . . Parliamentary taxation, like an Indian attack in earlier years, was thus both a danger to be resisted and an act of providence to recall Americans from declension.

Danger as saving providence, disaster leading to renewal — these strategies of the colonial jeremiad appear even more forcefully in Gordon Wood's description of moral complaint in the decade before the Revolution:

> [The] prevalence of vice and corruption that many Americans saw in their midst . . . became a stimulus, perhaps in fact the most important stimulus, to revolution. . . . The calls for independence thus took on a

tone of imperativeness. . . . Only this mingling of urgency and anxiety during their introspective probings at the height of the crisis could have given their revolutionary language the frenzied quality it acquired. Only profound doubts could have created their millennial vision of a new society, their idealized expectation that "on the morrow" there would be a "new thing under the sun, that hath not been already of old time."[36]

Only the jeremiad form, I would add, as this was developed from the Puritans through Edwards, could have sufficed for the occasion. And as Wood observes, it was a form that generated millennial frenzy out of the very process of self-doubt. Increasingly during the 1760s and the early 1770s, patriot leaders drew on the image of a "chosen band, removed from the depravations . . . of Europe," going forth to receive "the heathen . . . for an inheritance and these uttermost parts of the earth [for] a possession." Increasingly, they invoked what they construed to be the libertarian legacy of the Puritan founders. And increasingly, they spoke of the emerging conflict for independence in apocalyptic terms. The colonists were still suffering in captivity, rightly "complaining of the severe treatment of Pharaoh, who *made their lives bitter with hard bondage*" — but *soon, speedily, shortly*, they promised, the English "dragon will be destroyed," and "the kingdom of our God will be established." When in 1774 Thomas Jefferson revived the fast-day ritual, he noted with some surprise that "the effect thru' the whole colony was like the shock of electricity, arousing every man & placing him erect." He learned the lesson well enough to return to those rhetorical devices on other important public occasions, from his exhortations during the Revolutionary era to his second inaugural address. Tom Paine must have learned the same lesson, to judge by his otherwise startling recourse to that language in *Common Sense*. I refer to his use of biblical precedents, his emphasis on providence, and above all the figural blueprint he presents for American exceptionalism, with due emphasis on the landmarks of early New England christianography: a fallen Old World (harboring Romish Antichrist), an Egyptian England (in bondage to a "hardened, sullen-tempered pharaoh"), and a New Canaan charged "by the design of Heaven" with "the cause of all mankind."[37]

No doubt these Enlightenment heroes capitalized on the work of the "black regiment," that "numerous, learned and respectable body," as the Revolutionary historian David Ramsay described the New England clergy, "who had a great ascendancy over the minds of their hearers. They connected religion and patriotism, and in their sermons and prayers represented the cause of America as the cause of Heaven." To varying degrees, most of the leading Revolutionaries responded in similar fashion. Their appeals for unity, sounded from military camp, scholar's study, and political platform, affirm the same typology of mission. "America," explained Washington's protégé, Colonel David Humphreys, "after having been concealed for so many centuries . . . was probably discovered in the maturity of time, to become the theatre for displaying the illustrious designs of Providence." Jacob Duché, examining those designs in a Congressional speech, hailed the future through the image of "the American vine." "I see new kingdoms and empires," he cried in the theopathic language of Edwards and the Mathers, "rushing forward, . . . eager to disclose their latent powers; whilst the old ones on the other side of the Atlantic, 'hide their diminished heads,' . . . I see the last efforts of a powerful Providence exerted, in order to reclaim our wandering race from the paths of ignorance and error."* All things considered, wrote Samuel Adams,

> it need not be asked, Are we able to support the measures which will secure independency? The answer is plain and easy. Though all the world may think we are not, yet, *God*, it appears, thinks otherwise. . . . I say, *God* thinks otherwise, because every part of his providential proceedings justifies the thought. We may then know what part we ought to take. God does the work, but not without instruments, and they who are employed are denominated his servants. . . . We may affect humility in refusing to be made the servants of Divine vengeance, but the good servant will execute the will of his master. *Samuel* will slay *Agag; Moses, Aaron,* and *Hur* will pray in the mountain; and *Joshua* will defeat the *Canaanites.*[38]

Nowhere is the figural import of these exhortations clearer than in the Revolutionary appeal to the example of the Bay planters. The appeal itself, as both Wood and Morgan suggest, was part of New England tradition. But in 1776 it assumed a special urgency. In what was surely the single most troubling ideological attack on independ-

---

*Duché eventually defected to the Loyalists, but as Perry Miller noted, this "does not make his *The American Vine* any less a spiritual jeremiad of the sort that most invigorated patriot courage" (*Nature's Nation* [Cambridge, Mass., 1967], p. 95). Much the same might be said about the sermons of the Loyalist Thomas Frink.

ence, the Tories charged that the radicals were violating a holy filial
bond — inciting their countrymen to an act of ingratitude that was
tantamount to patricide. The patriots, we know, had a ready reply:
the country had evidently come of age; continued dependence was
either unnatural or tyrannous. But we also know that their reply,
however persuasive to others, left them profoundly disquieted. An
anti-authoritarian spirit was abroad in the land, and they had too
much at stake in the status quo to undo traditional metaphors of
deference. In retrospect, their recourse to filiopietism seems well-
nigh inevitable. It allowed them not only to deny the Tory charge,
but (as it were) to usurp it for themselves — and in usurping it, to
sanctify the basic premises of their culture. By definition, they
pointed out, the fathers of the country were not Englishmen, but
Americans — emigrant heroes (like Aeneas' band, or the wandering
Israelites) who had left a fallen civilization to unveil the promise of
the New World. That promise was figural — at once sacred and
historical. Calling both on Danforth's concept of the "wilderness-
condition" and on the more recent rhetoric of liberty, the Revolutionaries pointed out that in fleeing the Old World, the emigrants
were abandoning a bankrupt monarchical order to establish a new
way of life, civic and economic as well as religious. It was to *their*
cause of liberty, rather than to some Old World despot, that filial
allegiance was due. In effect the Whig leaders, in what was clearly
an extension of earlier techniques, turned the jeremiad into a lesson
in national genealogy. The lesson led to the familiar figural imperative: what the fathers began, the sons were bound to complete.
Revolution meant improvement, not hiatus; obedience, not riot; not
a breach of social order, but the fulfillment of God's plan. As an act
of filiopietism, independence was America's long-prepared-for, reverently *ordered* passage into national maturity.*

---

*This Revolutionary genealogy eventually helped in many ways to fortify the
myth. It enabled nineteenth-century historians to represent the Revolutionary leaders
as a model of fraternal consensus, to stress the inevitability of their uprising, and to
acclaim the unprecedented pace of "national" progress. It gave substance to the
rhetoric about an American "people," providing as it did a substitute for what European nationalists termed "folk culture." Not least important, this Revolutionary
genealogy helped to project the movement from colony to republic forward to the
transition from Jeffersonian fathers to Jacksonian sons, and later to celebrate the Civil
War as a confirmation of the revolution begun in New England over two hundred
years before.

The rite of passage centered, as we might expect, on the *figura*: Israel's exodus, New England's errand, America's mission. Athens and Rome were horological antecedents for the republic; they offered incentives or warnings in various temporal, conditional matters. As before, sacred history provided the controlling metaphor. And as before, the American Jeremiahs described England as a "worse than Egyptian darkness" — its "rulers . . . madly rushing, like Pharaoh and his host, through a sea of blood, on their utter destruction" — using this ritual exorcism of foreign demons (once again) to rededicate the American Israel to its mission. I refer now not only to the leading clerics of the period, but to such disparate political thinkers as Washington, Hamilton, and Tom Paine. Various historians have reminded us that the first proposals for the seal of the United States, submitted by Franklin and Jefferson, featured Moses leading the chosen people from Egypt; it might be added that the symbol adopted instead was widely interpreted in just this way. "If any should be disposed to ask," said Edwards's disciple David Austin in 1794, "what has become of the eagle, on whose wings the persecuted woman [Revelation 12:14] was borne in to the American wilderness, may it not be answered, that she hath taken her station upon the Civil Seal of the United States"? So indeed it had been answered (to no one's surprise) by Samuel Sherwood on the eve of revolution. Invoking the same text from Revelation,* Sherwood proceeded to link this to the corresponding commemorative and proleptic passages in the Old Testament:

> Ye have sene what I did unto the Egyptians, and *how* I caryed you upon egles wings, and have broght you unto me.
> Now therefore if ye wil heare my voyce in dede, & kepe my covenant, then ye shalbe my chief treasure above all people, thogh all the earth be mine.

> *And when the dragon sawe that he was cast unto the earth, he persecuted ye woman which had broght forthe the man *childe*.
> But to the woman were given two winges of a great egle, yt she might flie into the wildernes. . . .
> Then the dragon was wroth with the woman, and went and made warre with the remnant of her sede, which kepe the commandements of God, and have the testimonie of Jesus Christ. (Revelation 12:13, 14, 17)

Traditionally, the woman means the church (or Mary, *figura ecclesiae*), the dragon means Antichrist or Satan, and the man child means Christ.

Ye shalbe unto me also a kingdome of Priestes, and an holy nation. (Exodus 19:4–6)

Why saiest thou, O Jaakob, and speakest O Israel, My waye is hid from the Lord . . . [?]

Knowest thou not? *or* hast thou not heard, that the everlasting God, the Lord hathe created the ends of the earth? . . .

But they that waite upon the Lord, shal renue *their* strength: they shal lift up the wings as the egles. (Isaiah 40:27, 28, 31)

Then, making explicit the figural import of all three texts, Sherwood announced to his election-day audience of May 1776:

When that God, to whom the earth belongs, and the fulness thereof, brought his church into this wilderness, as on eagles' wings by his kind protecting providence, he gave this good land to her, to her own lot and inheritance forever. He planted her as a pleasant and choice vine; and drove out the Heathen before her. He has tenderly nourished and cherished her in her infant state, and protected her amidst innumerable dangers. . . . God has, in this American quarter of the globe, provided for the woman and her seed. . . . He has wrought out a very glorious deliverance for them, and set them free from the cruel rod of tyranny and oppression . . . leading them to the good land of Canaan, which he gave them for an everlasting inheritance.[39]

Sherwood's election-day address, *The Church's Flight into the Wilderness*, was the most popular and most inflammatory sermon of 1776, the clerical counterpart of Tom Paine's *Common Sense*. As such, it may be said to signal a transition in the history of the American jeremiad. Its instant and widespread effect attests to its timeliness. Sherwood had absorbed all the relevant progressivist, libertarian, and Enlightenment sentiments. He puts due emphasis on civil and religious liberty, condemns tyranny in the language of Locke, denounces mercantilism with the vehemence of Adam Smith, eulogizes the doctrine of natural rights, and gives close attention to current affairs.* And at the same time he draws upon all the

---

*For example, the popular belief in a Catholic conspiracy — supported by "the corrupt system of . . . Great Britain, which appears so favourable to popery" (Samuel Sherwood, *The Church's Flight* [New York, 1776], pp. 14–15) — or as the colonists had put it in the Andros revolt, a "horrid *Popish Plot*" designed for nothing "less than the extinction of the *Protestant Religion*" (Cotton Mather, *The Declaration of the Gentlemen* [1689], in *Tracts*, ed. Peter Force [New York, 1947], Vol. IV, no. 10, p. 6). Similar charges were later made against republican France (and Tom Paine in particular), on the basis of what seemed to New England clerics the obvious parallels between Catholicism and atheism, and still later (during the elections at the turn of the century) against the party of Jefferson.

strategies of the American Puritan jeremiad. In this respect, his use
of the eagle recalls John Cotton's great sermon of 1630. God has
given you the good land across the Atlantic, Cotton had then instructed the *Arbella* passengers,

> As in Exod. 19.4. *You have seen how I have borne you as on eagles wings,
> and brought you unto my self.* So that though [you] meet with many diffi-
> culties, yet [He will carry you, as in Revelation 12:14] . . . high above
> them all, like an eagle, flying over seas and high rocks, and all hinder-
> ances. . . . Though there be many difficulties, yet God hath given us
> hearts to overlooke them all, as if we were carried upon eagles' wings
> [cf. Isaiah 40:31]. . . . He gives [you] the land by promise; others take
> the land by His providence, but Gods people take the land by promise.
> And therefore the land of Canaan is called a land of promise. [40]

Gods Promise to His Plantations marked a rite of passage into the New
World theocracy. It was a plea for order based on the Bible, on a
scriptural mode of identity, and on a traditional interpretation of the
eagle as Christ. Assuming the authority of tradition, Cotton used the
tradition to justify the venture.* Sherwood takes that justification,
rather than the tradition behind it, as his authority. Ultimately, he
appeals not to church tradition, and not even to the Bible, but to the
American experience; and in doing so he virtually reverses the hermeneutical process — turns figuralism inside out. Sherwood's authority is the country's progress, his text the Puritan past, his exegetical framework the typology of America's mission. Hence the ease
with which he interprets the eagle as the Puritan spirit of liberty,
figura of the spirit of '76. The radical Whigs, he is saying, are the

---

* I do not mean to suggest that Cotton was here setting out the entire figural scheme
of Puritan New England. *Gods Promise*, as I said, is a prototypical American jeremiad,
and at times inconsistent in its vision. But insofar as it anticipates the errand it bears
an important historical as well as literary relation to Sherwood's sermon. A group of
volatile nonconformists were hoping to set up a model state in a strange and unknown
land. Clearly, they required some extraordinary mode of cohesion, and Cotton offered it to them in a sweeping redefinition of their identity. Henceforth, he told them,
they were another chosen people, summoned by God to a new Canaan. English
Puritans might have to revolt in order to reform society. The emigrants, like the
ancient Hebrews, had channeled revolt into an act of exodus and rededication. By
filial bond, they were pledged to a form of progress through submission. This vision
Samuel Sherwood adapted to the volatile conditions of May 1776, but his adaptation
carries far more assurance, both in the assertiveness of its language and in the scope of
its application.

children of promise, as Joshua was the heir to Moses: it is all one grand spiral of fulfillment from theocracy to democracy.

As a summons to exodus and conquest through order, Sherwood's election-day address bears the same relation to the republic that *Gods Promise to His Plantations* does to the infant church-state. *The Church's Flight into the Wilderness* is the prototypical jeremiad of the new nation. The figural outlook it sets forth centers wholly on secular history. Though he includes the Reformation and forecasts the millennium, as Cotton does, Sherwood describes the main redemptive events in terms of the growth of American society. The sacred point of origin is the Puritan settlement; its climax, the impending war of independence. Danforth had similarly posited a figural unfolding from the Great Migration, but his pre-millennial view precluded a secular process of fulfillment. Edwards had opened the way for identifying local progress with the work of redemption, but the Northampton awakenings failed to serve as antitype of the Great Migration. The development of the Anglo-American colonies, as Edwards conceived this, stretched indefinitely into the universal age of the spirit. For Sherwood and his compatriots, the typology of America's mission took on a distinct, self-enclosed American form. Drawing out the logic of their Puritan forebears to a conclusion undreamt of by Danforth or Edwards (much less by Cotton and Winthrop), they announced that the often-prophecied, long-expected apocalyptic moment had arrived with the American Revolution. The patriot Whigs, "acting for the benefit of the whole world and of future ages," were sounding the same clarion call "as that of the heavenly host that announced the birth of the Saviour." The Revolution, they explained, marked the full and final "accomplishment of the *magnalia Dei* — the great events . . . designed from eternal ages to be displayed in these ends of the earth."[41]

The flowering of that figural scheme, as we shall see, appears in the major histories and orations of the Jacksonian era. But we can follow the process of growth through countless patriotic addresses of the post-Revolutionary period — Nicholas Street's *The American States Acting over the Part of the Children of Israel in the Wilderness* (New Haven, 1777), Samuel Langdon's *The Republic of the Israelites an Example to the United States* (Exeter, N. H., 1788), Abiel Abbot's *Traits of Resemblance in the People of the United States of America to*

Ancient Israel (Haverhill, Mass., 1799). In these republican jeremiads, terms like "acting over," "example," and "resemblance" denote a biblical reality thrice removed. For the Puritans, the errand carried forward the biblical exodus; for Edwards, the revival brought to fruition the Puritan errand; for the Whig preachers, the Revolution unveiled the meaning of exodus, errand, and revival. The flight of Noah, the wanderings of Abraham, the desert march of Israel, the formation of the early church, the revolt of Luther and Calvin against Rome: to all this the Revolution stood as antitype. When "OUR FOREFATHERS laid the foundation of this NEW WORLD," they did more than fulfill the ancient prophecies; they also prepared for "all those surprising scenes which have [just] taken place — as well as those still greater ones which . . . will succeed them, to the end of time." [42]

Like the Incarnation, then, the Revolution marked a qualitative change in the spiral of human history. A new era had begun with the discovery of the New World, as Chandler Robbins (for one) argued, and the Revolution confirmed it, precisely as Christ had confirmed the new era of faith. In both cases, the "surprising scenes" were at once definitive in their own right and a confirmation of "still greater ones" to come. This was also Samuel Cooper's message, when in 1780 he elucidated the parallel with Israel (for the benefit of the Massachusetts legislature) according to the "plain dictates . . . [of] reason and common sense." Having risen against tyranny, Cooper observed, our fathers miraculously escaped by sea and flourished in their wilderness refuge; but when subsequent generations angered the Lord, He imposed a king upon them. Of course, God's anger was meant only to correct and purify: "contrary to our deserts, and amidst all our troubles, the blessings promised . . . to the afflicted seed of Abraham is come upon us; 'Their Nobles shall be of themselves, and their Governor shall proceed from the Midst of them.'" [43] Cooper's reference (from Jeremiah) to the Conversion of the Jews and the renovated Zion could hardly have escaped his audience.* But the point of the application was not, as it had been in

---

*Thus saith the Lord; Beholde, . . . the citie shalbe buylded upon her own heape. . . .

And out of them shall procede thanksgiving. . . .

And their noble *ruler* shalbe of themselves, and their governour shal procede from the middes of them. . . .

the early jeremiads, that a new biblical theocracy was being established in Christ's name. For Cooper's audience, as for Robbins's and Sherwood's, the biblical precedent was consecrated by the achievement of America. Christ had invoked the authority of Scripture, but it was His mission that confirmed, defined, and explicated the prophecies. Such too was the relation between Old and New Israel. Now that the Americans had fulfilled the covenant, their *magnalia Dei* would continue, in the image of the Revolution, "to the end of time."

It would be another generation or so before this typology of mission could be fully rendered — before Washington could be enshrined as savior, his mighty deeds expounded, his apostles ranked, the Judas in their midst identified, the Declaration of Independence adequately compared to the Sermon on the Mount, the sacred places and objects (Bunker Hill, Valley Forge, the Liberty Bell) properly labeled, the Constitution duly ordained (in Emerson's words) as "the best book in the world" next to the New Testament, and the Revolution, summarily, "indissolubly linked" (as John Quincy Adams put it) with "the birthday . . . of the Savior," as being the social, moral, and political correlative of "the Redeemer's mission on earth," and thus "the first irrevocable pledge of the fulfillment of the prophecies, announced directly from Heaven." But the pattern was well established by the last decades of the eighteenth century. And fittingly enough, a key figure in its establishment was Edwards's grandson, Timothy Dwight, a leading member of the black regiment, signer of

---

And ye shalbe my people, and I wil be your God. (Jeremiah 30:18, 19, 21, 22)

The text was a favorite of the New England Puritan clergy in applying the doctrine of National Conversion to their own situation. It is also used, for example, in James Dana's election-day *Sermon Preached before the General Assembly* (Hartford, 1779), which argues that before 1776 "the only form of government expressly instituted by heaven was that of the Hebrews, . . . a confederate republic with JEHOVAH at the head" (p. 17), and in Joseph Huntington's *Discourse Adapted to the Present Day* (Hartford, 1781), which notes further that Israel was really a republic of "Thirteen United States or Tribes," since "the tribe of Joseph was subdivided . . . which made thirteen united, free and independent states" (pp. 9–10), a notion earlier advanced by Cotton Mather. Mather would also have recognized his rhetoric in the Revolutionaries' use of the story of Mordecai and Esther, as he himself had used it, to identify Haman with the English court and the colonists with the Jews (e.g., *The Present State of New England* [Boston, 1690], pp. 3–6), and in their widespread adoption of the Joachite image of the "stone cut out of the great mountain."

the Declaration of Independence, Enlightenment intellectual, Connecticut Wit, libertarian, Calvinist, patriot Whig, and Federalist. "This great continent," Dwight exclaimed, "is soon to be filled with the praise, and piety, of the Millennium; *here*, is the stem of that wonderful tree whose topmost boughs will reach the heavens."

> The period is now on the wing in which "the knowledge of the LORD shall fill the earth as waters fill the sea." Another sun, rolling around the great Centurial year will, not improbably, have scarcely finished his progress, when he shall see the Jew "reingrafted into the olive, from which he was broken off." . . . Think of the manner in which God *bare* your fathers in this land *on eagles wings*. Recal[l] their numerous deliverances. . . . [And now recall the still greater wonders of our War of Independence.] A work, thus begun, and thus carried out, is its own proof, that it will not be relinquished.[44]

Dwight expressed these hopes most fully in *The Conquest of Canäan*, an epic jeremiad that builds on constant crises (rebellion, backsliding, treachery, holy war) toward a celebration of the New World republic — America, the second "blissful Eden bright," "by heaven design'd." Dwight's hero is Joshua; his subject, the battle for the promised land. But the action itself, he makes clear, is part of a grand figural process culminating in the Revolution. The Israelite leader serves finally as harbinger of a "greater dispensation," to reveal Washington as the Christ-like "Benefactor to Mankind," directing a "*more* fateful conflict" on "*new* Canaan's promised shores." Ultimately, that is, Israel's conquest of Canaan is confirmed and consecrated by what it tells of America's mission:

> To nobler bliss yon western world shall rise,
> Unlike all former realms. . . .
>
> .   .   .   .   .
>
> Here union'd choice shall form a rule divine;
> Here countless lands in one great system join;
> The sway of Law unbroke, unrivall'd grow.

Some twenty years later, Washington's successor to the role of the American Joshua, John Adams, contemplated the meaning of that more fateful conflict, and he decided, in a justly famous passage, that the motives behind the Revolution "ought to be traced back for Two Hundred Years, and sought in the history of the Country from the first Plantations. . . . This produced, in 1760 and 1761, AN AWAKENING and a REVIVAL of American Principles and Feelings, with an Enthusiasm which went on increasing till in 1775 it burst out in open violence."[45] Adams's use of the Great Migration as precursor to the War of Independence is a significant testament to the secular-sacred typology developed through the eighteenth century. Significantly, too, his key terms remind us, whether by intention or not, of the Northampton millennium: *enthusiasm*, *awakening*, *revival*.

5

Ritual of Consensus

By all accounts, the jeremiad played a central role in the war of independence, and the war in turn confirmed the jeremiad as a national ritual. The Whig sermons and tracts express a rite of passage into nationhood, an official coming-of-age ceremony, which had long been in rehearsal. It was a ritual replete with a special set of symbols, a communal myth, and a sophisticated form of socialization — all of these now focused upon a single, comprehensive, distinctly American event. For as the Whig Jeremiahs explained it, independence was not the spoils of violence, but the harvest of Puritanism. It was not some sudden turbulent challenge to the system, but the consummation of a process of uprising that began aboard the *Mayflower* and *Arbella* and matured in the struggles of 1776. In short, the Revolution was the movement linking the two quintessential moments in the story of America — the twin legends of the country's founding fathers — the Great Migration and the War of Independence. In that development lay the sacred drama of American nationhood.

I have already discussed the Puritan origins of this outlook, but it may be well here to specify its meaning for the concept of revolution. Historically considered, revolution has two entirely different meanings, secular and religious. In secular tradition, revolution means a forcible change of government. It highlights discord, contradiction, and discontinuity, and has lent itself, in these terms, both to progressive and to cyclical views of history. For radicals, it proved that men could improve their conditions — that indeed, they might found a new paradise of reason by overthrowing the institutions of the past. For conservatives, revolution meant the treacherous, repetitive wheel of fortune. "Eadem, sed aliter," in Schopenhauer's famous phrase: despite its rhetoric of progress, it brought the same old thing in new dress. In either case, revolution was an issue in and of this world; and in either case, it had little or no bearing upon the course of sacred history. Whether or not man would improve his earthly lot, believers could feel secure in speaking of their spiritual destiny. In this context, the meaning of revolution was emphatically and unequivocally progressive. Individually, every true Christian had the promise of heaven, through what Augustine termed the *revolutio* of the soul toward God. Collectively, the church was advancing toward New Jerusalem through a series of revolutionary upheavals. Each upheaval constituted a revolution in itself, but all were linked in an ascending spiral. Thus Abraham was said to have revolted against the idolatry of Ur; thus Richard Hooker spoke of "the revolution begun by our Saviour" against the Hebraic Law;[1] thus Reformers spoke of Luther's revolution against Papal Antichrist, and anticipated the revolutions of the apocalypse.

The New England Puritans applied this vision directly to their own enterprise. As we have seen, they used it to obviate traditional distinctions — in this instance, the distinction between secular and sacred revolution.* They bequeathed their peculiar figural mode to Enlightenment America, and ultimately to the patriot Whigs, who mystified secular change as divine progress, and redefined the errand as a rite of passage into the sacred meaning of the American Revolu-

---

*The ritual of baptism, for example, accents the contradictions between worldly and spiritual commitments, between social revolution and the soul's *revolutio* to God. The Puritans invoked the example of John the Baptist to enforce a *social* conversion rite. They, too, used anxiety to inculcate a special symbolic habit of mind, but whereas baptism seeks to invert the meanings of secular discourse ("wilderness," "promised land," "revolution" itself), the Puritan Jeremiahs inverted the standard meanings of Christian discourse in order to enlist support for their tribal errand — to direct the rising generation toward the building of New Canaan and the revolutions that would usher in the Theopolis Americana. Their ritual techniques appear everywhere in the eighteenth century; in revival sermons, in military speeches, in exhortations to moral purification and commercial development, and finally, as Emory Elliott has shown, in the sermons of the Revolutionary pulpit.

tion. In doing so, they contributed in two important ways to the rhetoric of the jeremiad. First, they amplified the Puritan distinction between the Old World and the New. European uprisings, they explained, were revolutions in the secular sense. Internal divisions and conflicts led to violence, and violence to discord and decay. Revolution in America was the vehicle of providence. It took the form of a mighty, spontaneous turning forward, both regenerative and organic, confirming the prophecies of Scripture as well as the laws of nature and history. And in all this it stood diametrically opposed to rebellion. The Revolution fulfilled the divine will. Rebellion was a primal act of disobedience, as Lucifer's was, or Adam's. Rebels sought to negate, thwart, and destroy; the Revolutionaries were agents of the predetermined course of progress.

This was the Whigs' second contribution to the rhetoric of the jeremiad: they intensified the Puritan emphasis both on process and on control.* In the ritual of revolution they instituted, radicalism itself was socialized into an affirmation of order. If the condition of progress was continuing revolution, the condition of continuity (the Whig leaders insisted) was control of the revolutionary impulse. The social norms encouraged revolution, but the definition of revolution reinforced authority.

It was a ritual particularly suited to the troubled mood of post-Revolutionary America. The overthrow of imperial power, we know, set loose a libertarian spirit that terrified moderate and propertied democrats. Their terror is evident everywhere in the literature: in nervous satires of an egalitarian world-turned-upside-down; in Gothic novels and tales of violated taboos (parricide, incest, idolatry); and most explicitly, in the Federalist jeremiads, warning against unbridled ambition and denouncing a long series of local insurrections, from the Whiskey Rebellion to the Antirent War, most of which invoked the slogans of the American Revolution. I need not dwell on how deeply the fear of democracy which these writings convey affected the theory of representative government.

*For example, whereas for Edwards and the Puritans the unfolding scheme of "dispensations" was circumscribed by Scripture, for the Whigs the Revolution opened into an indefinitely self-renewing rite of passage. At the same time, the contrast which the Whigs constantly urged between American and European revolution placed special emphasis on conformity and order. Revolution was for them first and last a *controlling* metaphor for national identity.

Clearly, the first aim of legislators after 1776 was to curb popular demands. They set out, accordingly, to mediate (rather than meet) the call for self-determination, to curtail (without crushing) the surge of democratic individualism, and to institute equality before the law while insisting on a minority "rule by the best," drawn from the propertied and educated classes. But their measures did not take hold at once. To many of them, indeed, an explosive conflict seemed imminent, between the minority in power — the leading merchants, lawyers, and landholders — and the majority they "represented," now newly emboldened by military success, and by the rhetoric of independence, to challenge established norms of control. The Federalist Jeremiahs saw their duty at once: they had to keep the Revolution on course by exorcising the demons of rebellion.

They went to work with a vengeance. "Oh my country!" wailed Jeremy Belknap in 1786. "To what an alarming situation are we reduced, that Congress must say to us, as Joshua did to Israel, 'Behold I set before you life and death.'" The lament arose from every part of the land, and swelled in volume with the Constitutional debates. A "contagion of liberty" become licence had infected the body politic. "Enterprising ambition" was stalking God's Country, like some "hideous and horrid monster" — Virgil's epic *monstrum horrendum, ingens*, trampling the American vine, challenging property rights, advocating "the liberty of Infidels," threatening to mislead New Israel into a "millennium of Hell." "Can the selfishness of the heart be tamed?" thundered Asa Burton in 1786. "Can cords bind this Leviathan . . . ?" It was the burning question of the decade. We "must make provision for curbing the lusts and bounding the riotous appetites of men," the clergy warned. "Unless they are restrained by some effectual expediency," the entire achievement of the Revolution will "vanish like the baseless fabrick of a vision." "The people of America," wrote John Adams in his defense of the Constitution, "have now the best opportunity and the greatest trust in their hands that Providence ever committed to so small a number since the transgression of the first pair; if they betray their trust their guilt will merit even greater punishment than other nations have suffered and the indignation of Heaven."[2]

The motive of these Federalist Jeremiahs is transparent in the momentous choice they posed: on one side, apocalyptic disaster; on the other side, millennial glory earned through a process of *taming, binding, curbing, restraint*. Like their predecessors, they were berating the present generation for deviating from the past in order to prod it forward toward their vision of the future. In ritual terms, they were asserting consensus through anxiety, using promise and threat alike to inspire (or enforce) generational rededication. Alarmed at the "rage for innovation" that swept the infant republic, David Ramsay ended his patriotic *History of the American Revolution* by summoning all "friends of order" to extirpate "the vicious principles and habits which have taken deep root during the late convulsions." The contrast between *convulsions* and *revolution* speaks for itself; and its meaning grew more ominous after the French Revolution. If prior to 1790 the unpropertied "rabble" seemed hell-bent on usurping due authority, what would they *not* do under the intoxication of Jacobin excess? George Washington, who recognized the link between pre- and post-Revolutionary unrest, warned sternly that "mob action, [though] necessary in monarchies, has no place in America." But the spirit of '76 lingered, and a host of clerical, literary, and civic "friends of order" arrayed themselves against the threat. Retooling the old anti-imperialist rhetoric to defend the status quo, the aging firebrand Sam Adams turned his oratorical cannons against the "boundless and insatiable ambition" of "king mob." Timothy Dwight's epic previews of New Canaan darkened into visions of "ignorant masses" wallowing in "corruption, anarchy, atheism!"[3]

It seems safe to say that all or most of this was hyperbole, and that it was more or less consciously designed to keep things in hand. Not that it was just a cunning fiction; the conflicts were real enough. Throughout the period, "insurgents" were protesting an actual stratification of power and wealth, and their protests represented powerful new economic developments. But these were developments within the system. The repressive measures prove neither that the Federalists were seeking "refuge from democracy," as certain historians have claimed, nor that they were contending against some fundamental challenge to the republic. The insurgents, too, from Paine through Shays, were middle-class rebels. Their protests did not entail a struggle between contending systems, but variant possibilities within the same social structures. Even as the Anti-Federalists denounced the Constitution-makers — accused them of usurping power on the pretext of "efficient government" (whereas all that was "needed was efficiency in the protection of the 'liberties, lives, and property of the people governed' ") — the very language of their accusations indicates that the problem was not ends but means. As Merrill Jensen notes, even the demagogues among them "were not political extremists at heart." Basically, they shared the free-enterprise values of their culture. They, too, wanted what Hamilton called "the good will of the commercial interest throughout the states." At heart, they sought no more than a government "capable of regulating, protecting and extending the commerce of the Union," a government that would "protect them against domestic violence and the depredations which the democratic spirit is apt to make on property."[4]

The Anti-Federalists expressed the frustrations of emergent sectors of the American economy. The Federalists' lament expressed the dangers inherent in social, technological, and economic growth. Like the Jeremiahs of old, they were supporting the system by calling attention to its current dysfunctions. The republican dream, they pointed out, presupposed mutuality (not conflict) between free enterprise and the common good. Personal independence was supposed to lead to corporate self-fulfillment. When they contrasted selfishness and benevolence, or attacked self-seekers who undermined "the common centre of gravity," they were reaffirming the norms upon which their culture was continuing to thrive. As Henry Cumings put it, the republic was "poised in an even balance, between extremes of arbitrary power and despotism, on the one hand, and of anarchy and unrestrained licentiousness, on the other." *Poised* was the jeremiadic *mot juste*. It suggested, as it were in one anxious breath, the cultural ideal and its disastrous alternative. *Despotism* meant the feudal (or quasi-feudal) ways of the Old World; *anarchy*, the dangers of unbridled laissez-faire; and *even balance*, finally, what John Adams and David Tappan called America's "middle way," the "happy union of liberty and order."[5]

This flat, rationalistic standard seems to take us a long way from the Puritans. Winthrop's model of Christian charity is framed in prophecy; Edwards's ideal of "happy union" is charged with apocalyptic hope. When Cumings tells us, at the end of his oration, that the republic has attained "as broad a base of liberty as can consist with the end of design of social compacts," we can hardly fail to sense that we are dealing with a new variation of the jeremiad. The Federalists, after all, had set forth the most pragmatic, anti-enthusiast program on record for realizing the dreams of mankind. The Declaration of Independence is hard enough to reconcile with the Puritan vision, but at least it invokes the Deity and radiates optimism. The *Federalist Papers* exclude a priori all recourse to the absolute. In opposition to Plato's utopia, let alone the Christian millennium, they propose a republic of the cave, a sort of fifth monarchy of horologicals, based on the assumption that "neither Philosophy, nor Religion, nor Morality, nor Wisdom, nor Intellect, will ever govern nations or parties, against their Vanity, Pride, Resentment or Revenge, or their Avarice and Ambition. Nothing but Force and Power and Strength can restrain them. . . . [Therefore,] power must be opposed to power, force to force, strength to strength, interest to interest, as well as reason to reason, eloquence to eloquence, and passion to passion." Americans, after all, like the citizens of any other country, were "already corrupt to the core." Here as elsewhere, to understand "the real disposition of human nature" was to recognize "our common misfortune." In the new republic, no less than in the Old World, society was "produced by our wants, and government by our wickedness."[6]

If this exaggerates the case, the exaggeration serves to emphasize an important cultural fact. Like earlier American Jeremiahs, our Constitution-makers were seeking a middle way that would encompass apparent opposites — in this instance, a Hobbesian view of human nature and a commitment to personal freedom. They wanted an "acceptable medium" for "grasping and contending interests," as Martin Diamond has observed; and "while they thought self-interest the most dangerous and unbrookable quality of man, they necessarily underwrote it in trying to control it." *Necessarily*, because as modern statesmen they had no other choice. By the end of the eighteenth century, the concept of selfhood had lost its grounding in community. Christic identity presupposed that every believer was a member of the society of saints. Every member of "traditionalist" society defined himself within a civic and spiritual hierarchy. But the modern theory of possessive individualism (to recall C. B. Macpherson's term) simply cut the self loose in a world of other independent selves. And the modern theory of government supplied no ready way to impose community. Appeals to classical virtue or moral imperative were purely academic. The guiding political philosophers were the masters of *Realpolitik* — not Plato or Aristotle, but Bacon and Machiavelli; not Aquinas or Calvin, but Hobbes and Locke. "Experience," our Federalist Plinlimmons pointed out, though fallible, "is the least fallible guide. . . . Have we not already seen enough of the . . . extravagance of those idle theories which have amused us with promises of an exemption from the imperfections, the weaknesses, and the evils incident to society in every shape? Is it not time to awake from the deceitful dream of a golden age . . . ?" Thus Hamilton in the Sixth Federalist; Madison as usual put it more tersely and tough mindedly. "If men were angels, no government would be necessary . . . ; but experience has taught mankind the necessity of auxiliary precautions." What he meant by precautions became enshrined in the Constitution as the federal system of self-protective multiplicity: a society "broken into so many parts . . . that the rights of individuals . . . [would] be in little danger from interested combinations of the majority."[7]

The contrast could not be sharper. The millennialist Whigs were urging a supernal unity of design. The Constitution-makers, invoking the harsh lessons of experience, were insisting on fragmentation in every area of life. Hamilton's attack on "idle theories" seems deliberately aimed at the former group. Madison was so far removed from those visionaries that he seems to have forgotten the very principle of cosmic hierarchy: his idea of heaven is a model free-enterprise society, where each self-interested angel acts for the general good without government interference. And yet (to repeat) the two groups were seeking to consolidate the same middle-class *via media*. The very concept of multiplicity, after all, was inspired by a dream of harmony.* Madison and his colleagues wanted to magnify

---

*The dream dates back to the seventeenth century, as recent historians have shown — e.g., Joyce Appleby, "Ideology and Theory: The Tension between Political and Economic Liberalism in Seventeenth-Century England," *American Historical Review*, 81 (1976), 499–515, and Albert O. Hirschman, *The Passions and the Interests: Political Arguments for Capitalism before its Triumph* (Princeton, N. J., 1977) — and of course it grows increasingly explicit through the eighteenth century. Franklin's well-known

the operation of factions in order to "cure . . . the fatal factionalism that opinion and passion generate." If they had no "illusions regarding the way men *ought* to live," they did have a clear idea about how society ought to be run.[8] And if they could not advocate disinterested love, as Edwards had, or aspire, with Cotton and Winthrop, to a community that was one in Christ, they could offer a pragmatic modern alternative: a laissez-faire polity, where the dream of personal freedom was *made to correspond* with Hobbesian *Realpolitik*, because the intensity of competition between the parts was directly proportionate to the harmony of the whole.

It was not enough. Modern communities, we have come to learn, have as much need for spiritual cohesion as did the communities of the past; and that need was particularly strong in the new republic: a nation without a past, a people without common customs, a territory without clear boundaries, and an economy without a stable center — variously agrarian, urban, pre-modern, and in transition toward modernization — but with extraordinary opportunities for personal aggrandizement. Surely a major reason for the triumph of the republic was that the need for a social ideal was filled by the typology of America's mission. As this was translated into the language of the times, it provided what we might call the figural correlative to the theory of democratic capitalism. It gave the nation a past and future in sacred history, rendered its political and legal outlook a fulfillment of prophecy, elevated its "true inhabitants," the enterprising European Protestants who had immigrated within the past century or so, to the status of God's chosen, and declared the vast territories around them to be their chosen country. The rhetoric of trial provided moral support for the Federalists' emphasis on deprav-

---

dictum, that "Light often rises from a collision of opinions" (*The Papers of Benjamin Franklin*, ed. Leonard Labaree et al. [New Haven, 1960–], IX, 61), was a truism of the times, and it was applied freely in the areas of religion, politics, and economics. Thus Ezra Stiles argued that the multiplicity of sects would "unavoidably" issue in a "mutual balance," a general and lasting "harmony and union" (*The Christian Union* [Boston, 1761], pp. 51, 54); thus William Livingston felt sure that "the Jealousy of all Parties combating each other would inevitably produce a perfect Freedom" (*The Independent Reflector* [1752], ed. Milton M. Klein [Cambridge, Mass., 1963], pp. 195–96); and thus James Lovell cited the opinions of New England merchants to prove that an unrestrained diversity of commercial interests invariably benefited the public at large (*Freedom, the First of Blessings* [Boston, 1754], pp. 31 ff.).

ity. The concept of American revolution transformed self-reliance into a function not only of the common good but of the redemption of mankind. In virtually every area of life, the jeremiad became the official ritual form of continuing revolution. Mediating between religion and ideology, the jeremiad gave contract the sanctity of covenant, free enterprise the halo of grace, progress the assurance of the chiliad, and nationalism the grandeur of typology. In short, it wed self-interest to social perfection, and conferred on both the unique blessings of American destiny.

The union proved to be a fruitful one. Its success is dramatically attested to by the persistence of millennialism throughout the nineteenth century. I do not refer only to marginal visionaries — the eccentric prophets who kept urging Americans (then as now) to "live and act for the millennium, for nothing less," or what Tocqueville termed the "innumerable" enthusiasts roaming the land. Such phenomena appear elsewhere in the nineteenth century as an expression of social dysfunction. In America they were symptomatic of the dynamics of the culture. One rather obvious proof of this is the tradition of July Fourth addresses. The tradition itself is said to begin with an oration delivered in 1778 at Charlestown, South Carolina, hailing "the Revolution as the beginning of a new age in human history"; and the theme continues unabated in the long procession of orations that followed through the Federalist period. "From their birth," cried Thomas Yarrow of New York, the American states were "designed to be the political redeemers of mankind!" To Alexander Wilson of Pennsylvania and Jonathan Maxcy of Rhode Island, the country was "the GREAT TEMPLE OF LIBERTY"; "Long streams of light emanate from its portals. . . . Its turrets will swell into the heavens . . . and the pillar of divine glory, descending from God, will rest forever on its summit." In Maine, Virginia, and South Carolina, July Fourth orators explained the correspondence between local progress and "the vast designs of providence" for "the universal redemption of the human race." Predictably, Massachusetts led the chorus. On July 4, 1790, David Foster assured Bostonians that America was "the theatre, where the latter day glory shall be displayed." Six years later, Francis Blake in Worcester and

John Lathrop in Boston declared that "Liberty descended from Heaven on the 4th of July, 1776," and with it "the grand POLITICAL MILLENNIUM." By 1799, Abiel Abbot could proudly announce to the inhabitants of Haverhill that "'OUR AMERICAN ISRAEL' is a term frequently used; and common consent allows it apt and proper."[9]

So, too, was the term "political millennium," and more frequently still "American millennium" — and the use of these terms, under the aegis of the Revolution, became virtually standardized in the early nineteenth century. Nourished and sustained by a growing number of Jeremiahs, American millennialism pervaded the entire spectrum of social thought. Educators planned for a "spiritual revolution" that would bring humanity to perfection. Political and moral reformers advertised their programs as the "revolutionary consummation of God's plan."* Prominent thinkers urged that technology would "revolutionize the land" into being a "human-divine paradise," where "mechanical power [would] be matched by a new access of vitality . . . imaginative, utopian, transcendent," and the acquisitive spirit would "typify" the "infinite" reaches of the soul. Labor leaders found in the Revolution a "post-millennial justification for trade-unionism." Social critics sought to reclaim America's prerogatives "to guide the nations . . . through the sea of revolution." Politicians justified annexation and the Westward movement as part of America's duty to "manifest to mankind the excellence of the divine principles of our Revolution": "For this blessed mission to the nations of the world, which are shut out from the life-giving light of truth, has America been chosen."[10]

Increasingly, from the Federalist into the Jacksonian period, these millennialists focused upon the events of 1776; and with good reason. In 1826, with the deaths of Jefferson and John Adams, the Revolution passed officially — that is, ideologically as well as actually — into the

---

*These range from millenarian extremists, like the Millerites and Campbellites, to such broadly based movements as Christian Socialism and Social Gospelism; and from recurrent, short-lived experiments, like Brook Farm and Hopedale — whose members hoped to "provide 'types' for the millennium" (Lewis Perry, "Adin Ballou's Hopedale Community and the Theology of Antislavery," *Church History*, 39 [1970], 16–17) — to enduring sects like the Mormons, the "latter-day saints" who believed they had literally discovered Zion in America.

possession of a new generation. It was a troubled succession. According to anti-Jacksonians, especially after they had witnessed the upheavals of 1830 in France, Belgium, and Poland, and then two years later suffered an unprecedented electoral defeat, the difference between generations was nothing short of sinister: on one side, the newly consecrated fathers of the Revolution (Washington, Franklin, Jefferson, Adams); on the other side King Andrew, the tyrant-demagogue, classical symptom of the breakdown of democracy. Theirs was the minority opinion, of course. Jacksonians defended their president as the heir of Washington and Jefferson. But both parties agreed that the nation was in a crisis of identity, and both parties, each from its own perspective, proposed the same solution. They sought to stabilize society by rallying their countrymen, once again, to the chronometer of continuing revolution. As the *Albany Argus* put it in 1828, at the height of the Adams-Jackson debates, "the American Revolution is the greatest political event in history — every thing that belongs to it is consecrated"; the issue is not the relative merits of two political parties, but the only sure way to make America the seat of New Jerusalem.[11]

The summons was sounded by representatives of every shade of the political spectrum. The war of independence, declared the "radical workingman" Robert Walker in 1830, "marks a new . . . era in the history of man"; the spirit of '76 shines "in the political wilderness, as a pillar of fire to light the way of the oppressed of every clime to the hallowed temple of liberty." Three years later, the left-wing Democrat Robert Rantoul explained that the "independence of the United States of America is not only a marked epoch in the course of time, but it is indeed the end from which the new order of things is to be reckoned. It is the dividing point in the history of mankind; it is the moment of the political regeneration of the world."[12] This was the message, too, of the Reverend Leander Ker, speaking before the Athenean Society of Missouri; of Edwin Forrest, the Shakespearean actor, addressing the Democratic Republican Convention in New York City; of Josiah Bent, celebrating the "National Jubilee" in Boston; and of the conservative Westerlo Woodworth, exhorting the Young Men's Association against urban evils. In all of these orations (and countless others like them), the Revolution stands at once as the

climax of history and the pattern of things to come.* On the one
hand, it brings to fruition the labors of the holy remnant God sent
"*here* to plant the principles that are to renovate the earth." On the
other hand, it reveals the future "empire of consolidated minds."[13]
With that double prospect in view, Daniel Webster declared (in his
widely reprinted eulogy to the martyrs of Bunker Hill) that, properly speaking, the

> great wheel of political revolution began to move [only] in America.
> Here its rotation was guarded, regular and safe. . . . [In Europe,
> Africa, and Asia,] from unfortunate but natural causes, it received an
> irregular and violent impulse; it whirled along with a fearful celerity;
> till at length, like the chariot-wheels in the races of antiquity, it took fire
> . . . and blazed onward, spreading conflagration and terror around.
> . . . [But here we may] cherish a confident hope for her final triumph.
> . . . The American Revolution is the wonder and the blessing of the
> world. . . . Human agency cannot extinguish it. . . . Its inherent
> unconquerable force will heave both the ocean and land, and . . .
> flame up to heaven. . . . In our day there has been as it were a new
> creation. . . . The last hopes of mankind . . . rest with us.[14]

The new creation arose, as of old, from the fires of probation.
There is no need here to describe the Jacksonian laments. Other
historians have done so in detail, and the detail makes abundantly
clear the persistence of Puritan techniques.† What I would like to

*The following is a brief example of the argument: "Long ere our Revolution
began, we trace [God's] hand in relation to our present glory. It was He that saved
this New world, so long unknown to the overloaded Old world, to be the theatre of
new scenery to our race." Thus the nation's true genealogy led directly from Old Israel
through the Reformation to "our ancestors," who had such a "decided influence . . .
on the Revolution," and whose high enterprise, because it was "*local* to America,"
made manifest "the immortal hope of Christianity, and the light of everlasting truth!"
Nonetheless, "Until the successful termination of our Revolution" — "the most august event which ever constituted an epoch in the political annals of mankind" —
"Liberty was an exile and a fugitive in the earth. . . . But that era in her history, the
most eventful and important in . . . the world, has changed [everything]." It is "a
land-mark to guide the nations, . . . an expansive principle, which no power can
confine." (Quotations respectively from Josiah Bent, Jr., *National Jubilee* [Boston,
1826], p. 10; Daniel Webster, "The Settlement of New England," in *Works* [Boston,
1857], I, 49–50; Edwin Forrest, *Oration Delivered* [New York, 1838], p. 5; and Westerlo Woodworth, *Oration before the Association* [Albany, 1834], pp. 22–23.)

† Rush Welter has observed that from 1820 to 1860 "most Americans" believed that
"history in the large sense ['macrohistory'] stopped with the American Revolution,
but history in a more restricted sense (. . . 'microhistory') did not. Rather, it con-

emphasize in this chapter is ritual form and intent. Let me begin, therefore, with a July Fourth oration. The ceremony itself has always served as a vehicle of socialization, and especially during the Middle Period, as Rush Welter has noted, it constituted something of "a religious observance, in which the Declaration of Independence (customarily read at the start of the day's festivities) served in lieu of a religious text, and the oration in lieu of a sermon." A characteristic example is the oration-sermon which a self-styled "plain young man," William Evans Arthur, delivered at Covington, Kentucky, on July 4, 1850. He had just earned admission to the bar, and was shortly to go on to Congress and a federal judgeship. His "beautiful, patriotic, and eloquent address," as a grateful Covington audience remembered it, was a pastiche of Middle Period clichés, and undoubtedly it helped launch his career.[15]

Arthur opens his address, as Danforth did in 1670 and Sherwood in 1776, by invoking the fathers. Each "return of this our National birth-day," Arthur intones,

> proves yet more fully the peculiar and the commanding power of the Constitution to shape the destiny of this great people, and to firmly guide them through all the trying emergencies and changeful events inseparable from the uncertainties of life, and the instability of human affairs, to the fullest happiness and to the broadest renown. Like a good spirit commissioned of high heaven, this ever memorable anniversary suddenly appears from time to time in our midst, reviewing the past, reciting the present, and revealing the future. Steadily in majestic defiance of the general wreck of surrounding empires the rock upon which our Fathers happily builded extends its surface, increases its density, and exalts its summit. Onward! Onward!

---

tinued as the setting in which Americans strove to keep faith with their special destiny. . . . By contrast with Europeans . . . the Americans of the Middle Period lacked a sense of time. In their own terms, however, they saw themselves as living at the end of one kind of time — Greenwich Mean Time, one is tempted to call it — and immersed in another. Time came to a focus in their national experience, and microhistory recorded their struggle to live up to their responsibilities in the New World. . . . If macrohistory taught Americans to be complacent, microhistory pressed them to locate themselves in an unending struggle between the forces of good and evil" (*Mind of America*, pp. 26–27). This is very much like Edwardsian postmillennialism, and it should not surprise us that Edwards's concept of revolution, in his *History of the Work of Redemption*, was cited by leading Jacksonians from Bancroft to Webster. But for them macro- and microhistory both had their model in the Revolution. Only in America, they insisted, did revolution combine the benefits of sacred and secular history.

Arthur's tone is at once anxious and incantatory; his theme, the problematic relation of the text (the Constitution) to experience. Our fathers built upon a rock, their legacy is sacred, perpetual; yet what they accomplished summons us onward. How are we both to recapitulate the past and improve upon it — "not only to emulate but to excel"? It is a problem designed (like Danforth's notion of the errand and Sherwood's of "the church's flight into the wilderness") to stress the perils of process. We still have far to climb before we reach the summit, Arthur reminds his audience; and what is more, we cannot fail to acknowledge the contrast between the fathers' greatness and our own "instability." In both cases, the distance accentuates the "trying emergencies" ahead. When he considers the "changeful" nature of things, Arthur recalls "the general wreck of surrounding empires." In acknowledging the differences between generations, he invokes various "persons endowed with the . . . gift of detecting . . . the most appalling portents."[16] And yet the tone of the passage is hopeful, even euphoric. Anxiety functions here to excite and fortify expectations. Divisions and conflicts serve as prelude to the assertion of continuity. Clearly, Arthur's purpose is simultaneously to raise tension and to dispel doubt.

His method is evident from the start. July Fourth, he explains, obviates the usual distinctions of time and place. It is an occasion for "reviewing the past, reciting the present, and revealing the future." And each of these activities ("commissioned of high heaven") involves the others. The reciting requires the reviewing, and both are implicit in the revealing, as the type in its fulfillment. "Poised as we may be considered at this moment, upon a nick of time, . . . with our vision running through the . . . unforgotten past and o'er the . . . unclouded future, . . . [we are] exalted alike by the retrospect and by the anticipation." This is the exalted mood of the American figural imagination: the mood, for example, of Arthur's New England contemporary, Henry David Thoreau — "anxious to improve the nick of time, . . . to stand on the meeting of two eternities, the past and the future, which is precisely the present moment" — or of Jonathan Edwards a hundred years earlier, or of Thomas Shepard, the major colonial Puritan influence on Edwards. Through our errand, Shepard wrote in 1640, God had revealed His "secret for time past" and His "performances for [the] future, as though they were accomplishments at present. . . . For our selves here, the people of *New-England* . . . two Eternities (as it were) meet together." Poised at that figural nick of time, William Arthur resolves the problem of text versus experience, Constitutional ideals versus American realities, by making the present a function of retrospect and anticipation. For so perceived, the very "differences between the present and the past," he observes, "affirm that in every thing which should be permanent and enduring, the present generation doubly proves its heroic paternity."[17] From the vantage point of the Revolution, in short, the past is prophecy postdated, and the future, prophecy antedated.

From that vantage point, Arthur unfolds the country's heroic paternity. "The sparks . . . of which the revolution was the resulting flame," he tells his fellow Kentuckians, were "borne to this land . . . in the inflexible bosoms of . . . the Puritans." "Flying from religious and political tyranny," they founded here "a land of freedom where they might think and act as freemen should." The first third of the oration is devoted to their achievements. The next third describes the completion of their errand by the Revolutionaries, the world's greatest "collection of wise heads, brave hearts and eloquent tongues," led by a Christ-like Washington, who "outshone the brightest examples in history."* The final third of the oration traces the establishment of the republic. "With a benignity imitating that so pre-eminently displayed by the God of the flying and homeless Israelites," Arthur declares, "the illustrious Apostles of the Constitution . . . have given to mankind that which will serve forever as a pillar of cloud by day and a pillar of fire by night to guide this chosen people. We have reached the Land they promised, and have fed upon the fatness of the vine and the fig-tree." Thus the long journey from Egypt through Nazareth is vindicated by Ameri-

---

*This includes not only the image of Christ triumphant — as in Arthur's descriptions of "the unconquerable American commander grappling with the British Lion" — but also the image of Christ *agonistes*, betrayed by Arnold-Judas ("a walking Pandemonium") and subject to doubt bordering on despair: "The resources of Congress, it would seem, totally failed — the army grew less and less. . . . It was then that the great soul of Washington was wrung with anguish by the fearful jeopardy of his country, and that he groaned from the depths of his sorrow . . . 'Whither shall we go?'" (*Oration* [Covington, Ky., 1850], pp. 29–30, 28).

ca's progress from forefathers to fathers, Winthrop to Washington, covenant to Constitution.

> How boldly and brightly the fourth day of July stands out upon the page of History! With what an electrical splendor it bursts upon the vision . . . towering into the mid-heaven, as it were the sun of a new system. . . .
> Illustrious day! . . . How vast and ennobling the change thou didst work on the face of the world, and in the progress and condition, present and prospective, of the whole wide spread race of man! Thou art indeed an epoch to date from — an immortal remembrancer — a museum of glorious relics . . . [and a book of revelations, forecasting] the universal diffusion of Christianity, Liberty and Science.[18]

Both in its present and prospective condition, the country would seem to be assured of success. But from the start, we recall, Arthur places special emphasis on "the *instability* of human affairs." And he sustains that emphasis by the very structure of his oration: pre-Revolution, Revolution, post-Revolution. For all his display of confidence, what he offers is an initiation through anxiety into further anxiety. To be post-Revolutionary is not to have left the Revolution behind. On the contrary, it is to exemplify (in one's life and in one's generation) the stormy course of its progress. In one sense, to be sure, the Revolution is over and done with, resolved *ad aeternum* in the "glorious Constitution under which we live, and move, and have our being. . . . American enterprise [is] now . . . unshackled and at liberty to indulge its impulses and its speculations"; we are constantly witnessing "new *stars* of the first magnitude, each supreme in its orbit, and all conducive to the glory and eternity of the great central *luminary*." This is indeed to celebrate American enterprise (and free enterprise in general) as the decree of Nature's God. But the decree itself, Arthur stresses, is processual, developmental. In its largest sense, it invites us not only to live at "the nick of time" — forever shuttling between sacred past and sacred future — but also (in Thoreau's words) "to *improve* the nick of time," forever advancing toward an always-imminent, never-present Circassia. It signifies an expanding cosmos, we might say, rather than a fixed Ptolemaic universe. We find our place now in 1850 (in Concord or in Covington) as the country did in 1776, by accepting process, declaring our independence, and then indulging our unshackled impulses, each one of us supreme in his orbit. "Society is composed of individuals," said Enos Hitchcock in a July Fourth oration in 1788 (advocating the Constitution), "and when each one moves in his own orb . . . the system will be complete." But for the individual, *when* and *will be* are terms fraught with "changeful events and the uncertainties of life." Someday, surely, the system *will be complete*; and meanwhile, Arthur reminds his audience, in reaffirming Hitchcock's vision, the "economy of the God of Nature" demands that we comply through self-assertion with the general "tendency of our people," which is "upward . . . towards perfectibility."[10]

Compliance, however, is something quite different from self-assertion. Even Arthur recognizes this, and accordingly he makes it a central aim of his oration to solve the problem through rhetorical ambiguity. We are new-born as individuals, he argues, only when we become one in the spirit of the "National birth-day"; and we partake of the spirit only after we have shackled our impulses to the expanding cosmos of the American enterprise. Each one of us can become supreme if his orb follows the "immutable law" of "the great central luminary." *Perfectibility*, after all, like *completion* or *destiny*, requires an ordered as well as a sustained process of growth. Hence the focus on stress and self-doubt. Insecurity proves the need for order, and order, as Arthur defines it, leads to constant improvement. Hence also the private/public ambiguities of the goals he proposes: "liberty," "aspiring," "fullest happiness," "broadest renown," "unclouded future," and above all "American." The promise forecloses all alternative avenues of reform and change, personal or collective. Process and essence merge in the symbols of the Revolution, teleology precludes dialectics, and progress and conformity stand revealed as the twin pillars of the American temple of freedom.

The revelation issues from July Fourth as the paradigmatic cultural moment. Although the ascent from Winthrop to Washington was providential — though it was the expression not "of rash rebellion," Arthur emphasizes, but "of *truth* and prophecy, heralding what time and justice would sanction" — nonetheless it demanded struggle, union, and self-denial. The colonists "had fought long and hard, amid cannon and carnage, for liberty," but no sooner was liberty won than a "thousand obstacles" arose, devised by "sinister and corrupt men . . . in the hope of plunging the States into anarchy." Precisely because the Constitution provided the "sacred confines" of progress, we must henceforth take heed, in fear and trembling, never

> to lose sight of that eternal vigilance . . . which will ever be requisite to preserve . . . our common inheritance! I hope this generation will never forget that if . . . by any misdoing upon their part harm comes to the glorious trust which they hold and enjoy, they will be sternly required . . . to solemnly answer and atone for the trust which they shall have abused, with black ingratitude and violated faith, to the ruin of millions born after them! . . . [For take the Constitution] from us — dot but an *i*, or cross but a *t*, contrary to the spirit it breathes, and like the bird which flew from Noah's ark, our liberties will then have gone, to return no more forever, and we have become a by-word and a scoff for . . . mankind.

Arthur's forebodings, which may have been directly inspired by Winthrop's *Arbella* sermon, resemble those of a long procession of Jacksonian jeremiads. "It belongs to you," Henry Clay warned Americans of 1832, "to decide whether [the] great blessings of Liberty and Union shall be preserved. . . . The eyes of all civilized nations are gazing upon us." If our experiment succeeds, said Charles Drake in 1837 and Abram Maury in 1847, "we will become a beacon . . . to the nations of the earth," and "the genius of America, like the star in the east, will lead the earth's people" to redemption. "But if we should become corrupt and unprincipled . . . no horoscope will be needed to forecast our destinies," for then "the expiring cries of Liberty shall be heard in accents of agony, bewailing the fate of her last and loveliest abode." These jeremiads differed in many respects from one another, but they all shared with Arthur's Covington address a basic ritual intent. In every case, the catastrophic alternative was a strategy for channeling revolution into the service of society. "Various causes may conspire to shake this proud fabric," Arthur concedes.

> Vexed political questions may rush into antagonism. . . . The rage of conquest and the thirst of warlike achievement may pervert and allure. Social interests may seem to be inimical and . . . will, occasionally, interrupt the order and harmony of the Union. But the . . . hallowed *motive* of the revolution . . . combined with the magnificent destiny of the Republic . . . constitute gordian knots of inseparability. . . . Our

past career is crowded with heroic and inspiring remembrances, our future resplendent with attainments the most unequalled! . . . The Republic is [indeed] without a parallel in the world's ample history![20]

Whatever omens we may discern here of an impending civil war, the rhetoric itself carries forward a long national tradition. What the Revolution prefigures calls our attention to present shortcomings; what it postfigures inspires our faith; and what binds all this together at our "nick of time" is the achievement, material and ideational, of American culture. Arthur expounds the material achievement at great length.* He concludes with a representation of national ideals that epitomizes the entire ritual:

The American is the ark of safety, the anointed civilizer, the only visible source of light and heat and repose to the dark and discordant and troubled World, which is heaving and groaning, and livid in convulsions all around him! He is Liberty's chosen apostle; he is a master workman, and universal space is his workshop, and universal perfectibility his hallowed aim. He has present and eternal reward for his exertions, and limitless expanse for his enterprise, his genius, his glory. He is more fertile in expedients, more steadfast in purpose, more indomitable of soul, more energetic, more bold and aspiring, than his European predecessors or their contemporaries. . . . Like the disc of the sun, his own system is without blemish, lustrous and vitalizing! Thus advised, he burns with generous rivalry, — emulation is a fire in his blood, . . . the magical aliment of his mounting spirit. . . . Rainbows of promise and visions of grandeur crowd upon his enraptured mind. . . . Faithful to that constitution by which [America] has risen so rapidly from bondage to sovereignty, from poverty to opulence, from obscurity to fame . . . her future must be more than her past, "one tide of glory — one unclouded blaze."[21]

Sacred and secular blend here with formulaic ease: *ark* and *safety*, *anointed* and *civilizer*, *Liberty* and *apostle*, the *glory* of *fertile expedients*,

---

*This was standard fare for July Fourth orations; and as I have noted elsewhere ("How the Puritans Won the American Revolution," *Massachusetts Review*, 17 [1976], 612), George Bancroft's *History of the United States* — which became the Jacksonian gospel of progress — repeatedly conflates the growth of capitalism with the growth of the country. The exodus of the commercial class from mercantile bondage, as Bancroft explains it, begins with their discovery of the New World; their rise to power parallels that of New England; and their struggle for liberty and property culminates in the Revolutionary War. Arthur's continual association of "American" with "middle class" is a main theme of Bancroft's narrative.

and the *eternal reward* of *enterprise*. The concepts linking the formulae are equally traditional. *Ark of safety* images the American chronometer in process; apocalyptic convulsions (duly drawn from the Book of Revelation) convey the climate of crisis; *rainbows of promise* light up the democratic vistas of *perfectibility*. And at the heart of this symbolic landscape lie the social norms toward which the ritual points: *mounting spirit, emulation* of *boldness, master workman, limitless expanse, generous rivalry* — all the *hallowed aims* of New Israel, bearing the Ark of Independence, in covenant with the God of the Protestant Ethic, and herself the chief example of the rise from *poverty to opulence* to which she summons all her children, leading them by the light of the Constitution, as by a pillar of flame, through the perils of continuing revolution.

I do not imply that "plain" William Arthur, the ambitious young lawyer rising to political prominence in 1850, was conscious of all the rhetorical devices he used. Let us say that by his time they were conventions of cultural self-definition. Throughout the Middle Period, American Jeremiahs considered it their chief duty to make continuing revolution an appeal for national consensus. Consensus was intrinsic to the meaning of errand, implicit in the notion of controlled process, and central to the Federalist vision of union through multiplicity. It was also, from the start, a crucial problem for the republic. The Puritans and Edwardsians, we have seen, rooted their concept of New Israel in Scripture, and however arbitrary their applications, the concept itself derived from common tradition. Whether it meant visible New England saints or blessed unions of American converts, the term *chosen people* conveyed an identity which (like the terms *New England Way* and *Great Awakening*) was at once consensual and exclusive. Neither the libertarian nor the Enlightenment rhetoric of "the people" had that clarity. On the contrary: it proved to be a major obstacle for revolutionaries throughout the period. The vagueness of "the people" led Robespierre, in George Rudé's words, to fall "victim to his own ideals," trapped between the bourgeoisie that controlled the French Republic and the sans-culottes he thought he represented.[22] Similar ambiguities in Hidalgo's rhetoric contributed to the collapse of the 1810 revolution in Mexico. Preaching the parallels between the gospels and the principles of democratic equality, Hidalgo had hoped to forge a coalition of creoles and Indians against Spanish colonialism. Instead, he incited a more basic conflict in which all the upper classes — *letrado* intellectuals, Spanish *gachupines*, and immigrant *Mexicanos blancos* — alarmed at the threat to property rights, allied themselves against the dispossessed "people." The same conflicts destroyed Bolívar's dream of a South American Republic. Having made himself the Liberator of too many of "the people" — blacks, Indians, and mulattoes, as well as the aspiring creole class he came from — having succeeded too well, that is, with the rhetoric of liberal democracy, Bolívar too, like Robespierre and Hidalgo, found himself betrayed by the realities of class conflict.*

This is to simplify, I know, but not so much as to invalidate the contrast I would suggest. One important reason for the success of the American Revolution was that its advocates had inherited a figural mode of consensus that could endorse Lockean universalism and yet exclude from it whatever then hindered the progress of the republic. The *American* was not (like the French *citoyen* or the Latin American *ciudadano*) a member of "the people." He stood for an errand that was limitless in effect, because it was limited in fact to a "peculiar" nation. Thus (in the notorious paradox of the Declaration of Independence) he could denounce servitude, oppression, and inadequate representation while concerning himself least (if at all) with the most enslaved, oppressed and inadequately represented groups

---

*The pattern held true also for the revolution in Brazil, where the "conspirators" advocated that "native born black and mulatto slaves would be freed. . . . [But] the Bahian mulattoes were as opposed to rich Brazilians as to Portuguese dominion. They . . . sought an egalitarian and democratic society where differences of race would be no impediment to social mobility . . . [so that by 1792] 'men established in goods and property' [became] wary of republicanism" (Kenneth Maxwell, "The Generation of the 1790's and the Idea of Luso-Brazilian Empire," in *Colonial Roots of Modern Brazil*, ed. Daniel Alden [Berkeley, 1973], pp. 120, 126, 140). Compare Victor Turner's analysis of the defeat of Hidalgo's revolt: "The criollos [were] clearly denying the colonial past . . . [but] some radicals, like Hidalgo, started going back too far. For the moderates, the 'people' were 'honest men' of a certain education and social standing. . . . However, the 'nation' which in *reality* acclaimed . . . [Hidalgo] was no longer the 'constituted bodies,' nor the representatives of municipal governments, but the Indian peasants, . . . 'the ancient and legitimate owners of the country'" (*Dramas, Fields and Metaphors: Symbolic Action in Human Society* [Ithaca, N. Y., 1974], pp. 144 ff.).

in the land. Those groups were part of "the people," perhaps, but not the chosen people; part of America, but not the America of the Revolution. Through the ritual of the jeremiad, the leading patriots recast the Declaration to read "all propertied Anglo-Saxon Protestant males are created equal." Through that ritual, they *bound* and *tamed* the potential excesses of the early republic — on the one hand, the social demands of groups outside their middle-class consensus; on the other hand, the anarchy of unfettered self-interest. In short, they used the jeremiad to confine the concept of revolution to American progress, American progress to God's New Israel, and God's New Israel to people of their own kind. It is no accident that the debate at the turn of the nineteenth century between the Federalists and the Jeffersonians turned on which party was the legitimate heir to the title of the American Israel.* Nor is it by accident that under Jefferson's administration the Revolution issued in an increasing violation — for blacks and Indians — of life, liberty, and the pursuit of happiness. Nor is it accidental, finally, that while France and Latin America degenerated into factional pandemoniums, the American republic generated a conformist spirit that foreign observers termed a "tyranny of the majority."

Middle-class majority would have been more precise. Nationalism has served elsewhere to unify modern communities, but always by recourse to secular continuities from the past. Even when the national ideal makes universal claims, its basis remains local, historical, and complex. European national heroes, for all their representative qualities, are circumscribed by class and genealogy; the messianic dreams of German and Russian nationalism are rooted in atavistic distinctions of race, religion, and geography. The "American" community, on the contrary, defines itself by its relation to the Revolution and the promised future; or, more accurately, by a continuing revolution based on "*a conception of the future as the present*." Especially when its adherents invoke the legend of the fathers, as William Arthur does in his July Fourth oration, "American" identity

---

*The Federalists, wrote Nathaniel Howe in a typical Jeffersonian attack, were modern "Pharaohs," seeking to return God's Country to an Old World bondage (*An Oration* [Portland, Me., 1805], p. 6). The characteristic Federalist response was that the Jeffersonians were, like Absalom, rebels in "the land of promise" (James Sloan, *An Oration Delivered* [Trenton, N. J., 1802], p. 22).

obviates the usual distinctions of national history — divisions of class, complexities of time and place — because the very meaning of "American" involves a *cultural*, not a national, myth of consensus.* It is a testament to the power of this myth that our major nineteenth-century writers through Henry James could complain about the lack of history and diversity in the land. "I have never seen a nation so much alike in my life, as the people of the United States," wrote Cooper in *Notions of the Americans* (1828). He knew well enough about Indians and blacks, about differences between the urban rich, emigrant laborers, and rural gentry, about the variety of customs in the North, South, and West. So, too, did Hawthorne when in 1860 he described the United States as "a country where there is no . . . antiquity, no mystery, no picturesque and gloomy wrong, nor anything but a commonplace prosperity, in broad and simple daylight."[23] It was not ignorance or insensitivity that led to these wry complaints. It was merely, astonishingly, that in terms of the myth which Cooper and Hawthorne shared, such differences did not count. *Nation* meant *Americans* for them, *Americans* meant *the people*, and *the people* meant those who, thanks to the Revolution, enjoyed a *commonplace prosperity*: the simple, sunny rewards of American middle-class culture.

It seems inadequate to say that all this was fictional. In this case (as in others) the evasion itself of the facts speaks a fundamental truth about the country's dominant patterns of belief and social organization. By its very distortions the myth helps us define what amounts to an extraordinary cultural hegemony. For the fact is that the views

---

*This mode of filiopietism, Arthur's oration makes clear, also carries in it a marked ambivalence. The examples of the past do not resolve problems, as in other national or tribal rituals. Instead, they heighten the anxiety of process. Sometimes this leads to a fear of betrayal: the past may prove an outmoded guidebook to the future, as Melville suggests in *Redburn* and other works. Arthur would not agree with Melville that, according to America's "express dispensation," it is "the part of wisdom to pay homage to the prospective precedents of the Future in preference to those of the Past" (*White-Jacket; or, The World in a Man-of-War*, ed. Hennig Cohen [New York, 1967], pp. 149–50); but this view was latent in the outlook both men inherited from the New England Puritans, with its overriding emphasis on emulation as fulfillment. Charles Sprague's July Fourth dictum, "In place of the fathers shall be the children" (*Oration* [Boston, 1825], p. 25), may be traced back to Cotton Mather and forward through Emerson into our own time.

which Hawthorne and Cooper express may be found throughout the popular literature. In virtually every one of the countless biographies of American heroes, for example, the author insists that "true individualism" is not something unique — not a Byronic or Nietzschean assertion of superiority —but an exemplum of American enterprise: a model of progress and control that typifies the society as a whole. The great American, as Parson Weems said of Washington, embodies the "guardian power of . . . the Revolution"; "guided by the hand of God," he "serves the people [that will] regenerate the rest of the globe." The poor boy who rises to wealth and power is neither extraordinary nor the representative of a certain class. He stands for the Revolutionary legacy of all *the people*. One envious English businessman observed that "the great difference" between America and his own country was that "In England a man is too apt to be ashamed of having made his own fortune, unless he has done so in one of the few roads which the aristocracy condescended to travel."* In America, one might say, the very term *aristocracy*, as a class defini-

*Compare Philip Lindsley's *Address at Nashville* (Nashville, Tenn., 1832), pp. 17, 34: "it is notorious that Englishmen seem absolutely incapable of comprehending the genius and practical operations of our government. When they speak of the *people*, they mean the populace — the rabble — the mob — and without an aristocracy, in some form, to control their anarchical and tumultuary tendencies, they cannot conceive of any stable security for life or property or law or religion. Now we have no *populace* in the European sense of the term — we never had a populace. . . . We have but one *order* — and all the people belong to it." And we have no aristocrats either; Washington, our greatest hero, was simply "*American* in all his feelings, sentiments, and policy." The ritual import of such statements is at once leveling and restrictive. It owes something to the English Whig theory of history, but that theory was based on evolution, not revolution: it reflected a society deeply at odds with itself (as Lindsley suggests), trying uneasily to accommodate to middle-class forms the outmoded but still potent traditions of peasantry, aristocracy, and crown. And the American view owes something, too, to the theory of Romantic Striving, but it is emphatically not the Promethean self-assertion we find in Protestant Europe, proclaiming the autonomy of the autonomous heroic self to civic and moral law. Romantic Prometheanism represented a dangerous extreme of individualism. Even as it fed on middle-class ideology, it threatened the structures of middle-class society. The concept of American revolution precluded extreme individualism as effectively as it did the complexities of "organic growth." Prometheus, after all, like Cain, Satan, Faust, and other romantic heroes, was a rebel, an individualist who defied providence and the divine plan. In America, self-assertion was legitimated only insofar as it represented the norms of the culture.

tion, was as pejorative as *bourgeois* was in Europe. But these biographies do not really extol the bourgeois. Instead, they transform the term into a comprehensive system of moral and spiritual values: their heroes are not bourgeois but independent, not parvenu or nouveau riche but adaptable, self-educated, and self-reliant. Was not the Revolution won by "self-made industrious men; those who, by their own exertion, had established or laid a foundation for establishing personal independence, [and so] were most successfully employed in establishing that of their country"?[24] To be *self-made* in America was more than to make one's own fortune; it was to embody a cultural metaphysics.

In these biographies the metaphysics pertains mainly to men; but women found their own means of joining the consensus. The cult of domesticity during this period was not merely, as we are often told, "an oasis of noncommercial values in an otherwise acquisitive society." As Kathryn Sklar has shown, it was "central to the national life." Thus Catharine Beecher, a leading proponent of the "domestic sphere,"

> paid ample homage to the role of women in shaping the future of the American experiment. . . . The millennium seemed [to her] to be coming in a social rather than a strictly religious form . . . "the beneficient influences of Christianity, when carried into every social, civil, and political institution." Since the future depended on "the . . . character of *the people*" [my italics], and the shaping of that character was in turn "committed mainly to the female hand," Catharine . . . insisted all American women were . . . "agents in accomplishing the greatest work that ever was committed to human responsibility." Besides [this, the American woman's] . . . voluntary and self-initiated submission to authority . . . acted as an archetypal example of how to achieve social order in a democracy.

Three points here warrant special comment: first, "voluntary and self-initiated submission to authority" was also a male ideal; second, in free-enterprise America careerism could provide as "archetypal" an example of submission as could the norms of domesticity (Catharine Beecher proved this by her own career); and third, the process of submission involved the familiar jeremiadic formula of affirmation through lament. "To American women," Catharine Beecher declared, in her influential *Treatise on Domestic Economy*, "more than to any others on earth, is committed the exalted privilege of extending over the world those blessed influences, that are to renovate degraded man." She began her treatise, accordingly, by citing the Declaration of Independence. Since "the principles of [American] democracy . . . are identical with the principles of Christianity," and since the "tendencies of democratic institutions, in reference to the rights and interests of the female sex, have been fully developed in the United States," it followed that "No American woman . . . has any occasion for feeling that hers is a humble or insignificant lot." Complying as they were with the principles of Christ and the Revolution, "all [American women] may be cheered by the consciousness, that they are agents in accomplishing the greatest work that ever was committed to human responsibility."[25]

From their own militant perspective, the leading feminists — advocates of women's rights like Antoinette Brown Blackwell, Elizabeth Oakes Smith, and Elizabeth Cady Stanton — subscribed to the same national vision. This is not to overlook the many differences between them and Beecher. Here as elsewhere, I assume that significant issues divided various segments of society, and that the antagonists differed significantly from each other in purpose, approach, and quality of mind. All this has been amply documented. My point is that these were divisions, antagonisms, *within the culture*. It is hardly surprising that the radical feminists opposed the majority view. What is surprising, or at any rate worthy of special attention, is that they too appealed to "principles cherished by all Americans." The cause they fought for, as Stanton said over and again, was no "foreign import." It was the "legacy of the Fathers," augmented now by a "new spirit of energy": open competition, free labor, equal opportunity under the law, and the sanctity of private property — all the values, in short, prefigured by Puritan New England, fulfilled by the Revolution, and now applied to the cause of feminism. It was not just for the sake of propaganda that the manifesto of the first women's rights convention, at Seneca Falls, July 1848, followed the form and phrases of the Declaration of Independence. Nor was it merely a coincidence that in the same year (the year of the Paris Commune and *The Communist Manifesto*) Elizabeth Lummis Ellet should have issued a two-volume panegyric entitled *Women of the American Revolution*. Not even Margaret Fuller, the most radical feminist of the time, really escaped this figural frame of mind. She may have felt, by 1845, that America's "name is no longer a watchword for the highest hopes to the rest of the world," but as Ann Douglas notes, her "standard was always that set by the American Revolution." Though she lamented that her contemporaries had "received the inheritance earned by the fathers of the revolution, without their wisdom and virtue to use it," she seems never to have questioned the inheritance itself. What inspired her participation in Mazzini's cause was her belief (to cite Douglas again) that "the Italian struggle for independence paralleled the American Revolution, . . . [and] she passionately redeemed the legacy of the founding fathers by translating it in terms of the socialism which had become her creed."[26]

To be sure, the feminist struggle shows that the rhetoric of the jeremiad not only allowed for but actually elicited social criticism. But it did so by and large to enlist the criticism in the cause of continuing revolution. Indeed, the very proliferation of dissidents and reformers — the endless debate during the Middle Period about the true meaning of America — served to confirm the norms of the culture. What higher defense could one offer for middle-class society than an American Way that sui generis evoked the free competition of ideas? — and what could make this freedom safer for society than to define it in terms of the American Way? For by the logic of continuing revolution, any term blessed by the adjective American was a positive good; but by the same logic not everything in America was so blessed. Margaret Fuller could represent the American spirit to her supporters insofar as they denied that spirit to her no less representative antagonists. Both Henry Thoreau and William Arthur defined themselves as revolutionary Americans, but for each the definition entailed a rejection of the other. The state of tension that ensued proved an inexhaustible (because self-generating) source of exultation through lament. Under the slogan of continuing revolution, the ritual of the jeremiad spawned an astonishing variety of official or self-appointed committees on un-American activities: "progressivist societies" for eradicating the Indians, "benevolent societies" for deporting the blacks, "Young Americans" for banning European culture, "populists" obsessed with the spectre of foreign conspiracy, voluntary associations for safeguarding the Revolutionary tradition, male and female "reform societies" for social regeneration through sexual purification.

In all cases, the ideal of *American* revolution ruled out any basic challenge to the system. In Europe and Latin America, the summons to "the people," precisely because it was generalized and unbounded, exposed the pretense of unity; there, revolution bared the dialectics of historical change. In the United States, the summons to dissent, because it was grounded in a prescribed ritual form, preempted the threat of radical alternatives. Conflict itself was rendered a mode of control: a means of facilitating process through which process became an aid to socialization. Again, the plight of the mid-nineteenth-century feminists is instructive. On the one hand, it reminds us that the jeremiad has always restricted the ritual of consensus to a certain group within the culture. When William Arthur spoke of "the American," he was not thinking of people like Margaret Fuller — or for that matter, of Frederick Douglass, Black Hawk, Rabbi Issac Meyer Wise, or John England, the Catholic Bishop of Charleston, South Carolina. But on the other hand, the feminist struggle reminds us that such restrictions were largely a matter of what Plotinus Plinlimmon called "virtuous expediency." For the fact is that the American consensus could also absorb feminism, so long as that would lead into the middle-class American Way. Blacks and Indians too could learn to be True Americans, when in the fullness of time they would adopt the tenets of black and red capitalism. John Brown could join Adams, Franklin, and Jefferson in the pantheon of Revolutionary heroes when it was understood that he wanted to fulfill (rather than undermine) the American dream. On that provision, Jews and even Catholics could eventually become sons and daughters of the American Revolution. On those grounds, even such unlikely candidates for perfection as Alaska, Hawaii, and Puerto Rico could become America.

All of these recent enlargements of the consensus are implicit in the nineteenth-century jeremiad. Indeed, they may be said to have begun with the changes which the jeremiad effected as the errand took on the implications of manifest destiny. The New England *Way*, we have seen, established a New World context for the theocracy, and Edwards read into the flourishing colonial economy the image or type of a millennial America. During the Revolutionary decade, radical and moderate Whigs joined in elaborating that vision into an argument for independence. The colonies, they pointed out, had outgrown their need for Britain's resources. They could rely on the manifest "genius of the people and the fertility of the soil." By *genius* they meant enterprise; by *fertility of soil*, the "open" territories; and by *the people*, of course, God's American Israel. Under Jefferson's administration, and then Jackson's, the expansion across Indian land proved beyond any doubt what all those terms implied — that America was not a territorial definition (except in the vague sense of "New World"), but the symbol of an ideological consensus. "From the analogy of reason and providence," as well as "from prophecy," said Thomas Blockway in 1784, in a sermon commemorating the Revolution, "it is apparent that [the] . . . three thousand miles of Western territory" constitute the "stage on which [God means] to exhibit the great things of His Kingdom." Forty-two years later, Daniel Webster declared that the "principle" of the Revolution "adheres to the American soil. It is bedded in it, immovable as the mountains." By 1856, Charles Dana could confidently announce that "the region which, commencing on the slope of the Alleghanies, broadens over the vast prairie" is "*the Land of Promise*, and the Canaan of our time"; if only the proper "New England minds" would direct the Westward migration — and if only they would keep "the enemies of our Revolution" from "making us a by-word and a scoff for mankind" — then the "wildest dreamer on the future of our race may one day see actualized a destiny far outreaching in splendor his most generous visions."[27]

Dana's appeal to "our race" was typically American in its synthesis of "the people," the New England forefathers, the Revolutionary fathers, and the landscape as it was and would be. It was also typical in its evocation of crisis as a spur to manifest destiny. "If the great enterprise fail here," charged Professor Benjamin Tefft, discussing the prospects of the Mississippi Valley, "the toil and struggle of six thousand years are lost, and lost forever." "If, from any cause," said Augustus Jewett on July 4, 1840, at Terre Haute, Indiana, "we forget the ages of struggles" and "the heaven directed events [of 1776] that brought us" this "new world" of the West, then the hopes of mankind "can never be restored." Inevitably the solution was continuing revolution. The "generous visions" Dana held out to prospective emigrants were a staple of the promotional writings and speeches of the Middle Period. In "this chosen land," ran the argument, God "has been for ages watching and preparing. . . . The elements of a glorious order of civilization are now ready"; "we have increased beyond all previous calculations; we are surrounded by all comforts"; man's "highest destiny" lies before us — "the untransacted destiny of the American people . . . to subdue the continent — to rush over this vast field to the Pacific Ocean . . . to carry the career of mankind to its culminating point" — and this divine "right of manifest destiny to spread will not be admitted to exist in any nation except the universal Yankee nation."[28] Implicit in all these statements — drawn from Jewett's July Fourth speech, Tefft's university lecture, and imperialist apologias by William Gilpin, friend of Andrew Jackson, and Representative Robert Winthrop of Massachusetts — is the vision first expressed in *Gods Promise to His Plantations*: "Others take the land by His providence, but God's people take the land by promise."*

The parallel is worth pursuing for a moment. Contrary to general opinion, the Puritans neither hated nor feared their environment. "By promise," they believed, the land belonged to them before they belonged to the land, and they took possession, accordingly, first by imposing their own image upon it, and then by seeing themselves reflected back in the image they had imposed. The wilderness/garden became their mirror of prophecy. They saw themselves revealed in it as the New Israel that would make the desert blossom as the rose. They also discerned in it those who did not belong to the land: Indians, heretics, opponents of the New England Way, adherents to the ways of the Old World. In the course of time, these

---

*It has been a widespread misconception that whereas in "the colonial era the image of wilderness prevailed," in the Jacksonian era "the familiar term was 'the Promised Land'" (Martin Marty, *Righteous Empire: The Protestant Experience in America* [New York, 1970], p. 46). First, the image of wilderness was prevalent through the nineteenth century, and in precisely the same conjunction with Canaan that the Puritans used. Second, the scriptural texts invoked by the frontier expansionists — e.g., "a nation will be born in a day," "the desert will blossom as the rose" — were precisely those invoked by the Puritans. From either perspective, the Puritan view fed directly into the nineteenth-century American rationale for expansion.

images blurred and expanded. On the one hand, the opposition came to include French Canadian Catholics, English royalists, anti-Federalists, "Jacobin conspirators," and the western Indian nations. On the other hand, both the sacred landscape and its "true inhabitants" took on somewhat different meanings. Romanticism added the dimension of the sublime to *wilderness* and *garden*. Furthermore, through the doctrine of "natural supernaturalism,"* the promise of the land (not only the territory but its sacred significance) became accessible to a growing number of Americans. By 1856, when Dana published *The Garden of the World*, America was "nature's nation." But all this served only to heighten the old jeremiadic distinctions. European romantics looked to nature as European Protestants had to Scripture, as a source of inspiration that in its effect transcended time and place. American romantics looked to nature, as the New England Puritan had to Scripture, as a confirmation of the destiny of the New World. What they saw there was the vast frontier, mirroring, *come iri da iri*, by the light of prophecy, "the universal Yankee nation."

Their concept of the frontier is a measure of their debt to the Puritans. Traditionally, *frontier* meant a border dividing one people from another. It implied an acceptance of differences between nations. In a sense, the Puritans recognized those differences — their "frontier" separated them from the Indian "outer darkness" — but they could hardly accept the restriction as permanent. America was God's Country, after all, and they were on a redemptive errand for mankind. In effect, their motive for colonization entailed a decisive shift in the meaning of frontier, from a secular barrier to a mythical threshold. Even as they spoke of their frontier as a meeting-ground between two civilizations, Christian and pagan, they redefined it, in a rhetorical inversion characteristic of the myth-making imagination, to mean a *figural* outpost, the outskirts of the advancing kingdom of

---

*I take this Carlylean term from M. H. Abrams, *Natural Supernaturalism: Tradition and Revolution in Romantic Literature* (New York, 1973) to suggest the secularizing effects of the doctrine of spiritual perception. In particular, I refer to the romantics' transformation of what Edwards called the sixth sense of grace into the realm of the imagination. Perry Miller treats this theme in *Nature's Nation*, esp. pp. 119–203, though when I use the term "nature's nation" (below), I do so in a different sense from that which Miller gives it.

God. It became, in short, not a dividing line but a summons to territorial expansion. And when after the Revolution the holy commonwealth spread westward across the continent, bringing light into darkness — or in one of Cotton Mather's favorite phrases, "irradiating an Indian wilderness" — the frontier movement came to provide a sort of serial enactment of the ritual of the jeremiad. It was the moving stage for the quintessentially American drama of destined progress, of process as order and control. By the time of Jackson, the Puritan-Revolutionary inversion was standardized. What in Europe signified history and restriction, came in America to signify prophecy and unlimited prospects. This reading of *frontier* altered the Puritan concept, to be sure, from threat to promise; but in doing so it amplified (rather than changed) the old sense of errand. In part at least, Jacksonians also regarded the frontier as a savage domain awaiting liberation, and they also invoked it, as we have seen, as a vehicle of the jeremiad: to create anxiety, to denounce backsliders, to reinforce social values, and (summarily) to define the American consensus.*

This vision of the frontier had its chronometrical side in the American sublime. The Puritans had sought correlations between their environment and Scripture; the Jacksonian romantics, expanding the outlook of the Revolutionary era, read the biblical promises in nature itself. The Alleghenies, the prairies, the Hudson and Mississippi rivers became their Book of Revelation. "Never before," David Huntington has observed, "had the landscape painter known such urgency. He had, for the first time in the world, been asked to paint the myth of human destiny," to find an "iconology" through

---

*John Juricek notes that Americans in the nineteenth century introduced a series of new meanings of *frontier*, signifying first a "military line," and then "a cultural confrontation between whites and Indians"; finally, *frontier* referred to "only one of these populations, the [white] Americans," and it was this meaning that Frederick Jackson Turner drew upon. Juricek suggests that "the fact that this concept appeared to be a uniquely American product contributed no small measure to the credibility of Turner's thesis" ("American Usage of the Word 'Frontier' from Colonial Times to Frederick Jackson Turner," *Proceedings of the American Philosophical Society*, 110 [1966], 15, 32–33). Another way of saying this might be that Turner persuaded because he was articulating a myth profoundly expressive of his culture. After all, the "conquest of the continent" was for him also an enterprise of the spirit. It was to "dream as our fathers dreamt and . . . [to] make their dreams come true" (*The Frontier in American History* [New York, 1920], p. 301).

which "the spectator could slough off the Old World psyche and be spiritually reborn into the New World."* And that new birth, be it noted, was not "Adamic" or "prelapsarian," as our literary critics have told us, but (like the "National birth-day") progressive and redemptive. Its purpose was precisely to turn the nostalgia for paradise lost into a movement toward the future. It was shaped not by Rousseau but by New England Puritanism. "The genius of our people," went the refrain,

> is required to declare itself after a fashion of its own — must be influenced by its skies, molded to an intense appreciation of our woods and streams, our forests and immeasurable mountains, our voluminous and tumbling waters. "Nature here presents her loveliest, sublimest aspects. This heritage of ours is without a parallel." It is a wondrous impulse to the individual, to his hope, his exertions and his final success, [thus] to be taught that there is nothing in his way; — that he is not to be denied because of his birth or poverty; — that he stands fair with his comrades, on the same great arena, — with no social impediments, — and that the prize is always certain for the fleetest in the race. This is the *natural* influence of the democratic principle of our Revolution.[29]

Our people in this passage is as ambiguous as the *frontier* is barrierless. It stands for a remnant of visible saints become a host of visible WASPs — an American consensus that has broadened, in accordance with the broadening American landscape, from non-separating congregationalists to include all denominations of *our* (Anglo-Saxon Protestant) *race*.

Sectarian diversity did not weaken the consensus, of course. Nor did it diverge fundamentally from the New England Way. When the emigrants reconstituted themselves a New Israel, they set out what was to become a new mode of cultural cohesion. The biblical Hebrews were nationalists. Although they claimed their land by promise, Canaan itself was a country (like any other) with fixed bound-

---

*Huntington is speaking in particular of the painter Frederic Edwin Church, who "painted the New World as Resurrection and Millennium," and who "was a mania in his day [because, as the *New York Illustrated News* put it,] 'we look [in his paintings] . . . for a still greater American people. . . . To travel over these United States and see . . . is to anticipate American history, and read in it a kind of apocalypse'" (*The Landscape of Frederic Edwin Church: Vision of an American Era* [New York, 1966], pp. 59, 72).

aries; and though they defined themselves as a chosen people, the definition itself was based (like that of any other people of their time) upon genealogy and a certain form of religion. The Christian concept of New Israel did away with genealogy; the Puritans' concept of wilderness and frontier allowed their "walled garden" to expand (after Washington-Joshua's "conquest of Canaan") into the Western "garden of the world"; and the ritual of consensus they established issued in a religious identity that was potentially as open-ended — potentially (and purposefully) as ambiguous in scope and in theological content — as was their geographical and genealogical identity. In their view, they represented not a particular sect, but the vanguard of Protestantism; and Protestantism was not just a religious movement for them, but the last stage of the work of redemption. For purposes of control, those universal claims were at first restricted to a scrupulously self-contained community. But once the community had assumed its redemptive role it could increasingly discard its scruples as it moved outward to fulfill its mission. Eventually, we have seen, the movement led from tribal covenant renewal to mass revivals, and thence forward to a flowering of sectarianism which provided the spiritual counterpart to territorial expansion.

The function of the jeremiad in this development may be simply stated. It provided a ritual leveling of all sects within the framework of *American* religion. *By their very contradictions they were made to correspond*, since each of them separately and all of them together corresponded to the chronometer of New Israel.* The result was a Babel

*The argument during the War of Independence was that, since Americans had "the support of heaven," all patriots, "no matter how they might differ in other respects, were on the side of the angels. . . . All could join hands in the belief that a benevolent God had . . . promised them a second Eden in the New World" (William G. McLoughlin, "The Role of Religion in the Revolution: Liberty of Conscience and Cultural Cohesion in the New Nation," in *Essays on the American Revolution*, ed. James H. Hudson and Stephen G. Kurtz [New York, 1973], pp. 202, 205). Later on, with "the decline of conservative churches, sectarian expansion, and renewed immigration," this sense of "common mission," as J. F. Maclear has shown, "gave American churchmen an opportunity for greater unity than that implied in the mutual recognitions of denominational theory. Like the tribes of Israel, the American churches shared a special relation with God and a special destiny on earth which conferred on them a singularity eclipsing their disparate origins, histories, and confessions" ("The Republic and the Millennium," in *Religion of the Republic*, ed. E. A. Smith [Philadelphia, 1971], pp. 194–95). As Ely Gladden put it, the "glowing promises made by

of religious doctrines, united by their common reverence for "the American enterprise and [a] common conviction of its millennial denouement."[30] As Tocqueville shrewdly observed, "Each sect worships God in its own fashion, but all preach the same morality in the name of God"; Americans "practice religion out of self-interest," but "religion prevents them from imagining and forbids them to dare" anything that might basically challenge the "public order." *Democracy in America* is a foreigner's inside view of the consensus, and, like D. H. Lawrence's *Studies in Classic American Literature*, it is profoundly in touch with the ritual dynamics of the myth.* Its cultural equivalent in this respect is Philip Schaff's *America*. Schaff was born in Chur, Switzerland, educated at Stuttgart, Tübingen, Halle, and Berlin, and came to the United States in 1844 to save emigrant Pennsylvania Germans from the dangers of pluralism. He stayed to join the consensus. His lectures on his adopted country not only defend the American way of church and state, but sound all the notes of the mid-nineteenth-century jeremiad:

> When history shall have erected its central stage of action on the magnificent theatre of the new world, the extreme ends of the civilized world will be brought together by the power of steam and electricity, the wonderful achievements of modern science, the leveling influences of the press and public opinion, and the more silent, but deeper and stronger workings of the everlasting Gospel. Then [will come] the millennium of righteousness. This [is] the distinctive mission of the *American* nation, to represent a compact, well defined and yet world-embracing. As the children of pilgrims, and of the sturdy Puritans, whose descendents are the chief pioneers in our western States and

---

the old prophets, of the triumphs yet to be won for the kingdom of God in the world, are made to the nation and not to the church" — and specifically to this "holy nation," America, "with all the majesty of numbers and the might of wealth behind it" (cited in Maclear, "Republic," p. 210).

*The influence of the myth upon Tocqueville requires a separate essay. Here I can only point to one representative theme in his work: "This continual, gradual advance . . . toward the Rocky Mountains has something providential in it: it is like some flood of humanity rising constantly and driven on by the hand of God . . . the scattering of the seed of a great people which God with His own hands is planting on a predestined shore. . . . North America was discovered, as if God held it in reserve and it had only just arisen above the waters of the flood. . . . One could still properly call [it] an empty land waiting for inhabitants" (*Democracy in America*, ed. J. P. Mayer, trans. George Lawrence [Garden City, N. Y., 1969], pp. 378, 37, 280, 284).

territories, we are the nation of the future. [We] must be magnificent as the Niagara Falls, lofty as the Rocky Mountains, vast as our territory, far-reaching as the highways of commerce. The first Adam was a type and prophecy of the second Adam; the very name of Abraham pointed to the Messianic blessings that should flow from [our] seed upon the nations of the earth.

Such high views ought to humble us with a deep sense of our responsibility, [but] there are fearful tendencies in our national life. There is a false Americanism as well as a true one. I need only remind you of the wild and radical tendencies of our youth; the piratical schemes of our manifest-destinarians, who would swallow, in one meal, Cuba, all Central America, Mexico and Canada; the growing rowdyism. [Still,] these various signs of degeneracy [are] merely the wild oats of the young giant, who will in due time learn better manners and settle down upon the sober discharge of his proper duties. God delivered us from greater dangers and will not forsake us, until He has accomplished all His purposes through our instrumentality.[31]

I have quoted this passage at length because it so vividly demonstrates what it meant (and means) to become acculturated into the American Way. Philip Schaff was perhaps the greatest church historian of his time, an emigrant deeply rooted in the traditions of German thought (his lectures were first delivered in German, to a German audience), familiar with the major European thinkers of the day, and an outspoken opponent of the more outrageous forms of Americanism. Nonetheless, by 1854 he was incapable of imagining an alternative to the Puritan vision. The very terms of his opposition attest to his commitment. In particular, he attacks "false Americans" in order to reinforce the system ("better manners," "proper duties"); in general, his rhetorical thunder and consolation remind us how far the myth reached, and how enveloping were its powers. It was a web spun out of sacred history and middle-class ideology which allowed virtually no avenue of escape. Technology and religion, politics and art, individualism and social progress, spiritual and economic values — all the fragmented aspects of thought, belief, and behavior in this pluralistic society flowed into *America*, the symbol of continuing revolution, and then, in a ritual fusion of process and control, outward again to each self-reliant unit of the culture. To celebrate the future was to criticize the present. To denounce either "radical tendencies" or "manifest-destinarians" was to endorse the national dream. Whether one felt "humble," "responsible," "fearful," "hopeful" or outraged, the sense of crisis that attended those feelings reaffirmed a single omnivorous mission.

Schaff's lectures, in short, are not polemical but incantatory. His purpose, like William Arthur's, was to exorcise, revitalize, and consolidate. Significantly, his phrases were commonplace in the rhetoric of those he denounced: filibustering Congressmen, "piratical" imperialists, populist "rowdies." They, too, advanced their claims through the polarity of "true" and "false Americans," and in their case, too, the scope of "sober" action was defined a priori by the meaning of America. The result was an endless, self-contained debate, as vehement as it was circular — in which the contending parties, as Tocqueville astutely noted, did "not publish books to refute each other, but pamphlets which circulate[d] at an incredible rate, last[ed] a day, and die[d]." Tocqueville's conclusion about this obsession with process is equally astute: "In France I had seen the spirits of religion and of freedom almost always marching in opposite directions. In America I found them intimately linked together in joint reign over the land." The contrast is a striking one (especially if we recognize the laissez-faire myth that informs Tocqueville's view of freedom) because it involves the two major revolutions of the modern world. What Tocqueville implies about France pertains more or less to all European countries of the time: the emergent middle class was everywhere being frustrated by the persistence of earlier traditions. Economically France had entered the era of democratic capitalism, but as a culture it was torn by rival interests and beliefs. America, on the contrary, developed "providentially," organically — *as a culture* — into "both a Puritan and a trading nation."[32]

I mentioned this contrast before, and I emphasize it here again, because it goes so far to explain the persistence of the American jeremiad. In France (as in all revolutionary European and Latin American countries) the vision of corporate unity, whether civic or religious, derived from a culture that was profoundly hostile to modern values. Long after the French Revolution, the national pantheon of regal heroes remained intact: Charlemagne, Roland, Henri IV, the Sun King Louis XIV. *Aristocracy* and *elite* retained their honorific meanings despite the triumph of the middle class. The vision of

American unity, both civic and religious, not only supported the ideals of free enterprise, but provided a rationale for the shoddiest actions performed in the name of those ideals. Here as nowhere else, the very hope of improvement led social critics to reject the idea of class struggle, since improvement was the American Way, and *American*, after all, was a consensual term.* Like biblical exegesis and the Puritan rhetoric of ambiguity, it encouraged multiplicity of meaning while precluding contradiction in fact. Here only, the legend of the fathers was an impetus to modernization: a call for progress that enhanced the glories of the past; a nostalgia for a golden age that enforced the values of the present; and most important, a restrictive mode of consensus that throve on the diversity of sectarian belief, precisely as those diverse sects throve on the competitive system they espoused. As a celebrant of that "joint reign of freedom and religion," the Swiss-born, German-educated Philip Schaff had no more hesitation in calling the Puritans *his* fathers than did the "manifest-destinarians" he despised.

Any survey of the literature makes it clear that the disputes of the time were simply variations on a theme. Even as they offered proof of the "spirit of liberty," they fostered the climate of crisis required for continuing the errand. The more bitterly they denounced "false Americans," the more sharply the disputants focused attention on the symbol of cultural hegemony. And they secured the symbol itself by grounding the ritual in an appeal to the Revolution, as embodied in the nation's mythical fathers — or better, in the fathers of their mythical nationhood. "Divisions may spring up," said Edward Everett, in his celebrated "Oration on the Peculiar Motives to Intellectual Exertion in America," "ill blood [may] arise, parties be formed, and interests may *seem* to clash, but the great bonds of the nation are linked to . . . the great men [of Puritan New England and the Revolution] to whom this country owes its origin and growth." Bound together in those filial bonds, the sectarian Jeremiahs transmuted their mutual antagonisms into a triumphal *con-*

---

*This applies directly, in our own time, to the reason that (in Warren Susman's words) "socialists in America have . . . so often found [themselves] playing the Americanism game, ending up ironically reinforcing the order [they] propose to change" ("Comment 1," in *Failure of a Dream? Essays in the History of American Socialism*, ed. John H. M. Laslett and Seymour M. Lipset [New York, 1974], p. 453).

cordia discors. Let me illustrate its pervasiveness by setting Schaff's strictures alongside those of two of his antagonists, selected virtually at random. The first is from the controversial liberal theologian Horace Bushnell:

> Our sublime fathers had a high constructive instinct, raising them above their age and above themselves. God made them founders of a social state under forms appointed by Himself. This was the star of the East that guided them thither. They came as to the second cradle-place of a renovated Messiahship. . . . The real greatness of our institutions consists in the magnificent possibilities that underlie [them]. . . . When I ponder, *not without fears*, this sublime distinction of our country, I am swallowed up in admiration of our fathers. . . . Building on the glorious achievements of the Revolution . . . [we will soon] be seen outstripping the old world in enterprise and the race of power.

My second example is from an apologia for congregationalism by Joel Hawes, an adamant opponent of Unitarians and Arminians, who at various times denounced the thought of Everett, Bushnell, and Schaff:

> [I do not] wish to detract from the merits of other denominations. . . . The founders of New-England were raised up of God, to open new sources of human improvement. They were not papists [but] . . . *enlightened freemen*, who lay the foundations of a mighty empire. . . . [Consider their] many striking points of resemblance . . . [to] the ancient Israelites. Like them, our ancestors were persecuted, delivered from their oppressors by the "arm of Jehovah," and planted, *a noble vine*, *wholly a right seed*, in . . . [this good] land. And like them, their descendents have forsaken the God of their fathers. . . . [Nonetheless,] God will *not* forget the children. The divine light will continue to expand, from generation to generation, till it mingles in the glories of millennial day.[33]

Schaff considered Everett a Brahmin aristocrat and Bushnell a "wild and radical" romantic. But he was particularly repelled by Joel Hawes because of Hawes's support for revivalism — the great awakenings of the nineteenth century which Schaff deemed the epitome of "false Americanism," and which constituted perhaps the most effective vehicle in his time of what he called "American Nationality." Appropriately, the movement began under the aegis of Edwards's grandson, the Calvinist Whig Timothy Dwight. And appropriately the leadership passed in time to an Arminian Americafirster, Charles Grandison Finney, who claimed the mantle of Edwards as passionately as Edwards, debating the Liberals of his time, had claimed the mantle of the Puritan orthodoxy. Under the banner of "national Religion," the nineteenth-century awakenings transformed the itinerant pulpit into a platform for the American jeremiad, and the itinerant preacher into an apostle of socialization. His summons to salvation promised a "paradise on earth" under Christ and the Constitution; his emphasis on personal experience openly enlisted possessive individualism (as "self-love") into a crusade for continuing revolution; his threats held out the prospect of doom ("If America fail . . . the *world* will fail"); and his alternative to failure — "The Gospel the Only Security for Eminent and Abiding National Prosperity" — offered the old figural key to the future: horologicals *and* (not *or*) chronometricals. "The way of the Lord," said Finney's leading opponent, Lyman Beecher, in *A Plea for the West* and again in *The Memory of Our Fathers*, depends upon "our march of revolution." It was a way fraught with danger, needless to say. There were Satanic conspiracies everywhere, omens that the Mississippi Valley was about to become "the great battle field of the world" (Americans versus "the combined forces of Infidelity and Popery"), labor agitators who "threatened nothing less than the cataclysmic destruction of the entire nation." But by heaven's decree America would yet "blow the trumpet and hold up the light," cheering "nation after nation . . . by her example . . . till the whole earth is free."[34]

The Great Awakening helped transform tribal into social consensus; the nineteenth-century awakenings undertook what amounted to a nationwide co-optation of the conversion experience — a purposeful inversion of spiritual *communitas* into a ritual of socialization. In 1858, William Conant brought the good news of "a revival of unprecedented power . . . in beautiful harmony with the nature of modern American existence." That vision of harmony had inspired evangelicals for half a century, but Conant had special warrant for his optimism. The year before, a wave of urban revivals had swept the country. It seems to have been brought on by an economic depression — which the preachers predictably interpreted as a season of probation — and it generated "a passionate longing for perfection, reform, and the millennial dawn." For men like Conant, there could be no mistaking its import. The Lord was "preparing his armaments, and marshalling his hosts" as He had in 1739 and 1776, but now surely for the last time. Religion and industry together had spurred the country's productive energies to unprecedented heights. "All that now exists of capital, of convenience, of comfort, and of intelligence . . . is the reward which God has bestowed upon us," and it only remained for Americans to "give free scope to the laws of Divine Providence."[35]* The fathers had provided the pattern and established the direction. It was time to complete the work of the Revolution.

By all historical accounts, the enthusiasm contributed directly to the Civil War. Some two hundred years earlier, speaking at a moment of social turbulence and sharp inner dissent, William Stoughton announced to an election-day audience that

> Antichrist is now displaying his Colours, setting up his Standard, and so is the Lord Jesus Christ. The field is large whereinto the Forces on both sides are drawing; but the fight will be very close, and there can be no *neutralizing* therefore in this day. This we must know, that the Lord's promises, and expectations of great things, have singled [us] out, above any Nation or people. And now it is not long before the Lord will *finish his great works in the world.*

Stoughton had no more doubt about the issue than did the minister who the following year, from the same election-day desk, offered *A Brief Recognition of New England's Errand into the Wilderness.* The Jeremiahs of the industrialized Northern states in 1860 had no doubt at all. In their case the ritual was fully matured, a vehicle of crisis and consensus that had virtually assumed a dynamic of its own. America was consecrated to the Revolution — that is, to progress, unity, and the middle class — and the South was not. Hence, once again, "God's judgment on His people was truly righteous," and once again "cleansing and purging were necessary . . . for the task of fulfilling His will in history." Calling on the authority of the fathers, extolling the sacred deeds of the Revolution, bewailing the harsh necessities of probation, and invoking the dream of "this last,

---

* Revivalists hailed this statement by Francis Wayland as the clearest, simplest, and most profound definition of the aims of American evangelicalism. A fair example of the persistence of those aims (rhetorically and ritually) may be found in Josiah Strong's best seller, *Our Country* (1886).

best hope of earth," Lincoln summoned God's New Israel to the "irrepressible conflict."[36]

According to Daniel Aaron, the Union leaders saw the Civil War in terms of the cosmic war in *Paradise Lost*. I would suggest that they also saw it as a dramatization of the national myth. "In Heaven," writes Aaron, in a fine summary of their outlook,

> a disgruntled Jehovah decides to rebuke the American people. . . . Repudiating the commandments of their fathers, they have become stiff-necked and luxury-loving. . . . After repeated warnings . . . God finally speaks through the pens and voices of His prophets, . . . [then] blasts the nation . . . but solicitous always, [He] frustrates the Satanic plotters . . . and preserves the Union.

To anyone acquainted with the typology of America's mission, the story was a familiar one. So was its happy ending, as the Union prophets told it once more ("the realization of the kingdom of God" in "this land of . . . millennial glory"); and the moral was spoken by Lincoln himself, on a national fast day in 1863: the war was "a punishment inflicted upon us for our presumptuous sins to the end that the whole people might be redeemed." *The whole people* meant (as of old) a developing middle class; and *redemption*, something equally formulaic: the capacity of the culture both to control the energies it unleashed and to continue unleashing those energies toward specific social ends. Now that the South had been made to correspond to the ideal, it too could join the revolution toward the American City of God. Addressing that *whole people*, North and South, James Russell Lowell praised the new "Promised Land" — "Among the Nations bright beyond compare" — which held "great futures in [its] lusty reign / And certif[ied] to earth a new imperial race."* And in Ohio, an obscure Union preacher commemorated the

---

*In 1861 Lowell had made explicit what he meant by this, and as Daniel Aaron notes, it amounted to "an up-to-date version of the Puritan Holy Commonwealth" (*The Unwritten War: American Writers and the Civil War* [New York, 1973], p. 30). Two similar attempts that year to bring the Puritan ideal up to date were Hollis Reed's *Coming Crisis of the World*, and Horace Bushnell's *Discourse on the Disaster of Bull Run*, both of which sound the old jeremiadic call for preparation through probation. This is of course the call of "The Battle Hymn of the Republic." It is also the main theme of John William De Forest's *Miss Ravenel's Conversion from Secession to Loyalty* (1865), where the war is seen as the climactic fifth act in the drama of sacred history, and the implicit message of Harriet Beecher Stowe's *Uncle Tom's Cabin*, where

victory by pointing out (in a sermon entitled *The American Republic and Human Liberty Foreshadowed in Scripture*) that "the written Constitution of the Decalogue" guaranteed "the fulfillment of liberty for mankind in the United States Constitution." Moreover, he explained, "the national apostasy of slavery and the . . . purge of that apostasy were foretold in [the] Old Testament." Then he invited his listeners to "come back to our solemn Life Covenant," whereby the "United States is to fill the earth." [37]

Christ-like Tom is succeeded by antitypal George, Eliza's "nearly white" husband, who saves the consensus (*a*) by leaving America, and (*b*) by carrying the errand into darkest Liberia, with a group of "picked men" who can "put in practice the lessons they have learned in America" — not slavery, of course, but Protestantism, "property, reputation, and education" (*Uncle Tom's Cabin; or, Life among the Lowly*, ed. Dwight L. Dumond [New York, 1974], pp. 494, 496).

6

Epilogue:
The Symbol of America

The ritual of the jeremiad bespeaks an ideological consensus — in moral, religious, economic, social, and intellectual matters — unmatched in any other modern culture. And the power of consensus is nowhere more evident than in the symbolic meaning that the jeremiads infused into the term America. Only in the United States has nationalism carried with it the Christian meaning of the sacred. Only America, of all national designations, has assumed the combined force of eschatology and chauvinism. Many other societies have defended the status quo by reference to religious values; many forms of nationalism have laid claim to a world-redeeming promise; many Christian sects have sought, in secret or open heresy, to find the sacred in the profane, and many European defenders of middle-class democracy have tried to link order and progress. But only the American Way, of all modern ideologies, has managed to circumvent the paradoxes inherent in these approaches. Of all symbols of identity, only *America* has united nationality and universality, civic and spiritual selfhood, secular and redemptive history, the country's past and paradise to be, in a single synthetic ideal.

The symbol of America is the triumphant issue of early New England rhetoric and a long-ripened ritual of socialization. Let me illustrate its literary dimensions by citing the famous passage on national destiny in Melville's early novel *White-Jacket*:

176

The Future is endowed with such a life, that it lives to us even in anticipation . . . the Future is the Bible of the Free. . . . [Thus] in many things we Americans are driven to a rejection of the maxims of the Past, seeing that, ere long, the van of the nations must, of right, belong to ourselves. . . . Escaped from the house of bondage, Israel of old did not follow after the Egyptians; to her were given new things under the sun. And we Americans are the peculiar, chosen people — the Israel of our time; we bear the ark of the liberties of the world. . . . God has predestinated, mankind expects, great things from our race; and great things we feel in our souls. . . . Long enough have we been skeptics with regard to ourselves, and doubted whether, indeed, the political Messiah had come. But he has come in *us*.[1]

The term *American* here involves a distinctive blend of the visionary, historical, and figural modes. As opposed to (say) Donne's or Blake's symbol of America,* Melville's carries in it the authority of Scripture. It offers itself neither as a conceit nor as a personal vision, but as a civic identity rooted in a prophetic view of history. And yet Melville's *American* clearly absorbs both civic identity and prophecy into what can only be called a symbolic outlook. "Egypt," "Israel," and "ark" gather meaning by reference to "the Bible of the Free," through an assertion of will and imagination. The "predestinated" future rests with a worldly enterprise — "our race," "the people," a "political Messiah" — but the rhetoric plainly substitutes symbolic for social analysis.

The substitution is a crucial one. Historical or social analysis is secular, relativistic, and therefore open to a consideration of radically different systems of thought and action. Symbolic analysis on

---

*Donne's famous conceit — "O my America! my new-found-land, / . . . How blest am I in this discovering thee!" ("To His Mistris Going to Bed," Elegie XIX) — reflects the sexual imagery in many seventeenth-century descriptions of America by non-Puritan colonists. Harold Bloom describes Blake's frontispiece illustration of *America* as "an epitome . . . of the torments of self-consciousness in relation to the contraries of nature and emergent imagination" (*Romanticism and Consciousness: Essays in Criticism*, ed. Bloom [New York, 1970]). Another difference between these uses of "America" and Melville's lies in Melville's association of America with Israel. For Donne, the *figura* of Israel enjoined the ritual of the church. For Blake, humanizing Scripture as Romantic symbology, the *figura* of Israel opened into a ritual of self-fulfillment. *White-Jacket* contains both these elements — it is at once a parable of sacred history and a Romantic conversion story — but it joins and transforms these, through the *figura* of Israel, into a summons to America's mission.

the contrary, confines us to the alternatives generated by the symbol itself. It may suggest unexpected meanings, but only within a fixed, bipolar system. Since every symbol unites opposites, or represents them as the same thing, we can understand what is being represented only by measuring it against its opposite, or by placing it within a series of comparable and related oppositions.[2] Thus the search for meaning is at once endless and self-enclosed. Any possibility we propose invites a host of different possibilities, all of these inherent in the symbol. Any resolution of opposites we discover is implicit in the dualisms with which we began. It is through this endless, self-enclosed process that the future reveals itself, in *White-Jacket*, by contrast with the present, and "American" by contrast with what Philip Schaff called "false Americanism." In both cases, the contrast closely resembles that between the sacred and the profane; and the resemblance is especially revealing of the uses of America as symbol.

As I noted earlier, in discussing the difference between revolution and rebellion, the sacred characteristically defines itself through antithesis. The significance of "holy land" depends on other lands not being holy; the chosenness of the chosen people implies their antagonism to the *goyim*, the profane "nations of the earth." Moreover, sacred history means the gradual conquest of the profane by the sacred. The believer cultivates the inner wilderness in prescribed stages of spiritual growth; the church as a whole wins the world back from Satan in a series of increasingly terrifying and triumphant wars of the Lord. Continuous conflict, then, and gradual fulfillment become mutually sustaining concepts, and as such they lend themselves powerfully to the strategies of the American jeremiad.

But there is a crucial distinction to be made — or more accurately, a crucial distinction was *not* made in this country. By all tradition, the war between sacred and profane accents the absolute, unbridgeable difference between the two. They confront each other not as greater and lesser antagonists, but as diametrically opposite ways of perception. Eden is forever the garden of our innocence through our willing suspension of geography. Jerusalem is the "holy city" insofar as we dissociate it from the cities of the earth. In short, sacred meaning is fixed, impervious to the vicissitudes of the pro-

fane, and essentially that meaning is progressive, leading upwards
from Eden to New Jerusalem. The American Jeremiahs obviated
the separation of the world and the kingdom, and then invested the
symbol of America with the attributes of the sacred.

So conceived, the symbol took on an entirely different function
from that of the religious symbols in which it was rooted. The
revelation of the sacred serves to diminish, and ultimately to deny,
the values of secular society. The revelation of America serves to
blight, and ultimately to preclude, the possibility of fundamental
social change. To condemn the profane is to commit oneself to a
spiritual ideal. To condemn "false Americans" as profane is to express one's faith in a national ideology. In effect, it is to transform
what might have been a search for moral or social alternatives into a
call for cultural revitalization. This had been the purpose of the New
England Puritan Jeremiahs as well; but in their case the symbolic
mode drew its authority from figural exegesis. Despite the secular-
sacred correspondences they asserted, some conflict remained in
their rhetoric (if only by sheer force of the tradition they invoked)
between *Christian* on the one hand and *New Englander* or *American* on
the other. And despite their insistent progressivism, the future they
appealed to was necessarily limited, by the very prophecies they
vaunted, to the ideals of the past. The American experience for them
was a new, last book of Scripture, but Scripture itself was the Book
of God, not "the Bible of the Free." As I noted earlier, New England
Puritan symbology, like the theocracy itself, was a transitional
mode, geared toward new forms of thought but trailing what Melville scornfully called the "maxims of the Past." For Melville, and all
the major writers of the American Renaissance, America as symbol
was its own reality, a totalistic bipolar system, sufficient to itself.

I do not mean to blur the differences between these writers, much
less to reduce their works to ideology. On the contrary, I invoke
them precisely because of their well-known divergence from "popular culture," in order to indicate the pervasive impact of the American jeremiad. Let me say at once, to avoid all misunderstanding, that
all our classic writers (to varying degrees) labored against the myth
as well as within it. All of them felt, privately at least, as oppressed
by Americanism as liberated by it. And all of them, however capti-
vated by the national dream, also *used* the dream to reach beyond the

categories of their culture. To speak of their cultural limitations may be no more than to speak of Chaucer's debt to the medieval world picture. Still, their case seems to me somewhat special. For one thing, critics of American literature have tended to ignore cultural limitations, or else to translate these into quasi-mystical terms, as though the American Renaissance were the embodiment of some New World spirit. Clearly, such terms have their source in the symbol of America — but in this case they seem to derive directly from the great works of our literary tradition. This points to the second, more important reason for insisting that that tradition was the expression of a particular society. Chaucer wrote openly from within his culture. American writers have tended to see themselves as outcasts and isolates, prophets crying in the wilderness. So they have been, as a rule: *American* Jeremiahs, simultaneously lamenting a declension and celebrating a national dream. Their major works are the most striking testimony we have to the power and reach of the American jeremiad.

For leaders of politics and industry in the nineteenth century, the symbol of America was the key to social control. For revivalists, it was the link between religion and middle-class values. For reformers it was a way of fusing the millenarian impulse (which tended elsewhere to challenge the status quo in basic ways) with the concept of gradual improvement. For our classic writers, the symbol of America functioned as an ancestral taboo, barring them from paths that led beyond the boundaries of their culture. It was not that they lacked courage or radical commitment, but that they had invested these in a vision designed to contain self-assertion. I mean *containment* in its double sense, as sustenance and restriction. The symbol set free titanic creative energies in our classic writers, and it confined their freedom to the terms of the American myth. The dream that inspired them to defy the false Americanism of their time compelled them to speak their defiance as keepers of the dream. It is true that as keepers of the dream they could internalize the myth. Like the latter-day Puritan Jeremiahs, they could offer *themselves* as the symbol incarnate, and so relocate America — transplant the entire national enterprise, en masse — into the mind and imagination of the exemplary American. The cultural polarities implied in this relocation have been discussed from various perspectives.* In general, the artist-hero is presented as an unsought Philoctetes, trying to win his way out of alienation by creating an "ideal world," a "mythic anti-history" designed "to halt, to stem the tide of the on-going process itself."[3]

The characterization seems to me a very partial one. Symbols, myths, and ideals no less than any other human artifacts or activities partake of the ongoing process of history; and the interaction between rhetoric and history is especially prominent in the work of our major nineteenth-century authors. To declare oneself a representative of the English, French, or Russian spirit may or may not show one's allegiance to modern English, French, or Russian society; in all these cases, the spirit of the nation (or "the people") antedates modern society. To declare oneself the symbol of America is by definition to retain one's allegiance to a middle-class culture. The isolation of our classic writers signifies neither an aesthetic withdrawal nor a romantic-antinomian declaration of superiority to history and "the mass." Those reactions describe the attitudes of writers in other modern literatures. What distinguishes the American writer — and the American Jeremiah from the late seventeenth century on — is his *refusal* to abandon the national covenant. His "polarized emotions," Newton Arvin has observed, alternate between defiance of the country and a "deep identification with it and with its meaning for the . . . future." More than that, these extremes reinforce one another in a kind of symbiotic antagonism. His identification with America as it ought to be impels the writer to withdraw from what is in America. When he retreats into his art, however, it is characteristically to create a haven for what Thoreau called "the only true

---

*Richard Chase, for example, has defined our nineteenth-century "romance" through the image of a broken circuit between the ideal and the real (*The American Novel and Its Tradition* [New York, 1957], p. 7); Leo Marx has found in the conflict between pastoral and technological ideas a "recurrent metaphor of contradiction" that reduces the writer's "inspiriting vision" to a token of individual survival (*The Machine in the Garden: Technology and the Pastoral Ideal in America* [New York, 1964], p. 364); and Roy Harvey Pearce has described the impulse toward antinomianism in American poetry ("the paradox of a Puritan faith at once reborn and transformed") as a decisive cleavage between author and audience (*The Continuity of American Poetry* [Princeton, N.J., 1961], pp. 41–42).

America."[4] In effect, the ideals that prompt his isolation enlist individualism itself, aesthetically, morally, and mythically, into the service of society.

Most explicitly, this process is manifest in Emerson's thought. No one made larger claims for the individual than Emerson did, no one more virulently denounced corruption in America, and no one more passionately upheld the metaphysics of the American system. His career exemplifies the possibilities and constrictions of the nineteenth-century jeremiad. "I dedicate this book to the Spirit of America," Emerson wrote at the start of his journal on July 11, 1822. He might have begun all his works this way.* When Unitarianism proved a dead religion, he remembered that America was bound to shape the religion of the future. If he doubted the "raw multitudes" of the West, he invoked the Western landscape to justify America's "errand of genius and love." In reaction against the Fugitive Slave Law he affirmed "the pilgrimage of American liberty." Confronted with a "riot of mediocrities and dishonesties and fudges" — corruption in politics, shallowness in art, "barbarism" in morals and manners — Emerson listened all the more intently to his prophetic inner voice, speaking of the Poet, Teacher, and Scholar to come, and of "the reformation of the world [which must] . . . be expected from America." "The destiny of this country is great," he remarked, and in itself ensures "the promise of better times and greater men." In the face of public discouragement and personal tragedy, he found solace in recalling that "Asia, Africa, Europe [were] old, leprous, & wicked" — that his "birthright in America" was "a preferable gift to the honours of any other nation that breathes upon the Earth" — and

---

*Much the same might be said for the Transcendentalists as a group. As George Hochfield has observed (Introduction to *Selected Writings of the Transcendentalists*, ed. Hochfield [New York, 1966], pp. xi, xxvii), they felt that they were "living on the threshold of profound and glorious change" and "wrote of America as though its destiny was to be a messiah among the nations." For Bronson Alcott and the young Orestes Brownson (before his disenchantment and conversion to Catholicism), the country had attained a "vantage ground to which no people have ever ascended before." America had been appointed "to unite the infinite and finite . . . [and] bind together the past and the future"; after some two hundred years success at last seemed at hand: "that cause which landed our fathers on Plymouth Rock" was drawing to its close; "Verily it is near. . . . Humanity awaits the hour of its renewal" (*Selected Writings*, pp. 93, 155–56, 175–76, 252–53).

he rededicated himself once more to "this new yet unapproachable America I have found in the West."[5]

In all these instances, Emerson was building upon the old jeremiadic ambiguities. America for him symbolized a state of soul, a mode of civic and moral identity, a progressive view of history, and a distinct but flexible concept of elect nationhood. Above all, "America" wed the ideals of individualism, community, and continuing revolution. It was a marriage, we have seen, that was particularly suited to Emerson's society. Many earlier laissez-faire theorists had recognized that open competition and upward mobility could endanger the very enterprise that nourished those values. Thus John Locke urged voluntary submission to authority in order to safeguard rights of property — including the property of the self — and thus in 1776 Adam Smith offered a rationale for self-interest that stressed the mutuality of independence and interdependence. Emerson, who counted Smith's *Wealth of Nations* a "book of wisdom,"* found in America the perfect symbol of that mutuality. America meant "self-trust," the "unapproachable" heights of revolutionary self-reliance. And in the same breath it meant trust in the social principles embodied in the American Revolution. "The only true basis of political economy," Emerson wrote, was the one that encouraged "freedom of trade," a "self-adjusting meter of supply and demand," "non-interference" by government, the primacy of "property as . . . the motive to industry," and the sanctity of

---

*Emerson had his doubts about Adam Smith, as John Gerber shows ("Emerson and Political Economists," *New England Quarterly*, 22 [1949], 344), but Gerber also notes that he admired Smith above all other economists, and that "though their terms are quite different, the arguments of Smith and Emerson at some points are surprisingly parallel" (p. 339). The same may be said about Emerson's view of the middle class. His disgust with the "pushing" Jacksonian "masses" is well known; his solution was to train a new leadership, essentially drawn from the "cultured" middle class, "to cope with the needs of . . . a new age" (William Charvat, *The Profession of Authorship in America, 1800–1870* [Columbus, Ohio, 1968], pp. 61, 65). He held up Robert Burns, the "poet of the middle class," as an avatar of the American Revolution (*Works*, ed. Edward Waldo Emerson [Boston, 1903–4], XI, 440), and he insisted that socialism was incompatible with self-reliance because it tended "to remove the motive to industry. If you refuse rent and interest, you make all men idle and immoral. As to the poor, a vast proportion have made themselves so, and in any new arrangement will only prove a burden on the state" (*Journals and Miscellaneous Notebooks*, ed. William H. Gilman [Cambridge, Mass., 1960–67], VII, 431).

"hard work, when labor is sure to pay." So conceived and so circumscribed, America stood for an "economic system" — as well as a moral, religious, and political way of life — that had "all of nature behind it." It was proof to the world that "all great men come out of the middle classes."[6]

My point in all this, to repeat, is not that Emerson was an apologist for the middle class. He was often its severe critic. But his jeremiads were couched in terms that reaffirmed the basic tenets of the culture. Far from pressing the conflict between individual and society, Emerson obviated all conflict whatever by defining inward revolt and social revolution in identical terms, through the bipolar unities of the symbol of America. His vision of the good society invited the individual to deny every secular distinction between himself and others and so to make individuation an endless process of incorporation. His call to self-transcendence closed all options to middle-class norms. True selfhood was the standard by which he gauged social failure or success. And true selfhood, as he conceived it, was the *summum et ultimum* of the American Way. On the one hand, he urged upon his countrymen the need for "persons of purer fire . . . the exciters and monitors; collectors of the heavenly spark, with power to convey the electricity to others . . . rare and gifted men, to compass, and verify out bearings from superior chronometers." On the other hand, Emerson's own "superior chronometer" kept time with the country's free-enterprise system. The blessings of nature and self-discipline, he wrote, derive from

> property and its filial systems of debt and credit. Debt, grinding debt, whose iron face the widow, the orphan, and the sons of genius fear and hate; — debt which consumes so much time, which so cripples and disheartens a great spirit with cares that seem so base, is a preceptor whose lessons cannot be foregone, and is needed most by those who suffer from it most. Moreover, property, which has been well compared to snow, — "if it fall today, it will be blown into drifts tomorrow," — is the surface action of internal machinery, like the index on the face of a clock. Whilst now it is the gymnastics of the understanding, it is hiving, in the foresight of the spirit, experience in profounder laws.[7]

The "surface action," we might say, is a horologue, the "internal machinery" works by "the foresight of the spirit," and through the "profounder laws" of Compensation the two are made to correspond.

As Emerson explained it, that correspondence taught Americans that they must

> Always pay; for first or last you must pay your entire debt. . . . Benefit is the end of nature. But for every benefit which you receive, a tax is levied. . . . The absolute balance of Give and Take, the doctrine that every thing has its price . . . is not less sublime in the columns of a ledger than in the budgets of state, in the laws of light and darkness, in all the action and reaction of nature. . . . Put God in your debt. Every stroke shall be repaid. The longer the payment is witholden, the better for you; for compound interest on compound interest is the rate and usage of this exchequer.

By this "absolute balance" in his "sublime" ledgers, Emerson assured his audiences that self-interest always flowed into the common good. Through these "gymnastics of the understanding," in his journals and essays, he explained the confluence in terms that recall Madison's laissez-faire heaven: "Every man comes at the common results with most conviction in his own way. But he only uses a different vocabulary from yours; it comes to the same thing. . . . I have only to translate a few of the leading phrases into their equivalent verities, to adjust his almanack to my meridian, and all the conclusions, all the predictions shall be strictly true."[8]

The man who most closely adjusted his almanac to Emerson's meridian was of course Henry Thoreau. His aversion to most aspects of American life is well documented, and nowhere more fully than in *Walden*, a conversion narrative that fuses the laws of nature, reason, and economics with the spirit of America. Leo Marx has observed that Thoreau transposes the national ideal "from history . . . [to] his own consciousnesss"; recognizing that his forest site could "not provide a refuge, in any literal sense, from the forces of change," he situated America "in his craft, in *Walden*." Edwin Fussell, discussing the influence of the frontier movement, has shown that for Thoreau "the West stands for . . . the future of the American continent and then by analogous transfer . . . [for] the soul of the American writer." All of this may be accurate with regard to Thoreau's intention. But the "analogous transfer" does not convey us into some pure realm of consciousness (whatever that is). Rather, it leads from misguided "forces of change" to a social ideal.

Thoreau's art is a mimesis of the higher laws of his culture. What makes *Walden* part of the tradition of the jeremiad is that the act of mimesis enables Thoreau simultaneously to berate his neighbors and to safeguard the values that undergird their way of life. If (as he claims) it was by accident that he made July Fourth the first day of his independence, it is no accident that he describes his life at Walden through a series of opposites which reaffirm the typology of America's mission: Concord's Puritan fathers versus its present profane inhabitants; America's sacred pioneer "economy" versus Franklin's secular Way to Wealth; the true American, Henry Thoreau, versus John Field, the emigrant bog-hoer, living "by some derivative old-country mode in this primitive new country."[9]

Clearly, the "new country" Thoreau speaks of is America, actually as well as ideally; but it excludes the industrialized North and East, the slavery-infested South, the land-grabbing, Indian-massacring West. It excludes, in sum, everything he considered un-American, from Washington bureaucrats to California gold-rushers to his Concord neighbors, John and Jonathan, stillborn in New Canaan, barred by their delegated functions from entering "the only true America," oblivious to the prospect of "a millennium . . . a total renewal . . . distinctly on the actual soil of New England" — and by extension across the continent at large — a period "more imaginative, . . . clearer, fresher, and more ethereal" than any since "Adam in Paradise." For if *Walden* was Thoreau's celebration of the kingdom within, his proof that the revolution of the soul corresponded to nature's revolutions, it was also, as Stanley Cavell notes, his "final proof of the nation's maturity, proof that its errand among nations had been accomplished," or at least was still in process.*

---

*Cavell refers here to the "call for the creation of an American literature" that would demonstrate the nation's "specialness" (*The Senses of "Walden"* [New York, 1974], p. 13). Elsewhere he discusses Thoreau's acceptance of that challenge, his role as America's "watchman" and "true prophet," and his use of denunciation as a goad toward the future. Let me emphasize again that it is no more my intention than it was Cavell's to present Thoreau as an ideologue. Thoreau believed in something like what Hegel called "the Law of the Heart," by which the individual affirms "the universal . . . immediately within [himself]." But for Hegel that act of self-liberation is essentially a tragic one. It stands opposed to "reality" — i.e., the demands of history and society — and in asserting himself, the individual comes to see in the law of the heart also the principle of self-destruction (*The Phenomonology of Mind*, trans. J. B.

With that national faith, Thoreau tells us that "We go eastward to realize history" and "westward as into the future," leaving behind us "the Old World and its institutions." As a frontiersman of the spirit, he enunciates the principles of his "extra-vagrant" mode of life. A decade before Thoreau began *Walden*, Cooper had personified the American middle class as Aristabulus Bragg, the "regular mover" who supports democracy because, for all its failings, it obviates history, along with every impediment to industry, enterprise, and self-fulfillment. "America may, indeed, be termed a happy and a free country . . . in this, as well as in other things," Bragg explains to a visitor from the Old World. "I am for the end of the road at least," and for all "onward impulses."[10] This is *not* Thoreau bragging lustily as chanticleer; but the very contrast in mind and purpose makes the parallels in rhetoric all the more remarkable. He and Aristabulus march to different drummers, but along the same free and enterprising American Way. The sun of the good that Thoreau saw reflected in the depths of Walden Pond was the same American sun that warmed Concord and the real West.

Walden embodies the myth of American laissez-faire individualism. It has been remarked that Thoreau wrote the book just as *The Communist Manifesto* was being published, and that the "same diseases of the profit system impressed the American recluse and the German scholar[s]." If so, the impression led to strikingly different conclusions. Marx and Engels proposed a new form of government, based on a wholly different social system. Thoreau lifted his motto for the ideal political order — "that government governs best which governs least" — from the masthead of the jingoistic *Democratic Review*, and though he certainly did it to protest jingoism, it was a protest from within, intended not to change the profit system but to cure its diseases. Like a biblical prophet, he hoped to wake his countrymen up to the fact that they were desecrating their own beliefs. *Walden* summons us toward what George Bancroft, an ardent jingoist and leading figure on the *Democratic Review*, called "the bright morning star that harbingered American independence."

Baillee [New York, 1967], pp. 391–96). This is the romantic-antinomian dilemma. Thoreau sometimes recognizes it as such, but characteristically he "transcends" it by adopting America as the symbol both of self and society in the New World.

The lessons it teaches echo those of the celebrated Homo Economicus of mid-nineteenth-century America. He, too (as Leggett, Lieber, Nichols, Rantoul, and other Jacksonian economists describe him), is a simple and simplifying man, mobile, self-employed, living by "seasonal rhythm" and the "order of nature," his "independence disciplined by virtue" and sustained by antipathy to government controls. He, too, denounces the "wicked spending," "soap-bubble business," and "wasteful acquisition," the "appalling . . . tugging, trying scheming to advance," that characterizes the "false American" life. He too, finally, exemplifies the American method for self-perfection: "true value of riches," usually learned in a "purifying" state of poverty; "free exercise of confidence between man and man," based on a "natural system in politics"; and "useful toil" toward the "highest excellences, physical, intellectual, and above all, moral."[11]

Again, this is not the hero of *Walden*, but enough like him to suggest the ideology behind the myth. And *Walden*, let me add, is enough like other classics of the American Renaissance to suggest the socializing effects of the myth. I think especially of their concern with rites of passage and of their peculiarly adolescent themes: their emphasis on freedom from prescribed roles, on confrontations with the absolute, on the disparity between social and "ultimate" values, even while they return insistently to the meaning of America. But in context the insistence upon America suggests that, in this case, to increase tension is to further the process of acculturation. Recent anthropologists have observed that the rite of passage, despite its ideological intent, may pose enormous dangers to society. By freeing the initiate, however briefly, from traditional structures, it directs him (to recall the Turnerian terms I used in chapter 5) to a state of *communitas*, whose values appeal to humanity at large, ràther than to particular communities: they speak of oneness as opposed to political or even sexual division; equality, as opposed to hierarchy; universality, as opposed to tribal or national exclusiveness. Many societies have paid homage to such values, and as a rule ideology seeks to justify social structures by integrating them, through symbol and myth, with the deeper human structures of ritual *communitas*. Nonetheless, it seems evident that the experience of *communitas* has often led individuals and groups to challenge their societies in basic ways. European novels like Dickens's *Great Expectations* and Balzac's *Lost Illusions* — or to select a work closer to *Walden*, Carlyle's *Sartor Resartus* — show how the rite of passage may issue in a sweeping criticism of middle-class dreams, not only in their deviance from the ideal but in their own right, as cultural norms. The symbol of America functions in our most idealistic, most communitarian literary classics to pre-empt that kind of challenge.

Walden is the example par excellence. Thoreau inherited the concept that an "invisible hand" orders "the divine economy in nature," and he made that order visible through a brilliant fusion of nature, economy, and the divine. He inherited the theory that "social process can best be studied as an aggregation of . . . [separate, independent] individuals," and he turned his study of process into "the discovery or projection of a fixed point — the center — [which] is equivalent to the creation of a world." He inherited "the assumption that individual subjective utility is commensurate with general market values," and he transmuted this into a "frontier . . . where passage from the profane to the sacred world becomes possible," and where "three cosmic levels — earth, heaven, underworld — have been put in communication." [12] From the vantage point of that Jacksonian *sancta terra*, that westering city on a hill, Thoreau condemned the evil practices in his society.* Significantly, he did not consider

*Thoreau makes it clear in his great essay "Walking" (in *Walden and Other Writings*, ed. Brooks Atkinson [New York, 1950], pp. 607 ff.) that the movement toward and away from society take the same "westering" direction for him, into the symbol of America. Indeed, what he means here by "westering" is as much an emblem of mass action as it is a gesture of Romantic quietism. Historically, the Westward movement signals a renascence of mankind, manifested in "the prevailing tendency of my countrymen" and the life of the American backwoodsman. Spiritually, Thoreau's westward walk — leading (as he says) towards Oregon and away from Europe — denotes the flowering of the soul, the Romantic journey into the "golden West of the imagination." Essentially, his strategy is to fuse the two levels of meaning by making his subject an *American* walker. With this double meaning, he praised Whitman's poetry as being "very brave and American" ("Concerning Walt Whitman," in *Literature in America*, ed. Philip Rahv [New York, 1960], p. 149), and defended John Brown as being a true son of the Puritans and "the most American of us all" (*Reform Papers*, ed. Wendell Glick [Princeton, N. J., 1973], p. 124). The same ambiguity underlies his famous passages in "Walking" (pp. 608, 612), on the sun as "the great Western Pioneer whom all nations follow" and on America's prospect of making real the utopian visions of the ancients. Both notions may be traced through (for example) Edward Johnson's *Wonder-Working Providence* (1654), Cotton Mather's *Wonders of the Invisible World* (1693) and *India Christiana* (1721), Edwards's *Thoughts on the Revival* (1742), Jacob Duché's *Observations* (1774), and J. Sullivan Cox's "Imaginary Commonwealths" (1846).

these to be a defect of the American Way. He saw them rather as an aberration, like the backsliding of a de facto saint or the stiff-necked recalcitrance of a chosen people. That is why his outrage is so vehement, his rejections so absolute, his ironies so didactic, and so resonant with biblical allusion. Thoreau speaks as Emerson does, under the aspect of the symbol of America. His denunciation is part of a ritual appeal to his neighbors to comply with the terms of their New World destiny. The higher laws he discovers by his July Fourth experiment in *communitas* transform the dangers of liminality into an invitation to continuing revolution.

Neither Thoreau nor Emerson was always happy in his compliance. Stephen Whicher has suggested about Emerson in particular that the "dogmatic" optimism he vaunted publicly was something of a makeshift cover for the void he felt in private, a too-much-protested (and therefore sometimes callous) faith thrust upon him by "the ghastly reality of things." Other critics have noted that Emerson's vision of the country tottered uncertainly between misanthropy and chauvinism, shrill condemnation and uncritical acclaim. That sort of vacillation, I have argued, was part of a national ritual mode. But the extreme to which Emerson's pessimism could reach demands special attention. "Ah my country! In thee is the reasonable hope of mankind not fulfilled"; "When I see how false our life is, . . . [all] heroism seems our dream & and our insight a delusion"[13] — such statements form a leitmotif of his notebooks, letters, and journals, and their parallels in the writings of his contemporaries suggest that they are not just a matter of temperament or chance, but intrinsic to the optative American mood. I speak now of a cultural reflex, an ingrained habit of mind. The symbol of America magnified the culture into a cosmic totality: hence the euphoria of its adherents. But the same process of magnification carried a dangerous correlative: if America failed, then the cosmos itself — the laws of man, nature, and history, the very ground of heroism, insight, and hope — had failed as well.

It was a danger to which our major romantics were particularly susceptible. Their European contemporaries, for whom democratic capitalism was one of several traditions, could be disillusioned in society without descending into despair, just as they could espouse the middle class while exposing the limitations of its ideals. Our classic writers tended to uphold those ideals even when they most bitterly assailed their society. Their very radicalism, we might say, forced that upon them, since they identified America, symbolically, with the ideals of art and the self. Hence their quickness to condemn and the hyperbole or desperation we sometimes feel in their condemnation. When they abandoned their faith in America, they had no other recourse. The result was what we might call the anti-jeremiad: the denunciation of all ideals, sacred and secular, on the grounds that America is a lie. I use the term anti-jeremiad to recall the ubiquity of the national symbol. In this country, both the jeremiad and the anti-jeremiad foreclosed alternatives: the one by absorbing the hopes of mankind into the meaning of America, the other by reading into America the futility and fraud of hope itself.

Melville's early writings are the great mid-nineteenth-century example of this cultural schizophrenia. Every student of Melville is familiar with Hawthorne's description of him as a man who could neither accept God nor rest content in his disbelief. The same might be said about his view of America. Before *Moby-Dick*, as I have indicated, he repeatedly invoked the dream, and there is no reason to doubt his candor when he wrote that America was "bound to carry republican progressiveness into Literature, as well as into Life." Yet the seeds of disbelief are there from the start. *Redburn* intimates that the chauvinism of its hero is an index of his immaturity. *White-Jacket* tells us that the U.S.S. *Neversink* has "a Sick-bay for the smitten and helpless, whither we hurry them out of sight. . . . Outwardly regarded, our craft is a lie." The review of Hawthorne's *Mosses* juxtaposes the Calvinist "power of blackness" with the Emersonian faith in "the coming of the literary Shiloh of America"* — and here the two extremes fail to correspond, as they are made to correspond in the writings of the New England Calvinists. The juxtaposition is

---

* "With a spark of prophetic devotion, I hasten to hail the Genius, who yet counts the tardy years of childhood, but who is increasing unawares in the twilight, and swelling into strength, until the hour, when he shall break the cloud, to shew his colossal youth, and cover the firmament with the shadow of his wings" (Emerson, *Journals*, II, 4). This is of course also the theme of Hawthorne's short story "The Great Stone Face," which affected Melville deeply and may well have influenced his conception of *Pierre*.

more threatening still in *Mardi*, where circular tautologies stop short of resolution, where ambiguities lead only to paradox, and where the search for the absolute is undermined by the very symbol of America — Vivenza, which "fools" have declared a "universal and permanent Republic," forgetting that "through all eternity the parts of the past are but parts of the future reversed." [14]

Moby-Dick is the culmination of Melville's unsuccessful effort to resolve these tensions. The basic conflict in the novel is neither "the Cod-God paradox," as A. N. Kaul has termed it, [15] nor is it the contest which other critics have described between a predatory social venture and a private mode of vision. The jeremiad was designed precisely to obviate such conflicts, and Melville uses its strategies with great effect. Through Ishmael, he criticizes the real America of Nantucket while upholding the values of self-reliance, mobility, and laissez-faire. And through the *Pequod* community that Ishmael represents, Melville affirms the democratic ideal by contrast with the actual tyranny that Ahab manages to enforce. Indeed, Melville underscores the affirmation by shifting his criticism from society to the individual. The problem does not lie with shipowners and shareholders, or with any middle-class frustrations to self-fulfillment. It lies with Ahab, an antinomian romantic turned "mogul," "czar," "sultan," "emperor." Thus the novel tends to divide our sympathies between two modes of individualism, American and false American. And in Ishmael's ambiguous gestures toward fulfilling the federal covenant it offers us a cultural rite of passage — a revolutionary American Way to exorcise the rebellious Ahab in our souls. Blasphemy may enchant when it takes the form of monomania. As a social alternative it can only argue the need for the containment of individualism.

But the argument is not wholly persuasive. Clearly, Melville identifies to some extent with Ahab; and to that extent Ahab reflects his growing disenchantment not only with actual America but with the ideal. If Ahab is a sinister example of the rugged pioneer free-enterpriser, that may be, the novel suggests, because free enterprise is itself something sinister. If Ahab is a distortion of the "political Messiah" celebrated in *White-Jacket*, that may be because the messianic promise, the dream of knowledge, power, and the spirit, is itself a distortion. If Ahab proves false to Father Mapple's vision of the "anointed pilot-prophet" who "ever stands forth his own inexorable self," it may be not Ahab who fails, but a certain vision of selfhood.[16] Inwardly, perhaps, as well as outwardly regarded, "our craft is a lie." From this perspective, the bipolar unity of Ishmael and Ahab tends to exacerbate, rather than obviate, the contradictions between them. It is not that Ishmael participates, in word and deed, in Ahab's fiery quest. It is that whether Ishmael knows it or not the quest is his own as well as Ahab's. In part at least, the hunt for the white whale is the metaphysical dimension of the day-by-day frustrations that drive him to sea. Ishmael embodies Melville's quarrel with America, Ahab his quarrel with what America symbolically represents. The result is an irresolvable paradox which, pressed to its end, invalidates all terms of discourse.

I do not mean to minimize the power of Ishmael's imagination and the implications of his "rebirth." My point is that short of these the novel offers no hope whatever. Melville's options, given his commitment to America, were either progress toward the millennium or regression toward doomsday. He simply could not envision a different set of ideals — an antinomian self-sufficiency, a non-American course of progress — beyond that which his culture imposed. When in *Pierre*, accordingly, he did press the paradox to its logical conclusion, he could only turn Ishmael's mode of ambiguity against itself, which is to say against all cultural norms, including the norms of rhetoric, will, and the mind. The dominant theme of his work from *Pierre* through "Bartleby the Scrivener" to *Billy Budd* is the mutual annihilation of horologicals and chronometricals.* Dur-

---

**Moby-Dick allows one lone witness to report the American apocalypse; *The Confidence Man* allows no witnesses at all; and *Clarel* extends the April-Fool's-Day voyage of the *Fidèle* into an errand backward across the Atlantic, through the wilderness of a once Holy Land, where Ungar, the American Jeremiah, is everything which the symbol of America is not: Southern, half-breed, a prophet of "class-war," bitterly anti-Protestant, anti-white, and anti-democratic. The mock-epithet for all of Melville's later heroes — from Pierre through Israel Potter (whose voyages lead from revolution to captivity to oblivion) to Billy Budd — might be taken from the Confidence Man's lecture to a critic of "free Ameriky": "'human government, being subordinate to the divine, must needs, therefore, in its degree, partake of the characteristics of the divine. That is, . . . to one who has a right confidence, final benignity is, in every instance, as sure with the one law as with the other'" (*The Confidence Man, His Masquerade*, ed. R. W. B. Lewis [New York, 1967], p. 105).

ing the Civil War, Melville may momentarily have regained some of his early faith. Brooding over "the world's fairest hope linked with man's foulest crime," he prayed that the country would "verify in the end those expectations which kindle the bards of Progress and Humanity." The utter bleakness of the anti-jeremiad, the sheer extremity of its doomsday vision, must have driven him to renew his hope at other times as well. But always the terms of renewal remained locked within the same symbolic structure: "world's fairest hope" or "man's foulest crime," American heaven or universal hell. Loren Baritz has commented that Melville's work became "so purely American because of the depths of his rejection of America."[17] It was through such rhetorical ambiguities, such endless, self-enclosed dualisms, that the American jeremiad succeeded as a ritual of socialization.

For finally the anti-jeremiad is not so much a rejection of the culture as it is a variation on a central cultural theme. Wherever it appears, from Cooper's *The Crater* and George Lippard's *The Quaker City* through Twain's *Connecticut Yankee*, it has served to confirm the cosmic import of the American Way. Perhaps the work that best illustrates the continuity of this genre is *The Education of Henry Adams*. At first glance, to be sure, Adams gives the opposite impression. He deals incisively with historical factors and seems to berate himself with an unrelenting masochistic tough-mindedness for his inability to adjust. In fact, however, he makes it clear that the problem lies not with himself but with reality. He insists on personal failure in order to demonstrate the failure of everything else. As student and educator, diplomat and historian, scientist and art connoisseur, Adams offers his futile education as a metaphor for a world without "absolute standards." He would have us believe that to be unprepared for "the surge of a supersensual chaos" — to feel "altogether alone," "suddenly cut apart" from a universe without "ultimate Unity" — shows the astuteness of his perceptions. His bewilderment is a function of his integrity. And what lends special poignancy to his bewilderment, he tells us, what makes "the question . . . personal," is "the word *America*."[18] In this context, his impassioned lament for the country's desecrated hopes almost becomes, like Mather's *Magnalia*, a massive, defiant vindication of his forebears' achievement.

But of course Adams's strategy reverses that of Cotton Mather. The affinities in this respect between the *Education* and the *Magnalia* stem from opposing applications of a common vision. Mather's work, like Sherwood's *Church's Flight into the Wilderness*, Arthur's July Fourth oration, and Schaff's *America*, dwells almost obsessively, to the point of deliberate distortion, upon the "vigorous unanimity" between fathers and sons of preceding generations. Adams places all emphasis on an America rushing toward self-destruction in an entropic inversion of the work of redemption. In the latter days, wrote Jonathan Edwards, God's purposes would "be fulfilled with ever-doubling acceleration by geometric enlargement of the saintly host." For Adams, the process of fulfillment leads downward with ever-doubling acceleration, through backsliding, betrayal, and "godless materialism," toward cataclysm and stasis. He dwells obsessively, virtually to the point of distortion, on the widening chasm between generations. The fathers' "really great and noble dream had become a good deal like a stampede of hogs to a trough." By 1870, "the American people had no idea at all; they were wandering in a wilderness much more sandy than the Hebrews had ever trodden about Sinai . . . [and] the American priest had lost sight of faith." Standing between the two worlds — the first of false illusions, the second of grim fact — Henry Adams keeps "repeating to himself the eternal question: — Why! Why!! Why!!!"[19] And he finds the answer, predictably, in the hastening apocalypse.

The distinctive quality of the *Education* is that it reverses all the effects of the jeremiad while retaining intact the jeremiad's figural-symbolic outlook. Adams is not a Victorian sage calling halt to a rampant industrial capitalism. He is a prophet reading the fate of humanity, and the universe at large, in the tragic course of American history. It is true that he never allows the reader to lose sight of the old faith, and that his condemnation of the Dynamo, accordingly, gains much of its substance from the counterforce of the national symbol. America is represented, for example, in the figure of his grandfather, the remote, majestic incarnation of "moral principle," or in Clarence King, "the ideal American," a "type and model . . . of what the American, as [Henry Adams] conceived, should have been and was not." But the calculated effect here is to emphasize what is not. To this end, Adams offers himself as chronometer, in a self-portrait which despite its many vivid personal touches evolves into something of a mythic representation of non-being. The protagonist of the *Education*, we learn in the Preface, is not an *"Ego"* but a *"manikin."* He is a pasteboard symbol, that is, standing for the great "inheritance with which [Adams] took his name," for the "pure New England stock" which had nourished the Adams dynasty, for the whole configuration of "ideal values" embodied in the Constitution (including those of the Puritan emigrants). That is why he must be, like his grandfather, "an estray," out of time and place, and, like King, must end a failure. The symbol he projects in himself deprives us of alternatives. One set of "real" clothes after another is discarded as useless, until we remain only with the manikin itself, a disqualified ideal that is nonetheless *"the only measure of . . . [the] human condition."* This "model," Adams insists, *"must . . . be taken for real; must be treated as though it had life,"* because we have nothing else.[20]

By comparison, Lear's "poor, bare, forked animal" is a consoling image. At least it situates man in time and history. Adams's manikin both prophesies the end and images that horror. Not a certain culture has failed, he tells us, but culture itself. "The moral law had expired — like the Constitution"; so, too, had every other hope that once duped mankind into a dream of progress. The "degradation of American democratic principles . . . [was] symptomatic of a massive dissipation of solar energy," of "mankind's physical and moral decay," and of the "inevitable cosmic decline [which] began on that instant the human race was inserted into the solar system." It is continuing revolution re-presented as the death urge, an errand into the abyss. By Adams's calculations, the process would be complete by about the year 1938. He ends the *Education* by imagining himself returned from the dead, in 1938, together with his friends Hay and King, to witness, perhaps, "for the first time since man began his education among the carnivores . . . a world that sensitive and timid natures could regard without a shudder." This is the humor of the anti-jeremiad, the sort of sick joke that abounds in *Pierre* and *The Confidence Man*. Adams calls it America's "vacant and meaningless derision over its own failure." Mark Twain calls it "the laughter of the grotesque," and it rings throughout his last works* — most

---

* Bernard De Voto calls these late works "Symbols of Despair." From a belief that "the American republic [was] perishing," he writes, Twain deduced the approach of "a general apocalypse" (Introduction to *The Portable Mark Twain* [New York, 1946],

memorably at the conclusion of *The Mysterious Stranger*, where Satan delivers an address which may be read, together with Adams's "summing-up," as the *terminus ad quem* of Danforth's *Errand into the Wilderness:*

". . . I, your poor servant, have revealed you to yourself, and set you free. Dream other dreams, and better!

"Strange! that you should not have suspected . . . that your universe and its contents were only dreams, visions, fictions! Strange, because they are so frankly and hysterically insane . . . a grotesque and foolish dream. Nothing exists but you. And you are but a *thought* — a vagrant thought, a useless thought, a homeless thought, wandering forlorn among the empty eternities!"

He vanished and left me appalled, for I knew and realized, that all he had said was true.[21]

Emerson's Scholar denounces the state of the nation while heralding a millennial future. Adams's manikin extols the national past while pointing steadily toward the cosmic void. They are equal and opposite expressions of the same symbol, antagonists in the same ritual drama, like the good and evil angels of the medieval psychomachy. And as I suggested earlier, the evil angels in our rituals, like Melville's Bartleby, Adams's manikin, and Twain's Satan, have also contributed toward the process of acculturation. In spite of themselves, our prophets of doom also helped persuade the American that the vision he inherited must be made to correspond to the fact. They too helped make him feel, if only out of desperation, that the distance between what is and what ought to be demanded his rededication to the spirit of America. Something of this reaction

---

pp. 23–24). This outlook informs many novels of the time including those of the "naturalists," and it underlies the *fin-de-siècle* flowering of utopian literature. Thus a primary text of Kenneth Roemer's *The Obsolete Necessity: America in Utopian Writings, 1888–1900* (Kent, Ohio, 1976) is Edward Bellamy's "Letter to the People's Party" (1892): "Let us bear in mind that, if it [America] will be a failure, it will be a final failure" (p. 3). In this case, as Roemer shows, the result was that virtually all utopian writers reaffirmed the cultural symbol. With Bellamy, they built their visions on a renovated United States which "would so amaze all nations that they would change their ways and imitate America" (p. 143). Significantly, however, they remained profoundly ambivalent, like Twain in *A Connecticut Yankee* — at once "distraught" and "enthralled" by American progress — so that their works served as "mirrors, not cures: they reflected more than they solved" (p. 6).

may underlie Thoreau's marked ambivalence toward the Westward movement, as well as his efforts, after *Walden*, to reconcile "simplicity and an economy of machinery and profit." Certainly, this determination not to surrender the dream, because the dream was the only option to despair, informs Whitman's work. "As America," he wrote, "is the legitimate result and evolutionary outcome of the past" — and as the Constitution is "the greatest piece of moral building ever constructed," a "Bible of the Free" for modern man, composed by "mighty prophets and gods" — "so I would dare to claim for my verse." But he could not avoid considering the possibility of self-deceit, "and if so," he noted, both America and his poetry would prove "the most tremendous failure of time," mutual victims of "a destiny . . . equivalent in its real world to that of the fabled damned."[22] He resolved his fears through the ambiguities of the American jeremiad.

Whitman's solution appears most directly in his towering state-of-the-covenant address of 1870, during what Adams termed the Neanderthal Grant Administration. *Democratic Vistas* has proved disappointing as political or social commentary because it is a work of symbolic interpretation. Its terms are doomsday or millennium, its text "the problem of the future of America." When Whitman considers the conditions actually prevailing in the country ("bribery, falsehood, maladministration") he can only conclude that "the lowering darkness falls . . . as if to last forever." By contrast with the "fervid and tremendous IDEA" of America, our "unprecedented materialistic advancement . . . [is] canker'd, crude . . . saturated in corruption." It threatens "to eat us up, like a cancer" — has already, indeed, shown "our New World democracy . . . [to be] an almost complete failure." *Almost complete*: considered as historical analysis, the qualification seems slight, even perfunctory. For Whitman, it serves as a rhetorical ploy, an ambiguity that elicits a total reversal of perspective. Shifting his focus from realities to "grandest results," he announces (from the "Pisgah heights of immortal prophecy") that America will triumph despite "all opposing proofs and precedents." It has the "certainty" of "unparallel'd success." Did not "the Almighty [Himself] . . . spread before this nation charts of imperial destinies, dazzling as the sun"? So the problem, it appears, is not the future after all, but only the gap between present and future; and

Whitman proceeds to resolve this through the figural-symbolic mode he inherited: "Though not for us [perhaps] the chance ever to see with our own eyes the peerless power and splendid *éclat* of the democratic principle, arriv'd at meridian, filling the world with effulgence and majesty . . . there is yet, to whoever is eligible among us, the prophetic vision."[23]

Poetically, of course, Whitman had sought to realize that vision long before. According to his 1855 Preface, the "I" of *Leaves of Grass* draws its "fullest poetical nature" from the inhabitants and geography of the United States. Modern critics have argued that Whitman's poetry works in precisely the opposite direction, that it transforms the world "by alienating it from itself and the crude, workaday, anti-poetic reality which characterizes it." We would do better, I think, to take him at his word. No doubt he seeks to protect the American ideal by abstracting it from the real America. But in this case, the ideal does not contradict the real (much less alienate the real from itself). "By indirections," and often directly enough, Whitman does contribute, as he says, toward sweeping "America's busy, teeming, intricate swirl . . . to the infinite future." His act of self-discovery does issue in a *"National Poem,"* as he insists, "for American purposes." Finally, his work serves to confirm the culture. As he points out summarily in *Democratic Vistas,* "the extreme business energy, and this almost maniacal appetite for wealth prevalent in the United States, are parts of amelioration and progress, indispensably needed to prepare the very results I demand. . . . My theory includes riches, and the amplest products, power, activity, inventions, movements, etc. Upon them, as upon substrata, I raise the edifice design'd in these Vistas."[24]

The theory had been propounded long before by the man Whitman called (for a time) his Master. "My estimate of America," Emerson confided in his journals, like "my estimate of my [own] means and resources, is all or nothing." Beyond America, *nothing*: it was the message of the jeremiad internalized, and made an avatar of the Self. And since Emerson refused to give up his "deep instinctive hope," since for him the Self "always affirms an Optimism, never a Pessimism," he gave *all* to America. Eventually, as Maurice Gonnaud has noted, he found in "the concept of national destiny the unifying factor, articulating the claims of power, morality, and universal change, for which he had been groping all along. Each individual found himself vicariously fulfilled in the present and future achievements of his community." It was a community of the spirit, a "Columbia of thought and act"; it was also, and with growing explicitness, a white Protestant consensus, joined together as one man in the Constitution — a community "growing like a cloud, towns on towns, States on States," where "wealth, always interesting, since from wealth power cannot be divorced, [was] piled in every form invented for comfort and pride." America, symbol and fact, was "a garden of plenty, . . . a magazine of power. . . . Here [was] man in the Garden of Eden; here the Genesis and the Exodus"; and' here was to be the Revelation. True, the prophecies remained yet to be fulfilled; but for Americans, after all, prophecy was history antedated:

> The American people are fast opening their own destiny. The material basis is of such extent that no folly of man can quite subvert it. Add, that this energetic race derive an unprecedented material power from the new arts, from . . . the railroad, steamship, steam-ferry, steam-mill. . . . Conceding [all] unfavorable appearances . . . we are persuaded [nonetheless] that moral and material values are always commensurate. Every material organization exists to a moral end, which makes the reason of its existence. . . . Certainly then . . . this freedom leads onward and upward. . . . Our whole history appears to be a last effort of Divine Providence in behalf of the human race.[25]

By 1860, Emerson had fewer qualms than even Whitman did about the Union cause. Though he had been slow to endorse the abolitionists, though he continued to believe in the inherent inferiority of blacks,* and though he had recently defended states'

---

*This is not to call into question Emerson's commitment to abolitionism and the Union cause, but to emphasize that his commitment was above all to a cultural consensus. He felt that "the black man . . . is created on a lower plain than the white" (James Eliot Cabot, *A Memoir of Ralph Waldo Emerson* [Boston, 1887], II, 429), so that no "candid person" could maintain "that the African race have occupied or do promise ever to occupy any very high place in the human family. . . . The Irish cannot; the American Indian cannot; the Chinese cannot. Before the energy of the Caucasion race all the other races have quailed and done obeisance" (*Journals*, II, 48, and XIII, 152). Such statements attest not only to Emerson's provinciality, but to the *mythic* limitations of his claims for representative individualism. The same might be said about most of our keepers of the dream. By the early twentieth century, for

rights against federal "centralism," Emerson never hesitated about the war itself. The South had betrayed the Revolution. It was "a country where . . . public debts and private debts outside of the States are repudiated, — where the arts, such as they have, are all imported . . . — where the laborer is not secured in the earnings of his own hands" — a country, in short, "not civil but barbarous." Destiny left the North no choice in the matter. "We must . . . redeem America for all its sinful years since the century began." Translating the logic of consensus into the laws of reason, Emerson declared that the war was simply the "human means through which nature crushed the effort to nullify its decree." It was "not a question whether we shall be a nation . . . but whether we shall be the new nation, the leading Guide and Lawgiver of the world." The Emancipation Proclamation confirmed his belief that "A new day which most of us dared not hope to see . . . seems now to be close before us." And in 1863, the year of Lincoln's fast-day declaration, Emerson issued the Transcendentalist counterstatement to the anguished ambivalence of Melville's *Battle Pieces*. "The Fortune of the Republic" is a summons to continuing revolution that joins New England's errand, the Great Awakening, the War of Independence, and the Civil War, through the typology of America's mission. As we might expect, the tone is one of ritual anxiety. Apocalyptic tremors signal the community's rite of passage. America, Emerson declares, is "just passing through a great crisis in its history, as necessary as . . . puberty to the human individual. We are in these days settling for ourselves and our descendants questions which, as they shall be determined in one way or the other, will make the peace and prosperity or the calamity of the next ages."[26]

Prosperity or calamity: the social purpose of the anxiety is no less transparent here than it was in William Arthur's oration thirteen years earlier. "Calamity" closes all options but the way to prosperity; "prosperity" closes all options but that of constant progress, where

---

example, the Irish had joined the consensus; and Isadora Duncan, a self-proclaimed descendant of the Transcendentalists, defined her "Vision of America dancing" ("a new great vision of life that would express America") in contradistinction to the Greeks, "the Redskins," and the "sensual convulsion of the Negro." "This rhythm of America" she explained "is too mighty for the ears of most" (*My Life* [New York, 1927], pp. 240–43).

the condition of progress is instant conformity to an America in transition; and the meaning of transition, finally, precludes the prospect of failure. Not all revolutions and wars, Emerson explains, lead to progress. For example, those made "in the interest of feudalism" have always degenerated into "barbarism." But the American Revolution marks "the culmination of the triumphs of humanity," from the Hebrew exodus through the Reformation to "the planting of America." Thus the

> Faults in the working . . . in our system suggest their own remedies. After every practical mistake [such as slavery] out of which any disaster grows, the people wake and correct it with energy. Nature works in immense time, and spends individuals and races prodigally to prepare new individuals and races. The lower kinds [like the native Indians] are one after one extinguished; the higher forms come in. Here is practical democracy; here is the human race poured out over the continent to do itself justice. The people are law-abiding. They have no taste for misrule and uproar. As the globe keeps its identity by perpetual change, so our civil system, by perpetual appeal to the people.
>
> The revolution is the work of no man, but the external effervescence of Nature. It never did not work. Never country had such a fortune, as this, in its geography, its history, and in its majestic possibilities. They [who] complain of the flatness of American life have no perception of its destiny. They are not Americans. Let us realize that this country, the last found, is the great charity of God to the human race.[27]*

It has been said that "The Fortune of the Republic" is part of Emerson's capitulation to the system. No doubt it shows a relaxation of standards, an indiscriminate admiration for manifest destiny, "our race," the "social unities embodied in the state," and the "order shaped by history" as this expressed itself in the burgeoning civic

---

*This reconciliation of national interest and international beneficence in a world of free trade is an important function of America as symbol. Melville's often-quoted panegyric, written some fifteen years earlier — "with ourselves, almost for the first time in the history of earth, national selfishness is unbounded philanthropy; for we cannot do a good to America but we give alms to the world" (White-Jacket; or, The World in a Man-of-War, ed. Hennig Cohen [New York, 1967], p. 150) — was a cliché of the times. Compare further the closing pages of Melville's novel with the image of the American ark in Emerson's "Lecture on the Times" and "The Fortune of the Republic" (Works, I, 287–88, and XI, 543). As I noted earlier, with respect to David Austin and William Arthur, that image was also a cultural cliché.

institutions of God's Country.[28] But in all this Emerson's address marks a change of emphasis rather than a betrayal of principle. And if the change seems to weaken his earlier, imperial assertions of selfhood, it also lays bare the basis on which he managed to sustain his faith for over forty years in the spirit of America. The individual, Emerson explains, must fulfill himself and yet represent the consensus — the "appeal to the people" is "perpetual," and yet "the revolution is the work of no man" — because *individualism*, *the people*, and *revolution*, considered in their highest aspect, political and spiritual, correspond to America. In "The American Scholar" (1837), the major address of his early career, Emerson had hoped to arouse "the sluggard intellect of this continent"; he concluded, accordingly, by predicting the time when a "nation of men will for the first time exist." Now in 1863, speaking as America's scholar laureate, Emerson was sure that "America is no log or sluggard" but "a nation of individuals. . . . I do not think we shall by any perverse ingenuity prevent the blessing." And in what may be taken as the motto of this discourse — one which he kept repeating through the remaining fifteen years of his public life, adapting it to a variety of occasions, including his Farewell Sermon (1878) at the Old South Church of the Mathers — he urged his countrymen: "We must realize our rhetoric and our rituals."[29]

In one way or another, the rhetoric and ritual of "The Fortune of the Republic" inform most of the great works of the American Renaissance. To be American for our classic writers was by definition to be radical — to turn against the past, to defy the status quo and become an agent of change. And at the same time to be radical as an American was to transmute the revolutionary impulse in some basic sense: by spiritualizing it (as in *Walden*), by diffusing or deflecting it (as in *Leaves of Grass*), by translating it into a choice between blasphemy and regeneration (as in *Moby-Dick*), or most generally by accommodating it to society (as in "The Fortune of the Republic"). In every case, "America" resolved a conflict of values by reconciling personal, national, and cultural ideals. Sometimes, of course, as with Whitman and Thoreau, the reconciliation had no immediate public effect — or rather the effect was belated, the product of a slow process of cultural absorption. But that process, I would argue, followed from, rather than belied, the content of the work. In every case, the defiant act that might have posed fundamental social alternatives became instead a fundamental force against social change.*

*This is conspicuously true of the anti-jeremiad, as I noted before in discussing Melville's later writing. Consider the tenacity of belief (however wistfully or laconically expressed) in twentieth-century American writing — for example, in our major novels from Fitzgerald's *Great Gatsby* through Dos Passos's *USA* and Pynchon's *Gravity's Rainbow*; or the social protest poems of the Beats and Hippies, those self-proclaimed Children of Whitman caustically "waiting / for them to prove / that God is really American" (Lawrence Ferlinghetti, *A Coney Island of the Mind* [Norfolk, 1955], p. 49); or again, the student manifestos of the late 1960s, denouncing the nation "in the name of the promise of America" (Dotson Rader, *I Ain't Marchin' Anymore* [New York, 1969], p. 6). As Greil Marcus writes in his study of rock-'n'-roll music, "America is a trap: its promises and dreams . . . are too much to live up to and too much to escape" (*Mystery Train: The Image of America in Rock 'N' Roll* [New York, 1975], p. 22). Most vividly, in our time, this self-enclosed bipolar vision finds expression in *The Armies of the Night*, Norman Mailer's "diary-essay-tract-sermon" about his "love affair with America." What he remembers and seeks, he tells us, is "the land . . . of magnificence unparalleled." What he finds instead is "a beauty with leprous skin," disfigured by madness. His "mythic plaint" returns us by various routes back through Whitman and Adams to seventeenth-century New England: "Brood on that country that expresses our will. She is America, . . . heavy with child. . . . Now the first contractions of her fearsome labor begin. . . . Rush to the locks, God writhes in his bonds" (*The Armies of the Night: History as the Novel, the Novel as History* [New York, 1968], pp. 172, 288). I mention these "counter-culture" examples to emphasize the ritual efficacy of the myth. In a recent essay, Victor Turner observes that post-industrial rituals are characteristically subversive of social order. Tribal rituals, he points out, are intrinsic to the "work" of perpetuating the culture; there, liminality tends to sustain the status quo. Modern rituals, on the contrary, are characteristically centripetal and diverse; here, liminality is an after-work (and sometimes an anti-work) form of "play" which may become a source of basic radical protest. As expressions of a heterogeneous, individualistic culture, such "liminoid phenomena" may take the form of "social critiques or even revolutionary manifestoes — books, plays, paintings, films, etc., exposing the injustices, inefficiencies, and immoralities of the mainstream economic and political structures and organizations" ("Liminal to Liminoid, in Play, Flow, and Ritual: An Essay in Comparative Symbology," *Rice University Studies*, 60 [1974], 86). I would suggest that one reason for this (alongside those which Turner outlines) is the problematic meaning of "mainstream" in modern society, due to the confluence within the mainstream of earlier modes of organization and belief. In post-industrial countries the tension between social structures and social ideals has usually been mediated by competing systems of values. And especially in the realm of "high culture," the subversive process of which Turner speaks has proceeded dialectically, through symbolic "play" between mediating and mainstream values. In this country, the *unmediated* relation between

Whether the writer focused on the individual or on history, whether he sought to vindicate society or to ingest society into the self, the radical energies he celebrated served to sustain the culture, because the same ideal that released those energies transformed radicalism itself into a mode of cultural cohesion and continuity.

In the preceding chapter I suggested the ideological advantages of this outlook. In this chapter I have tried to indicate briefly how this outlook is expressed, through the symbol of America, in the work of the self-proclaimed isolatoes who formed our literary tradition. Of these, Hawthorne was the most resistant to the symbol. By temperament he was not a Jeremiah. He was too much of an ironist to adopt outright the Puritan mode of ambiguity, too good a historian wholly to espouse the American teleology, too concerned with personal relations to entertain the claims of the American self. Yet he was too much a part of his time and place to remain unaffected. His lifelong struggle with the typology of mission is a measure both of his own integrity and of the power of the myth. That struggle has not yet been adequately described. But its intensity is implicit in the controversies that characterize Hawthorne scholarship — concerning his views of the Puritans, the Revolution, and the country at large. Did he believe that "the nation had betrayed its promise," or that it was growing towards "a millennium . . . of Christian love"? And if his views changed after 1850, as most critics agree, what new direction did he take? Was he increasingly disillusioned (sickened eventually just "to look back to America," as being a country "not fit to live in"), or did he come "to accept uncritically" that "the Future was America's"? [30]

The controversies reflect Hawthorne's own irresolution. The tensions in his early stories expand rather than resolve themselves in his novels, and the process of expansion attests not only to his capacity to live in doubt, as Melville and Emerson could not, but to his inability to escape the cultural categories which those tensions expressed. Whether or not, as Hugo McPherson argues, *The House of the Seven Gables* and *The Blithedale Romance* are versions of the national myth, the novels clearly center on the meaning of American

---

social structure and social ideal has made the very exposure of social flaws part of a ritual of socialization — a sort of liminal interior dialogue that in effect reinforces the mainstream culture.

progress. Whether or not, as Leo Levy says, *The Marble Faun* presents America as the new promised land, Hawthorne at least flirts here with a figural-symbolic view of history. Despite his dissent from the Northern cause, his views have remarkable affinities with those of Emerson and Whitman. The abolitionists, he argues in his biography of Franklin Pierce, are bent upon "tearing to pieces the Constitution" and "severing into distracted fragments that common country which Providence brought into one nation, through a continued miracle of almost two hundred years, from the first settlement of the American wilderness until the Revolution." He urged them to adopt a different course of action — to consider "slavery as one of those evils which divine Providence" will settle "in its own good time . . . when all of its uses shall have been fulfilled." The figural uses of slavery! But there is no reason to think that Hawthorne was insincere, or that what he meant by "divine Providence" differed significantly from Emerson's "fortune of the republic," or that the consensus he believed in was not the same one that Whitman invoked in his Civil War poems. In *The Ancestral Footstep*, Hawthorne's last, abortive romance, the hero speaks with the fervor of Aristabulus Bragg about the democratic vistas ahead: "press on to higher and better things. . . . Onward, onward, onward!"[31]

Often enough, we know, Hawthorne ridiculed this view; but he could not let it alone. It was as though he felt that for all the delusions of American progressivism, no other mode of progress was available. This is the moral, I think, of the contrast he repeatedly makes between rebellion and revolution: between Miriam's blasphemous urge to overcome the past, for example, and Hilda's flight from the deprivations of Europe; or earlier, between Holgrave the anarchist, who wants to tear up society — sever it into distracted fragments — and Holgrave the hero, who joins the consensus, marries a daughter of the Puritans, and transforms class-conscious radicalism into suburban self-improvement. Most strikingly and complexly, the contrast appears in the two images, antinomian and American, of Hester Prynne. The American Hester (if I may call her so) sounds much like the Hawthorne of the Pierce biography. "Patience," she counsels the injured and insulted women who seek her advice: "at some brighter period, when the world shall have grown ripe for it, in Heaven's own time," the "revelation" will set things right. She speaks this sadly, remembering that once, be-witched by antinomianism, she "vainly imagined that she herself might be the destined prophetess."[32] Nonetheless, her vision is a hopeful one — or as hopeful as we can expect from a rebel who has become an agent of socialization. She discovered that her love did indeed have a consecration *of its own*, but that Puritan society had the consecration of the Lord of history. Now, having abandoned all personal and social alternatives — having come home to America — she can at last allow the scarlet letter to perform its ritual office, molding her dream of love to an indefinite rite of passage that confirms the national future.

I am not forgetting the ambiguities that permeate the scene. What I would suggest is that they may be part of a distinctive social-sym-bolic outlook. *The Scarlet Letter*, we recall, opens with a long, acerbic, and very troubled preface about Jacksonian America; the narrative itself begins, like a tribal rite, with a description of the country's origins ("a new colony" projecting a "Utopia of human virtue and hap-piness"); and in the penultimate scene, Hester seeks to reconcile the conflicts between self and society, love and justice, by anticipating a New World Eden to be. The movement is remarkably similar to that of the jeremiad. And like the jeremiad, it turns our attention to what Whitman called "the problem of the future of America." For if Hawthorne looks back (in the "Introductory") to Puritan times, Hes-ter looks forward (in the "Conclusion") to the age of Jackson; and though Hawthorne leaves us with the problem, rather than with the future, nonetheless the process of fulfillment may be implicit in the development from theocracy to democracy. It is a rather question-able development, as the "Introductory" makes plain. Yet we are offered some basis for hope in the novel's climactic episode — the most vivid rendering we have of the Puritan ritual of the jeremiad — and particularly in the chapter entitled "The Revelation of the Scar-let Letter," which records the effect of Dimmesdale's election-day address, delivered (like Samuel Danforth's *Errand into the Wilderness*) before Governor Richard Bellingham. Dimmesdale's subject, we learn, is

the relation between the Deity and the communities of mankind, with a special reference to the New England which they were here planting in the wilderness. And as he drew to a close, a spirit as of prophecy had

come upon him, constraining him to its purpose as mightily as the old
prophets of Israel were constrained; only with this difference, that,
whereas the Jewish seers had denounced judgments and ruin on their
country, it was his mission to foretell a high and glorious destiny for the
newly gathered people of the Lord. But throughout it all, and through
the whole discourse, there had been a certain deep, sad undercurrent of
pathos, which could not be interpreted otherwise than as the natural
regret of one soon to pass away.[33]

The passage is shot through with ironies. Arthur Dimmesdale's
vision is much like William Arthur's, in *his* "patriotic and eloquent
address" of 1850 (the year of *The Scarlet Letter*); but Hawthorne hints
that Dimmesdale's "spirit of prophecy" may be as deceptive as Hester's vision in the forest.* The colonists interpret the occasion as
Arthur does the Fourth of July — "a good spirit commissioned of
high heaven . . . reviewing the past, reciting the present, and revealing the future" — but Hawthorne remarks that they may be reading into their minister's speech and bearing only what they want to
hear and see. That possibility has been commented on often enough.
It may be, however, that its sheer bleakness is meant to lead us to
consider a different alternative. After all, the same force that con-
strains Dimmesdale also enables him (for once) to break free of his
own dilemma; and besides, what the colonists see is substantially accurate: their minister *is* about to die. In this sense Dimmesdale stands
before them as another Moses on Pisgah, overlooking the promised
land that he will never enter. They do not yet know of the sin that
bars him from New Canaan; some of them will never know, others

---

*Michael Bell notes that, in an "ironic sense," Dimmesdale's sermon "might bear
some relation to . . . Daniel Webster's first great assertion of the glorious future of
the Republic . . . on the occasion of the deaths of Adams and Jefferson" (*Hawthorne
and the Historical Romance of New England* [Princeton, N. J., 1971], pp. 143–44). Hester's vision might similarly bear some ironic relation to various Transcendentalist
paeans to the future — for example, to the "Ideal person" described by Bronson
Alcott: "She must have retained the purity, the innocence, the spirituality, the humble wisdom and seraphic love of infancy, and, at the same time, have suffered the
trials of terrestrial existence, to bring forth and render hardy and vigorous the virtues
of fortitude, self-dependence, self-control. An Angel is, indeed, wanted" ("Observations on the Spiritual Nurture of My Children" [MS], quoted in Bruce Ronda, "The
Transcendental Child: Images and Concepts of the Child in American Tran-
scendentalism," Diss. Yale 1975, p. 111). In neither Dimmesdale's case nor Hester's,
however, does the irony undermine the symbolic configuration I speak of.

will know but hide it from themselves, and still others will know and rejoice, believing with Hester (and their Jeremiahs) that affliction and promise are entwined in New England's "high and glorious destiny." But during the sermon itself all of them would surely recall the "prophetical song" that Moses delivered at Pisgah just before his death, containing the covenant of the work of redemption, with special reference (their ministers had often told them) to their own errand into the wilderness:

> Now . . . all these things shal come upon thee, *ether* the blessing or the curse [or "both the blessing and the curse," A.V.] which I have set before thee. . . .
> And the Lord thy God wil bring thee into the land which thy fathers possessed, and thou shalt possesse it, and he wil shewe thee favour, and wil multiplie thee above thy fathers. (Deuteronomic 30:1,5)

Surely, too, some of the colonists would recall that John Winthrop had used that text to conclude his lay sermon aboard the *Arbella* in 1630. Now, nineteen years later, Winthrop was dead, widely mourned as the Moses of the new chosen people, and Dimmesdale's election-day address was serving as the rite of passage to a new administration. In the novel's central chapter, Hawthorne tells us that at Winthrop's death, in March 1649, a meteor had flashed across the midnight sky, with "the appearance of an immense letter, — the letter A, — marked out in lines of dull red light." To Dimmesdale it seemed an emblem of his sin; to the community, a sign for "Angel," in honor of Winthrop's ascent to heaven. Hawthorne himself remarks of the "red letter in the sky" that "it seemed to give another moral interpretation to the things of this world than they had ever borne before . . . as if it were the light that is to reveal all secrets and the daybreak that shall unite all who belong to one another."[34] On all these levels of seeming, the incident foreshadows the message of Dimmesdale's jeremiad. And on all these levels, too, Dimmesdale's jeremiad ambiguously illuminates the long tradition that begins at the absolute Greenwich time of the Great Migration — with the chronometer carried from Babylon to the ends of the earth — that last and greatest of human dreams which launched the *Arbella*:

> Also I wil appoint a place for my people Israel, and wil plant it, that they may dwel in a place of their owne, and move nomore. . . .

I wilbe his father, & he shalbe my sonne: & if he sinne, I wil chasten him with the rod of men, and with the plagues of the children of men.

But my mercy shal not departe away from him, as I toke it from Saul whome I have put away before thee.

And thine house shalbe stablished and thy kingdome for ever before thee, *even* thy throne shalbe stablished for ever,

According to all these wordes, and according to all this vision. . . . (2 Samuel 7:10, 14–17)

NOTES
INDEX

Notes

CHAPTER 1   Introduction: The Puritan Errand Reassessed

1 John Winthrop, *A Model of Christian Charity* (1630), in *Puritan Political Ideas, 1558–1794*, ed. Edmund S. Morgan (New York, 1965), pp. 90–91.
2 John Cotton, *Gods Promise to His Plantations* (London, 1630), in *Old South Leaflets* (Boston, [1896]), Vol. III, no. 53, pp. 4, 13.
3 Perry Miller, "Errand into the Wilderness," in *Errand into the Wilderness* (Cambridge, Mass., 1958), pp. 8, 15.
4 Thomas Shepard, *Election Sermon* (1638), in *New England Historical and Genealogical Register*, 24 (1870), 363, and *The Parable of the Ten Virgins* (1636–40), ed. Jonathan Mitchel and Thomas Shepard, Jr. (London, 1660), Pt. II, p. 5; Increase Mather, Preface to Eleazar Mather, *A Serious Exhortation* (Cambridge, Mass., 1671), sigs. A2ᵛ–A3; Increase Mather, *An Earnest Exhortation* (Cambridge, Mass., 1678), p. 23.
5 Perry Miller, *The New England Mind: From Colony to Province* (1953; rpt. Boston, 1961), p. 29.
6 Hannah More, letter to Mrs. Boscawen, in William Roberts, *Memoirs of the Life and Correspondence of Mrs. Hannah More* (London, 1835), I, 186; Samuel Willard, *Useful Instructions* (Cambridge, Mass., 1673), p. 12.
7 Winthrop, *Model*, pp. 90–91; Cotton, *Gods Promise*, p. 3; Loren Baritz, *City on a Hill: A History of Ideas and Myths in America* (New York, 1964), p. 31; Jesper Rosenmeier, "VERITAS: The Sealing of the Promise," *Harvard Library Bulletin*, 16 (1968), 33.
8 Miller, "Errand," pp. 8–9.
9 Samuel Danforth, *A Brief Recognition of New England's Errand into the Wilderness* (1670), in *The Wall and the Garden: Selected Massachusetts Election Sermons*, ed. A. William Plumstead (Minneapolis, 1968), p. 57.
10 Ibid., pp. 60, 62.
11 Nicholas Noyes, *New-Englands Duty* (Boston, 1698), p. 43.
12 Danforth, *Brief Recognition*, pp. 75–77, 64–65.
13 Alexis de Tocqueville, *Democracy in America*, ed. J. P. Mayer, trans. George Lawrence (Garden City, N. Y., 1969), pp. 34–35, 56, 279.

14 Douglass C. North and Robert Paul Thomas, eds., *The Growth of the American Economy* (New York, 1968), p. 5; Ralph Barton Perry, *Puritanism and Democracy* (New York, 1944), p. 297; Robert E. Brown, *Middle-Class Democracy and the Revolution in Massachusetts, 1691–1780* (Ithaca, N. Y., 1955), p. 82.

15 Cotton, *Gods Promise*, p. 5 (see also p. 14).

16 Cotton Mather, "Biblia Americana," quoted in Cheryl Rivers, "Cotton Mather and the Traditions of Puritan Scholarship," Diss. Columbia 1976, pp. 86–87; Danforth, *Brief Recognition*, pp. 59, 72; John G. Cawelti, *Apostles of the Self-Made Man* (Chicago, 1965), p. 4.

17 Christopher Hill, *The Century of Revolution: 1603–1714* (Edinburgh, 1961), p. 97; Emery Battis, *Saints and Sectaries: Ann Hutchinson and the Antinomian Controversy in the Massachusetts Bay Colony* (Chapel Hill, N. C., 1962), p. 255; Edmund S Morgan, "The Revolutionary Era as an Age of Politics," in *The Role of Ideology in the American Revolution*, ed. John R. Howe, Jr. (New York, 1970), p. 11.

18 Victor Turner, *The Forest of Symbols* (Ithaca, N. Y., 1967).

19 Johan Huizinga, *America*, trans. Robert H. Rowen (New York, 1972), pp. 8–9; Larzer Ziff, *Puritanism in America: New Culture in a New World* (New York, 1973), pp. 189–90 (citing Bellingham and the committee report).

20 Miller, *Colony to Province*, p. 400.

21 Herman Melville, *Pierre; or, The Ambiguities*, ed. Harrison Hayford, Herschel Parker, and G. Thomas Tanselle (Evanston, Ill., 1971), pp. 33, 13, 211–13.

22 Perry Miller, *The New England Mind: The Seventeenth Century* (1939; rpt. Boston, 1961), p. 462.

23 Melville, *Pierre*, pp. 214, 211–12.

CHAPTER 2   The Blessings of Time and Eternity

1 Alan Charity, *Events and Their Afterlife: The Dialectics of Christian Typology in the Bible and Dante* (Cambridge, 1966), pp. 32–33 (see further pp. 75–76, 78–79).

2 Clement Cotton, Dedication to John Calvin, *Two and Twenty Lectures Upon Jeremiah* (London, 1620), sigs. A2–A2ᵛ; John Cotton, *The Covenant of Grace* (London, 1655), p. 40, and *A Treatise of Grace* (London, 1659), p. 18 (see also pp. 19–21).

3 Andrew Willet, *Hexapla* (London, 1620), p. 3 (paraphrasing Calvin); John Calvin, *Commentaries on the Prophet Jeremiah*, trans. and ed. John Owen (Grand Rapids, Mich., 1950), IV, 127.

4 Martin Luther, "Preface to the Prophet Jeremiah," in *Works*, ed. Henry

Eyster Jacobs and Adolph Spaeth (Philadelphia, 1915–32), VI, 409–10 (see also pp. 488–89); George Joye, Preface to *Jeremy* (Antwerp, 1534), sig. A^v (citing Luther).

5 John Milton, *Areopagitica* (1644), ed. William Haller, in *Works*, ed. Frank Allen Patterson (New York, 1931), IV, 341; John Bale, *The Image of Both Churches* (1548), in *Select Works*, ed. Henry Christmas (Cambridge, 1849), p. 252 (see also pp. 410 ff.); Thomas Beard, *The Theatre of Gods Judgements* (London, 1597), p. 460; Thomas Fuller, *The Church History of Britain*, ed. J. S. Brewer (Oxford, 1845), I, 7, 2 (Dedication).

6 Robert Dowglas, *A Phenix; or, The Solemn League and Covenant* (Edinburgh, [1662]); pp. 38–39, 3; Joseph Mede, *Works*, ed. John Worthington (London, 1677), p. 370; Herschel Baker, *The Race of Time: Three Lectures on Renaissance Historiography* (Toronto, 1967), p. 38 (citing various Renaissance historians).

7 Heinrich Bullinger, *A Hundred Sermons Uppon the Apocalipse*, trans. John Dawes (London, 1573), p. 32; John Canne, *A Necessity of Separation* (1634), ed. Charles Stead (London, 1849), p. 194; John Robinson, *A Justification of Separation* (1610), in *Works*, ed. Robert Ashton (London, 1851), II, 304, 311, 473.

8 Robinson, *Justification*, in *Works*, II, 116, 126–27.

9 William Haller, *The Elect Nation: The Meaning and the Relevance of Foxe's "Book of Martyrs"* (New York, 1963), p. 109; Thomas Shepard and John Allin, *A Defence of the Answer* (London, 1648), p. 8; Joy B. Gilsdorf, "The Puritan Apocalypse: New England Eschatology in the Seventeenth Century," Diss. Yale, 1964, pp. 120, 133 (citing Hooker); John Winthrop, letter of May 15, 1629, quoted in Peter N. Carroll, *Puritanism and the Wilderness: The Intellectual Significance of the New England Frontier, 1629–1700* (New York, 1969), p. 19; John Winthrop, "Conclusions" (1629), in *Old South Leaflets* (Boston, [1896]), Vol. II, no. 60, pp. 3–4, 6.

10 Richard Mather, *An Apologie of the Churches in New-England* (London, 1643), p. 12; John Milton, *Of Reformation*, ed. Harry M. Ayres, in *Works*, ed. Patterson, III, 4; Robinson, *Justification*, in *Works*, II, 134; John Cotton, *Gods Promise to His Plantations*, in *Old South Leaflets* (Boston, [1896]), Vol. III, no. 53, p. 15; John Winthrop, *A Model of Christian Charity* (1630), in *Puritan Political Ideas, 1558–1794*, ed. Edmund S. Morgan (New York, 1965), pp. 87, 93.

11 Nathaniel Ward, *The Simple Cobler of Aggawam in America* (1647), ed. R. M. Zall (Lincoln, Neb., 1969), p. 6.

12 Roger Williams, *Complete Writings*, ed. Perry Miller (New York, 1963), IV, 403, 181; I, 76; III, 322.

13 John Cotton, *The Bloody Tenent, Washed* (London, 1647), pp. 68, 126 (see also pp. 61–64).

14 Cotton Mather, quoted in Mason I. Lowance, "Typology and the New England Way: Cotton Mather and the Exegesis of Biblical Types," *Early American Literature*, 4 (1969), 30–31; Jonathan Mitchel, *Nehemiah on the Wall* (Cambridge, Mass., 1671), p. 9; Nicholas Noyes, *New-Englands Duty* (Boston, 1698), p. 43; William Adams, *Gods Eye on the Contrite* (Cambridge, Mass., 1685), p. 1; Urian Oakes, *New England Pleaded With* (Cambridge, Mass., 1673), p. 19.

15 Larzer Ziff, "The Social Bond of Church Covenant," *American Quarterly*, 10 (1958), 455–62; Edmund S. Morgan, *Visible Saints: The History of a Puritan Idea* (New York, 1963), pp. 83 ff.; R. Mather, *Apologie*, pp. 26, 6; Peter Bulkeley, *The Gospel-Covenant* (London, 1651), p. 39.

16 Samuel Hudson, *The Essence and Unitie of the Church* (London, 1645), p. 7; Geoffrey F. Nuttall, *Visible Saints: The Congregational Way, 1640–1660* (Oxford, 1957), p. 69 (citing Owen); Perry Miller, *The New England Mind: From Colony to Province* (1953; rpt. Boston, 1961), p. 70; John Cotton, *A Sermon Delivered at Salem* (1646), in *John Cotton on the Churches of New England*, ed. Larzer Ziff (Cambridge, Mass., 1968), pp. 44–45, 55–56 (ellipses deleted); R. Mather, *Apologie*, pp. 1–3 (ellipses deleted).

17 William Hooke, *New-Englands Sence* (London, 1645), p. 23.

18 Edward Winslow, *Good Newes from New-England* (1624), in Alexander Young, ed., *Chronicles of the Pilgrim Fathers* (Boston, 1841), p. 372.

19 John Higginson, *The Cause of God* (Cambridge, Mass., 1663), p. 10.

20 John Davenport, *A Sermon Preached at the Election* (Cambridge, Mass., 1669), p. 16; Richard Mather and William Tompson, *An Heart-Melting Exhortation* (London, 1650), p. 7.

21 Norman Pettit, *The Heart Prepared: Grace and Conversion in Puritan Spiritual Life* (New Haven, 1966), pp. 19, 219.

22 Bulkeley, *Gospel-Covenant*, pp. 17, 35, 361 (see also pp. 314–15, 326–27).

23 Bulkeley, *Gospel-Covenant*, p. 105; Cotton, *Covenant of Grace*, pp. 48, 100; Bulkeley, *Gospel-Covenant*, pp. 29–30 (see also pp. 75, 102, 325, 373, 390, 411); Thomas Hooker, *The Saitns* [sic] *Dignitie* (London, 1651), p. 38.

24 Ziff, Introduction to *Cotton on the Churches*, ed. Ziff, p. 28; Edmund S. Morgan, *The Puritan Family: Essays in Religion and Domestic Relations in Seventeenth-Century New England* (Boston, 1944), pp. 90, 94; Bulkeley, *Gospel-Covenant*, pp. 276, 279, 281 (ellipses deleted).

25 Thomas Shepard, *The Sincere Convert* (London, 1669), p. 110; John Cotton, *Gods Mercie Mixed with His Justice* (1641), ed. Everett H. Emerson (Gainesville, 1958), p. 17; Bulkeley, *Gospel-Covenant*, p. 75.

26 William Stoughton, *New-Englands True Interest* (Cambridge, Mass., 1670), pp. 16–17.

27 Richard Mather, *A Farewel Exhortation* (Cambridge, Mass., 1657), p. 23;

Increase Mather, *David Serving His Generation* (Boston, 1698), p. 22; Cotton Mather, *Wonders of the Invisible World* (Boston, 1693), p. 9, and *A Pillar of Gratitude* (Boston, 1700), pp. 13–14.

28 R. Mather, *Farewel-Exhortation*, p. 23; Increase Mather, Preface to Samuel Torrey, *An Exhortation unto Reformation* (Cambridge, Mass., 1674), sig. A2ᵛ; Oakes, *New-England Pleaded With*, pp. 13, 27; Samuel Whiting, *The Way of Israel's Welfare* (Boston, 1686), p. 7; John Oxenbridge, *New-England Freemen* (Boston, 1673), p. 18; John Norton, *The Evangelical Worshipper* (1663), in *Three Choice and Profitable Sermons* (Boston, 1669), p. 35; Samuel Torrey, *A Plea For the Life of Dying Religion* (Boston, 1683), pp. 43–44.

29 Torrey, *Plea*, p. 42; John Wilson, *A Seasonable Watch-Word* (Cambridge, Mass., 1677), p. 9; Miller, *Colony to Province*, p. 33; Stoughton, *New-Englands True Interest*, p. 27; Samuel Hooker, *Righteousness Rained from Heaven* (Hartford, 1677), p. 17; Cotton Mather, *The Everlasting Gospel* (Boston, 1700), pp. 71–72; William Williams, *The Great Salvation* (Boston, 1717), pp. v, 1.

30 Cotton Mather, *The Serviceable Man* (Boston, 1690), pp. 13–14, and *Things to Be Look'd For* (Cambridge, Mass., 1691), pp. 57, 59–60; Thomas Shepard, Preface to Samuel Danforth, *A Brief Recognition of New Englands Errand* (Cambridge, Mass., 1671), sig. A2; Mitchel, *Nehemiah*, pp. 25, 33; Torrey, *Plea*, pp. 28, 40–41 (ellipses deleted).

31 Higginson, *Cause of God*, p. 24; William Hubbard, *The Happiness of a People* (Boston, 1676), p. 53; John Davenport, *Gods Call* (Cambridge, Mass., 1669), pp. 24, 27.

32 Torrey, *Plea*, pp. 42–45; Samuel Willard, *The Checkered State of the Gospel Church* (Boston, 1701), p. 193; Oxenbridge, *New-England Freemen*, pp. 19, 47; Whiting, *Way of Israel's Welfare*, p. 16; Urian Oakes, Preface to Increase Mather, *The Day of Trouble Is Near* (Cambridge, Mass., 1674), sigs. A1–A1ᵛ.

33 Gurdon Saltonstall, *A Sermon before the Assembly* (Boston, 1697), p. 55; Hubbard, *Happiness*, p. 60; Samuel Wakeman, *Sound Repentance* (Hartford, 1685), p. 11; Thomas Thacher, Preface to Thomas Shepard, *Eye-Salve* (Cambridge, Mass., 1673), sig. A2ᵛ; Increase Mather, *Ichabod* (Boston, 1701), pp. 83–84.

34 Bale, *Image*, p. 295; Increase Mather, *The Times of Man* (Boston, 1675), pp. 16, 19–20; John Sherman and Thomas Shepard, Jr., Preface to Oakes, *New-England Pleaded With*, sig. A2.

35 John Norton, *The Heart of N-England Rent* (Cambridge, Mass., 1659), p. 5.

36 Cotton, *Covenant of Grace*, p. 102; Thomas Hooker, *The Soules Preparation*

for Christ (London, 1638), pp. 131–32 (see also John Norton, *The Believers Consolation*, in *Three Choice Sermons*, p. 26); C. Mather, *Things to Be Look'd for*, p. 25 (see also Hubbard, *Happiness*, pp. 59–60, and Stoughton, *New-Englands True Interest*, p. 19).

37 Cotton Mather, *Things for a Distressed People to Think Upon* (Boston, 1696), p. 27; I. Mather, Preface to Torrey, *Exhortation*, sig. A4; Danforth, *Brief Recognition*, p. 20; Torrey, *Plea*, p. 45.

38 I. Mather, *Day of Trouble*, pp. 4–5, 12–14, 26–28 (ellipses deleted).

39 William Williams, *A Plea for God* (Boston, 1719), p. 34 (see also Cotton Mather, *The Way to Prosperity* [Boston, 1690], p. 23, and Torrey, *Exhortation*, p. 6); Charles L. Sanford, *The Quest for Paradise: Europe and the American Moral Imagination* (Urbana, Ill., 1961), p. 83.

Chapter 3   The Genetics of Salvation

1 Norton, quoted in Increase Mather, *The First Principles of New England* (Cambridge, Mass., 1675), p. 17; Edmund S. Morgan, *The Puritan Family: Religion and Domestic Relations in Seventeenth-Century New England* (Boston, 1944), p. 103; Increase Mather, *A Discourse concerning Baptism* (Boston, 1675), pp. 7–8, 26.

2 Cotton Mather, summarizing the position of the emigrants, in *Magnalia Christi Americana* (1702), ed. Thomas Robbins (Hartford, 1853–55), II, 8, and *The Duty of Children* (Boston, 1703), p. 28.

3 Peter Bulkeley, *The Gospel-Covenant* (London, 1651), p. 36; Richard Mather, *A Farewel-Exhortation* (Cambridge, Mass., 1657), p. 12; John Cotton, *The Covenant of Grace* (London, 1655), p. 56; Cotton Mather, *Parentator* (Boston, 1726), p. 26, and *Duty of Children*, p. 20.

4 Increase Mather, *A Discourse concerning Apostasy* (Boston, 1685), p. 65, and *Pray for the Rising Generation* (Cambridge, Mass., 1678), pp. 14–15.

5 John Higginson, *Cause of God* (Cambridge, Mass., 1663), p. 12; Joshua Scottow, *Narrative of Massachusetts* (Boston, 1694), in *Collections of the Massachusetts Historical Society*, 4, 4th ser. (1858), 311, 305; William Stoughton, *New-Englands True Interest* (Cambridge, Mass., 1670), pp. 19, 33; James Fitch, *An Holy Connexion* (Cambridge, Mass., 1674), pp. 12–13; Cotton Mather, *The Wonders of the Invisible World* (Boston, 1693), p. 10.

6 Gerald R. Cragg, *Puritanism in the Period of the Great Persecution* (Cambridge, 1957), p. 258.

7 C. Mather, *Magnalia*, I, 42; Jonathan Mitchel, *Nehemiah on the Wall* (Cambridge, Mass., 1671), p. 9; John Goodwin, *Imputatio Fidei* (1642), quoted in A. S. P. Woodhouse, ed., *Puritanism and Liberty* (London, 1938), p. [46]; John Bale, *The Image of Both Churches*, ed. Henry Christmas (Cambridge, 1849), pp. 598, 252; Samuel Sewall, *Phaenomena quaedam Apocalyptica* (Boston, 1697), pp. 2, 40.

8 Samuel Torrey, *An Exhortation unto Reformation* (Cambridge, Mass., 1674), p. 1; Cotton Mather, *Things for a Distressed People to Think Upon* (Boston, 1696), pp. 32–33 (see also pp. 35–36, 38); Increase Mather, *Morning Star*, appended to *The Righteous Man* (Boston, 1702), p. 81.

9 Scottow, *Narrative*, pp. 286–87; Torrey, *Exhortation*, pp. 7, 31–32; Increase Mather, *The Day of Trouble Is Near* (Cambridge, Mass., 1674), p. 27; Urian Oakes, *New-England Pleaded With* (Cambridge, Mass., 1673), pp. 17, 20, 23.

10 Oakes, *New-England Pleaded With*, pp. 21, 23 (ellipses omitted); Cotton Mather, *The Serviceable Man* (Boston, 1690), p. 28; Sewall, *Phaenomena*, p. 2.

11 Abba Hillel Silver, *A History of Messianic Speculation in Israel, from the First through the Seventeenth Centuries* (New York, 1927), p. 150.

12 Gorton, quoted in Charles Sanford, *The Quest for Paradise: Europe and the American Moral Imagination* (Urbana, Ill., 1961), p. 82; Increase Mather, Preface to *A Discourse concerning Prayer* (Boston, 1710), p. i; Mitchel, Preface to Thomas Shepard, *The Parable of the Ten Virgins* (London, 1660), sigs. A3–A3ᵛ (the parable itself [Matthew 25], according to traditional interpretations, speaks of the Parousia); John Cotton, *A Briefe Exposition of Canticles* (London, 1642), pp. 182, 200; Sewall, *Phaenomena*, pp. 27–28; Cotton Mather, *Things to Be Look'd For* (Cambridge, Mass., 1691), pp. 3, 10; Thomas Shepard, *The Clear Sun-shine of the Gospel* (London, 1648), p. 30.

13 Increase Mather, *The Mystery of Israel's Salvation* (London, 1669), p. 52 (see also pp. 80, 90, 171, 177); Bulkeley, *Gospel-Covenant*, pp. 22–24 (ellipses deleted); William Williams, *The Great Duty* (Boston, 1726), p. 2.

14 Peter Folger, *A Looking Glass for the Times* (1676), in *Rhode Island Historical Tracts*, 16 (1883), 16; Samuel Willard, *The Fountain Opened* (Boston, 1700), pp. 7–9.

15 Cotton Mather, *A Pillar of Gratitude* (Boston, 1700), pp. 4 ff.

16 John Eliot, Preface to *The Christian Commonwealth* (London, 1659), sig. B4ᵛ; Mitchel, *Nehemiah*, p. 9; Edward Johnson, *The Wonder-Working Providence of Sion's Savior*, ed. J. Franklin Jameson (New York, 1910), pp. 203, 238–39, 256, 271–73 (ellipses deleted).

17 Increase Mather, *A Discourse concerning Prayer* (Boston, 1710), p. 96; Joy Gilsdorf, "The Puritan Apocalypse: New England Eschatology in the Seventeenth Century," Diss. Yale 1964, p. 142 (citing I. Mather); Oakes, *New-England Pleaded With*, p. 25; Samuel Willard, *The Perils of the Times* (Boston, 1700), p. 78; Perry Miller, *The New England Mind: From Colony to Province* (1953; rpt. Boston, 1961), pp. 187–88; Cotton Mather, *Theopolis Americana* (Boston, 1710), pp. 43–44.

18 Cotton Mather, *Decennium Luctuosum* (1699), in *Narratives of the Indian Wars, 1675–1699*, ed. Charles H. Lincoln (New York, 1913), p. 184; Increase Mather, *Renewal of Covenant* (Boston, 1677), p. 13; Thomas Thacher, *A Fast of God's Chusing* (Boston, 1678), p. 7.

19 William Adams, *The Necessity of the Pouring Out of the Spirit* (Boston, 1679), p. 13; I. Mather, *Renewal of Covenant*, p. 7.

20 I. Mather, *Renewal of Covenant*, p. 7, and *An Earnest Exhortation* (Boston, 1676), p. 13; William Williams, *A Plea for God* (Boston, 1719), p. 40; C. Mather, *Serviceable Man*, p. 14; Cotton Mather, *The Everlasting Gospel* (Boston, 1700), p. 28.

21 John Norton, *Sion the Out-Cast*, in *Three Choice and Profitable Sermons* (Cambridge, Mass., 1664), pp. 6–7; Samuel Danforth, *A Brief Recognition of New England's Errand into the Wilderness* (Cambridge, Mass., 1671), pp. 19–21.

22 Torrey, *Exhortation*, pp. 6, 10.

23 Samuel Torrey, *Man's Extremity, God's Opportunity* (Cambridge, Mass., 1695), pp. 2–3; W. Adams, *Necessity*, pp. 6–9 (on the representative quality of this sermon see William DeLoss Love, Jr., *The Fast and Thanksgiving Days of New England* [Boston, 1895], p. 214).

24 Urian Oakes, *The Soveraign Efficacy of Divine Providence* (Boston, 1682), p. 17 (see also p. 19); Higginson, *Cause of God*, p. 24; Nicholas Noyes, *New-Englands Duty* (Boston, 1698), pp. 63–64 (ellipses deleted).

25 Cotton Mather, *A Midnight Cry* (Boston, 1692), pp. 29–30, 22, 24, *Eleutheria* (London, 1698), pp. 87, 27, and *Magnalia*, I, 44, 46, and II, 579.

26 C. Mather, *Magnalia*, I, 330–31; Shepard, *Parable*, II, 8; James Allin, *New-Englands Choicest Blessing* (Boston, 1679), p. 5; Increase Mather. *The Surest Way to Greatest Honour* (Boston, 1699), p. 24.

27 Cotton Mather, *Diary*, ed. Worthington C. Ford (New York, 1957), I, 358 (July 4, 1700); Norton, *Sion the Out-Cast*, p. 6; Stoughton, *New-Englands True Interest*, p. 21; I. Mather, Preface to Samuel Torrey, *A Plea* (Boston, 1683), sig. A2; C. Mather, *Magnalia*, I, 36, 27.

28 Darrett B. Rutman, "Local Freedom and Puritan Control," in *Puritanism in Seventeenth-Century Massachusetts*, ed. David D. Hall (New York, 1968), p. 118; Joseph Morgan, *The History of the Kingdom of Basaruah* (1715), ed. Richard Schlatter (Cambridge, Mass., 1946), p. 110; Thomas Prince, *Chronological History* (Boston, 1736), I, Dedication, sig. A2–A2ᵛ, pp. 170, 104, 98, 103, 199, and Preface, p. iii.

29 Prince, *Chronological History*, p. 1; Thomas Prince, *The People of New England* (1730), in *The Wall and The Garden: Selected Massachusetts Election Sermons, 1660–1776*, ed. A. W. Plumstead (Minneapolis, 1968), pp. 199, 219, 205, 220; Darrett B. Rutman, *Winthrop's Boston: Portrait of a Puritan Town, 1630–1649* (Chapel Hill, 1965), pp. 278–79.

CHAPTER 4 The Typology of America's Mission

1 William Clebsch, *From Sacred to Profane America: The Role of Religion in American History* (New York, 1968).

2 David E. Smith, "Millenarian Scholarship in America," *American Quarterly*, 17 (1965), 530 (see also pp. 537, 541–42).

3 William Hubbard, *The Happiness of a People* (Boston, 1676), p. 61.

4 William Adams, *The Necessity of the Pouring Out of the Spirit* (Boston, 1679), p. 35.

5 John Cotton, quoted in Cotton Mather, *Magnalia Christi Americana* (1702), ed. Thomas Robbins (Hartford, 1853–55), I, 325; Joy B. Gilsdorf, "The Puritan Apocalypse: New England Eschatology in the Seventeenth Century," Diss. Yale 1964, pp. 97, 99 (see also p. 125); James Allin, *New Englands Choicest Blessing* (Boston, 1679), p. 13; Increase Mather, Preface to Samuel Torrey, *An Exhortation unto Reformation* (Cambridge, Mass., 1674), sig. A2; Cotton Mather, *Things to Be Look'd For* (Cambridge, Mass., 1691), pp. 26, 33; John Higginson, "Attestation" to C. Mather, *Magnalia*, I, 14–17 (ellipses deleted).

6 Jonathan Edwards, letter of March 1744, in *The Great Awakening*, ed. C. C. Goen (New Haven, 1972), p. 560, and *Works*, ed. John Erskine (New York, 1849), III, 316.

7 Edwards, quoted in Stephen J. Stein, "A Notebook on the Apocalypse, by Jonathan Edwards," *William and Mary Quarterly*, 29 (1972), 623; Edwards, *Works*, I, 354, 481–83; Cambridge Synod, *The Cambridge Platform* (Cambridge, Mass., 1649), p. 10.

8 C. C. Goen, "Jonathan Edwards: A New Departure in Eschatology," *Church History*, 28 (1959), 32; Edwards, *Works*, I, 484–86.

9 Edwards, *Works*, I, 469, and III, 308–9.

10 Edwards, *Works*, III, 310–12, I, 486–87, and III, 299 (see also I, 488–94, and III, 313–19).

11 Alan Heimert, *Religion and the American Mind, from the Great Awakening to the Revolution* (Cambridge, Mass., 1966), pp. 64, 66; Edwards, *Works*, III, 291, 483 (see also III, 334, 492); Samuel Buell, *The Excellence of Saving Knowledge* (New York, 1761), pp. 12–13.

12 Edwards, *Works*, I, 481, 469, 487, and III, 316, 322–24 (see also III, 458–61).

13 Edwards, *Works*, III, 458–59.

14 Heimert, *Religion*, p. 55 (citing Edwards); Edwards, *Works*, III, 410, 417–18, and I, 487 (see also III, 424, 431, 433, 457, 454).

15 Mather, *Magnalia*, I, 42–43; David Austin, "Advertisement" to Jonathan Edwards, *History of Redemption*, ed. Austin (New York, 1793), p. iv.

16 William Ellery Channing, quoted in H. Richard Niebuhr, *The Kingdom*

of God in America (Hamden, Conn., 1956), p. 144; Charles Chauncy, *Seasonable Thoughts* (1743), in *The Great Awakening*, ed. Alan Heimert and Perry Miller (New York, 1967), pp. 299, 302n., 302–3.

17 Alan Heimert, Introduction to Edwards's *Humble Inquiry*, in *Great Awakening*, ed. Heimert and Miller, p. 424; "A Letter from the Ministers of Windham" (1745), in *Great Awakening*, ed. Heimert and Miller, p. 401; Heimert, *Religion*, pp. 123–24 (citing Edwards and the Separates; see also pp. 125–30).

18 Perry Miller, *Jonathan Edwards* (New York, 1949), p. 62; David Lyttle, "Jonathan Edwards on Personal Identity," *Early American Literature*, 7 (1972), 165; Clebsch, *From Sacred to Profane*, p. 144; Roland Delattre, "Beauty and Politics: A Problematic Legacy of Jonathan Edwards," in *American Philosophy from Edwards to Quine*, ed. R. W. Shahan and K. R. Merrill (Norman, Okla., 1977), pp. 21–22; Clebsch, *From Sacred to Profane*, p. 185.

19 Cushing Strout, *The New Heavens and New Earth: Political Religion in America* (New York, 1975), p. 113; Edwards, *Works*, I, 10, and *Images or Shadows of Divine Things*, ed. Perry Miller (New Haven, 1948), p. 102.

20 Richard Bushman, *From Puritan to Yankee: Character and the Social Order in Connecticut, 1690–1765* (New York, 1967), p. 259.

21 Timothy Dwight, *The Conquest of Canäan* (Hartford, 1785), Bk. VI, l. 83 (my italics); Heimert, *Religion*, pp. 287, 284; John Barnard, *The Throne Established by Righteousness* (1734), in *The Wall and the Garden*, ed. A. William Plumstead (Minneapolis, 1968), p. 280; Jonathan Mayhew, *A Sermon Preach'd* (1754), in *Wall and Garden*, ed. Plumstead, pp. 299, 302; Ebenezer Thayer, *Jerusalem Instructed* (Boston, 1725), pp. 41–42.

22 Heimert, *Religion*, pp. 350, 438; William Smith, "Sermon VIII," in *Works* (Philadelphia, 1803), II, 170–72.

23 Smith, "Sermon VIII," in *Works*, II, 172–73; Thomas Foxcroft, *Observations on the Rise of New England* (Boston, 1730), p. 5; Thomas Frink, *A Sermon Delivered at Stafford* (Boston, 1757), pp. 4–5, and *A Sermon Preached before His Excellency* (Boston, 1758), pp. 30–31, 38.

24 George Duffield, quoted in Strout, *New Heavens*, p. 69; Edwards, *Images or Shadows*, p. 92; Ezra Stiles, *The United States Elevated to Glory* (Worcester, Mass., 1785), pp. 7–9; John Adams, *Familiar Letters of John Adams and His Wife Abigail Adams*, ed. Charles Francis Adams (New York, 1876), p. 403.

25 John Murray, *Nehemiah; or, The Struggle for Liberty* (Newburyport, Mass., 1779), p. 56; Ebenezer Baldwin, *The Duty of Rejoicing* (New York,

1776), p. 39; Charles Turner, *Due Glory Given to God* (Boston, 1783), p. 28; John Mellen, *A Sermon Delivered before the Governor* (Boston, 1797), p. 28.

26 Michael McGiffert, *The Question of '76* (Williamsburg, Va., 1977), pp. 10–12 (citing various eighteenth-century writers); Mercy Austin Warren, *The History of the American Revolution* (Boston, 1805), III, 435–36; William Smith, *A Sermon on the Present Situation* (Philadelphia, 1775), p. 28; Joel Barlow, "The Prospect of Peace" (1778), in *Works*, ed. William K. Bottorff and Arthur L. Ford (Gainesville, Fla., 1970), pp. 11, 10; anon. [Timothy Dwight?], *America; or, A Poem on the Settlement of the British Colonies* (New Haven, 1780), pp. 9, 11–12; Philip Freneau and Hugh Henry Brackenridge, "A Poem, on the Rising Glory of America," in *Colonial American Poetry*, ed. Kenneth Silverman (New York, 1968), pp. 440–42.

27 John Burt, *The Mercy of God* (Newport, R. I., 1759), p. 4; Nathaniel Appleton, *A Sermon Preached* (Boston, 1760), p. 36; Samuel Davies, *The Crisis*, in *Sermons on Important Subjects* (Philadelphia, 1818), pp. 257–58; Nathan O. Hatch, "The Origins of Civil Millennialism in America: New England Clergymen, War with France, and the Revolution," *William and Mary Quarterly*, 31 (1974), 417; Jonathan Mayhew, *Two Discourses* (Boston, 1759), p. 61; Mather Byles, *A Sermon, Delivered* (New London, Conn., 1760), p. 13; Charles Chauncy, *Marvellous Things* (Boston, 1745), p. 21. The sermon referred to in the text is Eli Forbes, *God the Strength and Salvation of His People* (Boston, 1761).

28 Jonathan Edwards, *Apocalyptic Writings*, ed. Stephen J. Stein (New Haven, 1977), pp. 254–57, 267, 261, 449, 459.

29 David Hall, *Israel's Triumph* (Boston, 1761), p. 11; Paul A. Varg, "The Advent of Nationalism, 1758–1776," *American Quarterly*, 16 (1964), 180–81 (citing Judah Champion).

30 Jonathan Mayhew, *A Sermon Preach'd* (Boston, 1754), p. 23; Samuel Cooper, *A Sermon before Thomas Pownall* (Boston, 1759), p. 48; Jonathan Bascom, *A Sermon at Eastham* (Boston, 1775), p. 19.

31 Theodorus Frelinghuysen, *A Sermon on the Late Treaty* (New York, 1754), p. 9.

32 Samuel Haven, *Joy and Salvation* (Portsmouth, N. H., 1763), p. 28; Matthias Harris, *A Sermon in Lewis* (Philadelphia, 1757), pp. 35–36.

33 Jonas Clarke, *A Sermon Preached before John Hancock* (Boston, 1781), p. 31; Samuel MacClintock, *A Sermon Preached before the Council* (Portsmouth, N. H., 1784), p. 35.

34 John Adams, *Adams Family Correspondence*, ed. L. H. Butterfield (Cambridge, Mass., 1963–73), II, 28; John and Abigail Adams, *Familiar Let-*

ters, pp. 306, 403 (see also Cecelia Tichi, "Worried Celebrants of the American Revolution," in *American Literature, 1764–1789: The Revolutionary Years*, ed. Everett Emerson [Madison, 1977], pp. 275–91); Thomas Chittenden, broadside, quoted in Mason I. Lowance, Jr., Introduction to *Early Vermont Broadsides*, ed. John Duffy (Hanover, N. H., 1975), p. xvii.

35 Chittenden, cited in Lowance, *Early Vermont Broadsides*, ed. Duffy, p. xvii; Strout, *New Heaven*, p. 12.

36 Edmund S. Morgan, "The Puritan Ethic and the American Revolution," *William and Mary Quarterly*, 24 (1967), 8–9; Gordon Wood, *The Creation of the American Republic, 1776–1789* (New York, 1969), pp. 107–8, 414.

37 Heimert, *Religion*, pp. 493–94 (citing various writers of the times; see also pp. 284, 396, 409–10, 543); David Griffith, *Passive Obedience Considered* (Williamsburg, Va., 1776), p. 14; Jacob Duché, *The American Vine* (Philadelphia, 1775), p. 26; Thomas Jefferson, *Writings*, ed. P. L. Ford (New York, 1892–99), I, 11; Thomas Paine, *Common Sense*, ed. N. F. Adkins (Indianapolis, 1953), pp. 27, 3, 23.

38 David Ramsay, *History of the American Revolution* (Lexington, Ky., 1815), I, 243; Humphreys, cited in Ernest L. Tuveson, *Redeemer Nation: The Idea of America's Millennial Role* (Chicago, 1968), p. 169; Duché, *American Vine*, pp. 17, 27; Sam Adams, cited in Stephen E. Lucas, *Portents of Rebellion: Rhetoric and Revolution in Philadelphia, 1765–1776* (Philadelphia, 1976), p. 195.

39 Anon., letter from Philadelphia, October 5, 1775, in *Letters on the American Revolution, 1774–1776*, ed. Margaret Willard (Boston, 1925), p. 213; David Austin, *The Millennium* (Elizabethtown, N. J., 1794), p. 415; Samuel Sherwood, *The Church's Flight* (New York, 1776), pp. 22–24.

40 John Cotton, *Gods Promise to His Plantations*, in *Old South Leaflets* (Boston, [1896], Vol. III, no. 53, pp. 4, 6–8.

41 Benjamin Rush to Granville Sharp (April 7, 1783), in "The Correspondence of Benjamin Rush and Granville Sharp, 1783–1809," ed. John A. Woods, *Journal of American Studies*, I (1967), 17; Stiles, *United States Elevated*, pp. 21–22.

42 Chandler Robbins, *A Sermon Preached at Plymouth* (Boston, 1794), p. 16.

43 Robbins, *Sermon at Plymouth*, pp. 6, 8; Samuel Cooper, *A Sermon Preached before John Hancock* (New York, 1780), pp. 43, 57.

44 Ralph Waldo Emerson, *Works*, ed. Edward Waldo Emerson (Boston, 1903–4), IX, 199; John Quincy Adams, *An Oration Delivered, July 4, 1837* (Newburyport, Mass. [1837]), pp. 5–6; Timothy Dwight, *A Discourse on the National Fast* (New York, 1812), pp. 54–56, and *A Discourse on Some Events of the Last Century* (New Haven, 1801), pp. 39–40, 42–43 (ellipses deleted).

45 Dwight, *Conquest of Canäan*, Bk. I, ll. 2–3, 755–57; and Bk. X, ll. 466, 524–30; John Adams, quoted in *The American Revolution: A Search for Meaning*, ed. Richard J. Hooker (New York, 1970), pp. 11–12.

CHAPTER 5   Ritual of Consensus

1 Richard Hooker, *Ecclesiastical Polity*, in *Works* (Oxford, 1807), I, 366.

2 Jeremy Belknap, letter of March 9, 1786, in *Massachusetts Historical Society Collections*, 5th ser., Vol. II, part 1 (1877), p. 431; Henry Cumings, *A Sermon Preached before Thomas Cushing* (Boston, 1783), p. 44; Timothy Dwight, *A Discourse on Some Events* (New Haven, 1801), p. 33; David Austin, *The Millennial Door* (East Windsor, Conn., 1799), p. 35; Asa Burton, *A Sermon Preached at Windsor* (Windsor, Vt., 1786), p. 13; William Symmes, *A Sermon Preached before His Honor* (Boston, 1785), p. 16; Zabdiel Adams, *A Sermon before His Excellency* (Boston, 1782), p. 48; John Adams, *A Defence of the Constitutions of the United States of America* (1787–88), in *The American Enlightenment*, ed. Adrienne Koch (New York, 1965), p. 257.

3 Ramsay, Washington, Samuel Adams, and Dwight, cited in Sacvan Bercovitch, "How the Puritans Won the American Revolution," *Massachusetts Review*, 17 (1976), 601.

4 Merrill Jensen, *The New Nation: A History of the United States during the Confederation, 1781–1789* (New York, 1962), p. 426; "Philadelphiensis" (Dec. 5, 1787), quoted in *The Declaration of Independence and the Constitution*, ed. Earl Latham (Lexington, Mass., 1976), p. 166; Merrill Jensen, *The American Revolution within America* (New York, 1974), p. 9 (see also pp. 10–11); Hamilton, quoted in *Declaration*, ed. Latham, p. 127.

5 Elizur Goodrich, *The Principles of Civil Union* (Hartford, 1787), p. 20; Henry Cumings, *A Sermon Preached at Billerica* (Boston, 1797), p. 16; John Adams, quoted in "The French and American Revolutions," *New Cambridge Modern History* (Cambridge, 1957–70), Vol. VIII, ed. A. Goodwin, p. 527; David Tappan, *Christian Thankfulness* (Boston, 1795), p. 20.

6 Cumings, *Sermon at Billerica*, p. 46; John Adams to Thomas Jefferson, Oct. 9, 1787, in *The Adams-Jefferson Correspondence*, ed. Lester J. Cappon (New York, 1971), p. xliv; Michael McGiffert, *The Question of '76* (Williamsburg, Va., 1976), p. 17 (citing Hamilton); Thomas Paine, *Representative Selections*, ed. Harry H. Clark (New York, 1961), p. 61.

7 Martin Diamond, "Ethics and Politics: The American Way" (MS), p. 12; Alexander Hamilton, Federalist 6, and James Madison, Federalist 51, in *The Federalist Papers*, ed. Clinton Rossiter (New York, 1961), pp. 57, 59, 322, 324.

8 Diamond, "Ethics," pp. 11, 25.

9 Alexis de Tocqueville, *Democracy in America*, ed. J. P. Mayer, trans. George Lawrence (Garden City, N. Y., 1969), p. 290; Wesley Frank Craven, *The Legend of the Founding Fathers* (Ithaca, N. Y., 1956), p. 71; Thomas Yarrow, *An Oration Delivered* (Mount Pleasant, N. Y., 1798), p.

10; Alexander Wilson, *Oration on Liberty* (Philadelphia, 1801), p. 11; Jonathan Maxcy, *An Oration in Providence* (Providence, 1795), pp. 19–20; Stephen Thacker, *An Oration Pronounced* (Boston, 1803), pp. 12–13; James Madison, *Manifestations* (Richmond, Va., 1795), p. 8; David Foster, *A Sermon before John Hancock* (Boston, 1790), p. 25; John Lathrop, Jr., *An Oration* (Boston, 1796), p. 5; Francis Blake, *An Oration at Worcester* (Worcester, Mass., 1796), p. 18; Abiel Abbot, *Traits of Resemblance* (Haverhill, Mass., 1799), p. 6

10 Ernest L. Tuveson, *Redeemer Nation: The Idea of America's Millennial Role* (Chicago, 1968), pp. 53–54, 171; Herbert G. Gutman, "Protestantism and the American Labor Movement: The Christian Spirit in the Gilded Age," *American Historical Review*, 72 (1966), 74; John L. Thomas, "Romantic Reform in America, 1815–1865," *American Quarterly*, 17 (1965), 673; William Cabell Rives, cited in Rush Welter, *The Mind of America, 1820–1860* (New York, 1975), p. 52; Cushing Strout, *The New Heaven and the New Earth: Political Religion in America* (New York, 1975), p. 229 (citing Joseph Bellamy); John O'Sullivan, "The Great Nation of Futurity," *United States Magazine and Democratic Review*, 6 (1839), 427, 430.

11 *Albany Argus*, cited in Welter, *Mind of America*, p. 3.

12 Walker and Rantoul, cited in Welter, *Mind of America*, pp. 4–5, 49.

13 Josiah Bent, Jr., *National Jubilee* (Boston, 1826), p. 10; Westerlo Woodworth, *Oration before the Young Men's Association* (Albany, 1834), p. 23.

14 Daniel Webster, "The Bunker Hill Monument," in *Works* (Boston, 1857), I, 78, 72–73, 75–77, 61.

15 W[illiam] E[vans] Arthur, *Oration* (Covington, Ky., 1850), p. 36 and inscription.

16 Arthur, *Oration*, pp. 3–5.

17 Arthur, *Oration*, p. 37; Henry David Thoreau, *Walden*, ed. Brooks Atkinson (New York, 1950), p. 15; Thomas Shepard, Preface to Peter Bulkeley, *The Gospel-Covenant* (London, 1651), sig. B2^v; Arthur, *Oration*, p. 32.

18 Arthur, *Oration*, pp. 11, 22–23, 34–35, 7.

19 Arthur, *Oration*, pp. 36, 40; Enos Hitchcock, *Oration at Providence* (Providence, R. I., 1788), p. 18; Arthur, *Oration*, p. 23.

20 Arthur, *Oration*, pp. 6, 9; Clay, cited in Welter, *Mind of America*, p. 24; Charles D. Drake, *The Duties of an American Citizen* (St. Louis, 1837), p. 27; Abram P. Maury, *Address on Advantages of the United States* (Nashville, Tenn., 1847), p. 24; Arthur, *Oration*, pp. 38, 40.

21 Arthur, *Oration*, pp. 38–40.

22 George Rudé, ed., *Robespierre* (Englewood Cliffs, N. J., 1967), p. 173.

23 William Appleman Williams, *America Confronts a Revolutionary World* (New York, 1976), p. 20; James Fenimore Cooper, *Notions of the Americans* (Philadelphia, 1828), II, 143; Nathaniel Hawthorne, *The Marble Faun*, ed. Murray Krieger (New York, 1961), p. vi.

24 Mason L. Weems, *A History of George Washington* (Philadelphia, 1800), p. 71; Sigmund Diamond, *The Reputation of the American Businessman* (Cambridge, Mass., 1955), p. 2 (citing an English newspaper account of 1853); David Ramsay, *History of the American Revolution* (Philadelphia, 1789), II, 321.

25 Kathryn Kish Sklar, *Catharine Beecher* (New Haven, 1973), pp. 159–61; Catharine Beecher, *A Treatise on Domestic Economy* (1841), ed. Kathryn Kish Sklar (New York, 1977), p. 13.

26 Susan P. Conrad, *Perish the Thought: Intellectual Women in Romantic America* (New York, 1976), pp. 123–24, 148 (citing Stanton and Smith); Ann Douglas, *The Feminization of American Culture* (New York, 1977), pp. 282, 285.

27 Charles Thomson to Benjamin Franklin, Nov. 26, 1769, in "The Papers of Charles Thomson," *Collections of the New York Historical Society*, 11 (1878), 23–24 (see also Richard Wells, cited in Stephen E. Lucas, *Portents of Rebellion: Rhetoric and Revolution in Philadelphia, 1765–76* [Philadelphia, 1976], p. 136); Thomas Blockway, *America Saved* (Hartford, 1784), p. 24; Daniel Webster, "Bunker Hill Monument," in *Works*, I, 79; Charles W. Dana, *The Garden of the World; or, The Great West* (Boston, 1856), pp. 13–15.

28 Benjamin F. Tefft, *The Far West* (Indianapolis, 1845), p. 35; M. Augustus Jewett, *An Oration, Delivered* (Terre Haute, Ind., 1840), p. 11; William Gilpin, quoted in Henry Nash Smith, *Virgin Land: The American West as Symbol and Myth* (New York, 1957), p. 40; Robert C. Winthrop, quoted in Julius W. Pratt, "The Origins of 'Manifest Destiny'," *American Historical Review*, 32 (1926–27), 797.

29 David C. Huntington, *The Landscapes of Frederic Edwin Church: Vision of an American Era* (New York, 1966), pp. x–xi, 10, 36–37; William Gilmore Simms, *Views and Reviews in American Literature, History, and Fiction: First Series*, ed. C. Hugh Holman (Cambridge, Mass., 1962), pp. 16, 20, 26 (ellipses deleted; see also pp. 17–19).

30 J. F. Maclear, "The Republic and the Millennium," in *The Religion of the Republic*, ed. Elwyn A. Smith (Philadelphia, 1971), pp. 194–95.

31 Tocqueville, *Democracy in America*, pp. 290, 530, 292, 530; Philip Schaff, *America: A Sketch of Its Political, Social, and Religious Character*, ed. Perry Miller (Cambridge, Mass., 1961), pp. 4, 15–16, 18, 20–24 (ellipses deleted).

32 Tocqueville, *Democracy in America*, pp. 470, 295, 592.
33 Edward Everett, "Oration on the Peculiar Motives to Intellectual Exertion in America" (1824), in *The American Literary Revolution, 1783–1837*, ed. Robert E. Spiller (New York, 1967), pp. 313–15; Horace Bushnell, "The Founders Great in Their Unconsciousness," in *Work and Play*, Vol. I of *Literary Varieties* (New York, 1881), pp. 129, 133–34, 150 (see also pp. 154, 163–65); Joel Hawes, *A Tribute to the Memory of the Pilgrims* (Hartford, 1830), pp. 60, 88, 183, 225–26 (see also pp. 62–63, 111–14, 145).
34 Lyman Beecher, *A Plea for the West* (Cincinnati, 1835), p. 177 (see also his *Memory of Our Fathers*, in *Works* [Boston, 1852–53], II, 176); Albert Barnes, quoted in Martin Marty, *Righteous Empire: The Protestant Experience in America* (New York, 1970), p. 129; Fred Somkin, *Unquiet Eagle: Memory and Desire in the Idea of American Freedom* (Ithaca, N. Y., 1967), p. 34; Francis Wayland, "Encouragement to Religious Efforts," *American National Preacher*, 5 (1830), 44.
35 William Conant, quoted in Perry Miller, *The Life of the Mind in America* (New York, 1965), p. 73; Francis Wayland, *The Elements of Moral Science* (1835), in *The American Evangelicals*, ed. William G. McLoughlin (Gloucester, Mass., 1976), p. 126 (see also p. 102); Maclear, "Republic and Millennium," p. 204; Miller, *Life of the Mind*, p. 93.
36 William Stoughton, *New England's True Interest* (Cambridge, Mass., 1670), pp. 17, 24, 32 (ellipses deleted); Maclear, "Republic and Millennium," p. 204.
37 Daniel Aaron, *The Unwritten War: American Writers and the Civil War* (New York, 1973), pp. xiii–xiv (italics deleted); Theodore Weld (abolitionist leader), quoted in H. Richard Niebuhr, *The Kingdom of God in America* (Hamden, Conn., 1956), p. 157; George M. Frederickson, *The Inner Civil War: Northern Intellectuals and the Crisis of the Union* (New York, 1961), p. 118 (see also pp. 7, 68, 82); Lincoln, quoted in Edward M. Burns, *The American Idea of Mission: Concepts of National Purpose and Destiny* (New Brunswick, N.J., 1957), p. 14; James Russell Lowell, "Ode Recited at the Harvard Commemoration" (1865), lines 232, 413, 421, 325, 327–28, in *Complete Poetical Works*, ed. Horace E. Scudder (Cambridge, Mass., 1925), pp. 345–47; George S. Phillips, quoted in William Clebsch, *From Sacred to Profane America: The Role of Religion in American History* (New York, 1968), pp. 190–91.

CHAPTER 6   Epilogue: The Symbol of America

1 Herman Melville, *White-Jacket; or, The World in a Man-of-War*, ed. Hennig Cohen (New York, 1967), pp. 149–50. In citing Melville, Hawthorne, Thoreau, and Whitman, I have used readily available editions of their works.

2 Victor Turner, *Dramas, Fields, and Metaphors: Symbolic Action in Human Society* (Ithaca, N. Y., 1974).

3 Warren I. Susman, "History and the Intellectual Uses of a Usable Past," in *The American Experience*, ed. Hennig Cohen (Boston, 1968), p. 93.

4 Newton Arvin, in "Our Country and Our Culture: A Symposium," *Partisan Review*, 19 (1952), 286; Henry David Thoreau, *Walden*, ed. Bruce Atkinson (New York, 1950), p. 279.

5 Ralph Waldo Emerson, *Journals and Miscellaneous Notebooks*, ed. William H. Gilman (Cambridge, Mass., 1960–77), II, 3, 114; Ralph Waldo Emerson, *Works*, ed. Edward Waldo Emerson (Boston, 1903–4), XI, 537–38, VIII, 233–34; XI, 205, 397; II, 218; I, 127; III, 71–72.

6 Emerson, quoted in John Gerber, "Emerson and the Political Economists," *New England Quarterly*, 22 (1949), 340; Emerson, *Works*, I, 156; VI, 105–6; *Journals*, X, 228, and VII, 431; *Works*, VI, 90, 93, 97.

7 Emerson, *Works*, II, 109, 111; *Journals*, II, 522.

8 Emerson, *Works*, II, 114; *Journals*, III, 382–83.

9 Leo Marx, *The Machine in the Garden: Technology and the Pastoral Ideal in America* (New York, 1964), pp. 253, 265; Edwin Fussell, *Frontier: American Literature and the American West* (Princeton, N. J., 1965), pp. 224, 229; Thoreau, *Walden*, p. 84.

10 James McIntosh, *Thoreau as Romantic Naturalist: His Shifting Stance towards Nature* (Ithaca, N. Y., 1974), pp. 223–24 (citing Thoreau); Thoreau, "Walking," in *Walden and Other Writings*, ed. Bruce Atkinson (New York, 1950), p. 612; Stanley Cavell, *The Senses of "Walden"* (New York, 1972), p. 13; Thoreau, "Walking," p. 612; James Fenimore Cooper, *Home as Found*, ed. Lewis Leary (New York, 1961), pp. 23–24.

11 H. S. Canby, "American Challenge: A Study of *Walden*," *Saturday Review*, 20 (1939), 16 (see also pp. 10–12); Henry David Thoreau, *Reform Papers*, ed. Wendell Glick (Princeton, N. J., 1973), p. 332n.; George Bancroft, *History of the United States* (Boston, 1876), IV, 411; Marvin Meyers, *The Jacksonian Persuasion: Politics and Belief* (Stanford, 1957), pp. 193, 172, 126, 170, 193 (citing various Jacksonian economists).

12 S. Todd Lowry, "The Archaeology of the Circulation Concept in Economic Theory," *Journal of the History of Ideas*, 35 (1974), 429–44, cited in Richard Berke, "Thoreau and the Jacksonian Homo Economicus," Diss. Columbia 1977; Mircea Eliade, *The Sacred and the Profane: The Nature of Religion*, trans. Willard Trask (New York, 1959), pp. 22, 25, 36.

13 Stephen E. Whicher, *Freedom and Fate: An Inner Life of Ralph Waldo Emerson* (New York, 1953), p. 11; Emerson, *Journals*, VII, 24, and *Works*, II, 346.

14 Herman Melville, "Hawthorne and His Mosses," in *The Portable Mel-*

ville, ed. Jay Leyda (New York, 1952), pp. 409–10; *White-Jacket*, p. 399; *Mardi; or, A Voyage Thither*, ed. H. Bruce Franklin (New York, 1964), pp. 436–37, 356 (see also p. 353).

15 A. N. Kaul, *The American Vision: Actual and Ideal Society in Nineteenth-Century Fiction* (New Haven, 1963), p. 259.

16 Herman Melville, *Moby-Dick; or, The Whale*, ed. Charles Feidelson (Indianapolis, 1964), p. 80.

17 Melville, quoted in Daniel Aaron, *The Unwritten War: American Writers and the Civil War* (New York, 1973), pp. 80, 88; Loren Baritz, *City on a Hill* (New York, 1964), p. 273.

18 Henry Adams, *The Education of Henry Adams*, ed. James T. Adams (New York, 1931), pp. 314, 232, 343, 5, 280, 92 (my italics).

19 Cotton Mather, *Magnalia Christi Americana* (1702), ed. Thomas Robbins (Hartford, 1853–55), II, 181 (see also I, 103); Edwards, paraphrased in Alan Heimert, *Religion and the American Mind: From the Great Awakening to the Revolution* (Cambridge, Mass., 1966), p. 67; James T. Adams, Introduction to Adams, *Education*, p. ix; Adams, *Education*, pp. 328–29, 91 (see also pp. 12–14, 21, 308).

20 Adams, *Education*, pp. 12–14, 308, x, 21, 343, 383, xi (see also pp. 238, 313).

21 Adams, *Education*, p. 280; Adams, quoted in Martha Banta, "American Apocalypses: Excrement and Ennui," *Studies in the Literary Imagination*, 7 (1974), 24; Adams, *Education*, pp. 505, 272 (see also pp. 273, 324, 337); Mark Twain, *The Mysterious Stranger*, in *The Portable Mark Twain*, ed. Bernard De Voto (New York, 1946), pp. 742–44.

22 Leo Stoller, "Thoreau's Doctrine of Simplicity," *New England Quarterly*, 29 (1956), 443; Walt Whitman, *The Eighteenth Presidency*, ed. Edward F. Grier (Lawrence, Kansas, 1956), pp. 34–35 (see also pp. 23–24, 39), "A Backward Glance O'er Travel'd Roads," and *Democratic Vistas*, in *Complete Poetry and Selected Prose*, ed. James E. Miller, Jr. (Boston, 1959), pp. 449, 500, 456.

23 Whitman, *Democratic Vistas*, pp. 456, 460–61, 478, 499, 476.

24 Whitman, 1855 Preface, in *Complete Poetry and Selected Prose*, ed. Miller, p. 411; Roy Harvey Pearce, *The Continuity of American Poetry* (Princeton, N. J., 1961), p. 170 (see also p. 82); Whitman, "Inscriptions," in *Complete Poetry and Selected Prose*, ed. Miller, pp. 8–9, and quoted in Edwin Fussell, *Lucifer in Harness: American Meter, Metaphor, and Diction* (Princeton, N.J., 1973), p. 53; Whitman, *Democratic Vistas*, p. 496, and quoted in John G. Cawelti, *Apostles of the Self-Made Man: Changing Concepts of Success in America* (Chicago, 1965), pp. 81–82.

25 Emerson, *Works*, VII, 417, and VI, 200; Maurice Gonnaud, "Emerson and the Imperial Self: A European Critique," in *Emerson: Prophecy*,

Metamorphosis, and Influence, ed. David Levin (New York, 1975), p. 127; Emerson, *Works*, IX, 199, and VII, 399; *Journals*, III, 14; and "Oration and Response," in *New England Society Orations*, ed. Cephas Brainerd and Eveline Warner (New York, 1901), II, 33; *Works*, VIII, 142–43; XI, 383, 385–87.

26 Emerson, quoted in Aaron, *Unwritten War*, pp. 34–35; Emerson, *Journals*, X, 195; *Works*, XI, 538, 319, 516.

27 Emerson, *Works*, XI, 514–15, 525–30, 534–37, 540, 544 (ellipses deleted).

28 George Frederickson, *The Inner Civil War: Northern Intellectuals and the Crisis of the Union* (New York, 1965), pp. 176–78.

29 Emerson, *Works*, I, 81, 115, and XI, 530.

30 Michael D. Bell, *Hawthorne and the Historical Romance* (Princeton, N. J., 1971), p. 23; Kaul, *American Vision*, p. 319; Gretchen G. Jordan, "Hawthorne's Bell: Historical Evolution Through Symbol," *Nineteenth-Century Fiction*, 19 (1964), 125–26; Charles L. Sanford, *The Quest for Paradise: Europe and the American Moral Imagination* (Urbana, Ill., 1961), pp. 183–84; Hawthorne, quoted in Arnold Rampersad, *Melville's Israel Potter: A Pilgrimage and Progress* (Bowling Green, Ohio, 1969), p. 97; Roy Harvey Pearce, *Historicism Once More: Problems and Occasions for the American Scholar* (Princeton, N. J., 1969), pp. 168–69.

31 Hugo McPherson, *Hawthorne as Myth-Maker: A Study in Imagination* (Toronto, 1969), p. 145; Leo Levy, "The Landscape Mode of *The Scarlet Letter*," Nineteenth-Century Fiction, 23 (1969), 375; Nathaniel Hawthorne, *The Life of Franklin Pierce*, in *Works*, ed. George P. Lathrop (Boston, 1883), XVII, 165–66; Hawthorne, *The Ancestral Footstep*, quoted in Pearce, *Historicism*, p. 170.

32 Nathaniel Hawthorne, *The Scarlet Letter*, ed. Harry Levin (Boston, 1961), p. 261.

33 Ibid., pp. 49, 247.

34 Ibid., pp. 153, 157, 153.

Index

233

DESIGNED BY IRVING PERKINS
COMPOSED BY THE NORTH CENTRAL PUBLISHING CO.
ST. PAUL, MINNESOTA
MANUFACTURED BY INTER-COLLEGIATE PRESS, INC.
SHAWNEE MISSION, KANSAS
TEXT IS SET IN JANSON, DISPLAY LINES IN NICOLAS JENSEN

Library of Congress Cataloging in Publication Data
Bercovitch, Sacvan.
The American jeremiad.
Includes bibliographical references and index.
1. American prose literature—History and criticism.
2. Preaching—United States—History.
3. Oratory—United States—History.
4. Puritans—New England.
5. Christianity and politics—History.
6. United States—Civilization.
I. Title.
PS362.B43   810'.9'38   78-53283
ISBN 0-299-07350-5